AUTHOR'S NOTE

This book is long overdue. It was written as a tribute to all of the FBI agents of Criminal Squad #1, more commonly referred to as the C-1 squad, who were assigned to the Chicago Division of the FBI from 1957 to 1976, a period of nineteen years. These agents were the original pioneers who were required to wage war against one of the most powerful organized crime syndicates in the nation since the infamous days of the notorious Al Capone era. Never before had the challenge been greater. This is a story of the unique challenges and adversity confronting these brave and dedicated agents who, despite great personal risk and hardship, accepted their immense responsibilities with resourcefulness, ingenuity, and determination. It was at a time when the FBI did not have the necessary tools or legislation to combat organized crime, but they accomplished their goals aggressively and tirelessly with whatever means were available. As pioneers in this field, they paved the way for other agents to follow. As a result of their relentless efforts, they were responsible for the incredible successes achieved, which resulted in severely curtailing, disrupting, and crippling the activities of the Chicago mob. Organized crime will never be the same in Chicago, thanks to the tenacity of the C-1 agents to whom we owe a huge debt of gratitude and thanks. I have had the honor and the privilege of having been a part of the C-1 squad for a period of nineteen years. Many of these agents have passed away, but their incredible accomplishments against the corrupt and destructive forces of the Chicago crime syndicate should never be forgotten.

Eliot Ness, the man behind the legend, was a federal prohibition agent, who formed a special group of US Treasury agents from about 1929 to 1931. They became famous for their efforts to enforce prohibition in Chicago. In 1957, Ness wrote a book entitled *The Untouchables*, which later became a popular TV series and a movie that glorified the role of Eliot Ness and his men. I don't wish to minimize in any manner the fine work of these prohibition agents. However, I firmly believe that there will never be another time in the history of Chicago to compare with the unprecedented task and challenges faced by the C-1 squad agents in 1957 and the following nineteen years, and the incomparable results achieved during that period against the Chicago mob.

C-1
AND THE
CHICAGO
MOB

For Mary Sue Smith,
With warm best wishes & Blessings

Vincent L. Inserra

10-23-14

VINCENT L. INSERRA

To order additional copies of this book, contact:
Xlibris LLC
1-888-795-4274
www.Xlibris.com
Orders@Xlibris.com
541435

CONTENTS

FOREWORD

There are three attributes that are essential to the character of every Special Agent of the FBI. They are:

Fidelity, Bravery and Integrity

Those words are emblazoned on the credentials of each agent and form the basis of all their actions, both professional and private. Nowhere were those virtues more apparent than in the Chicago FBI field office during the time that I was prosecutor in the Justice Department and Racketeering section. I had the unique opportunity to work closely with those excellent investigators.

Every agent that I have met has consistently demonstrated their devotion to the safety of this country, and the remarkable ability to work as long and as hard as necessary to achieve their purpose. The most extraordinary of all were those agents that constituted the squad known to everyone as, "C-1" and that squad was under the direction of SA Vincent L. Inserra, the author of this book.

For anyone who is the least interested in the recent history of organized crime in the Chicago area, this book is a "must read." It takes you inside the FBI during a relentless battle against the Chicago mob, told by the man who was both the leader of, and the driving force behind, those honorable and courageous members of C-1.

You will read for many years how the Chicago crime syndicate held a virtual stranglehold on the city and its suburbs. It seemed that the hoodlums were untouchable by law enforcement. Then along came Inserra and the C-1 squad. As a direct result of their unselfish dedication to duty and their total commitment to the success of the task before them, the tables were turned and the arrogant La Cosa Nostra, as they called themselves, were called to account and were securely and irrevocably on the defensive.

I consider it a singular honor to write this foreword. In my entire career as an attorney, I have never known a more honorable and finer group of men, and SA Vincent L. Inserra is the finest of them all.

David P. Schippers, Esq.
Former Chief of the Organized Crime
Strike Force, Chicago (1964-1967)
June, 2014

How It All Began:
Top Hoodlum Program

It all started on November 14, 1957, following the discovery of a large gathering of individuals at the palatial estate of Joseph Barbera in Apalachin, New York. About sixty-three persons were arrested in this history-making raid by Sergeant Ed Croswell and officers of the New York State Police. Approximately fifty others fled and escaped detection and arrest. These people were from all parts of the country, some were prominent members of organized crime and others not so prominent. The one thing they all had in common was that they were all of Italian descent. During the identification process, the police found that many had no criminal record. One person, John Montana, had been voted "Man of the Year" in the Pennsylvania-New York area. Another man, virtually unknown, was later identified as Frank DeSimone, an attorney who was reported to be the mob boss from the Los Angeles, California, area.

The magnitude of the meeting and the people involved shocked many law enforcement officials. Questions were asked about this prominent hoodlum gathering and the purpose of the meeting, and the FBI and other state and federal law enforcement agencies had no specific answers to many of the questions. The Chicago office of the FBI was asked by FBI headquarters to explain why a Frank Zito, a minor character from Springfield, Illinois, was in attendance with so many prominent hoodlums because he was the only person apparently representing Illinois at this meeting. We did not know then what we know now, that Frank Zito was not representing the Chicago mob but was representing the organized crime family in Rockford, Illinois, because Rockford area boss Tony Musso was too ill to attend and his underboss, Jasper Calo, was not available. We didn't know then that Salvatore "Momo" Giancana, a.k.a. Sam Giancana, was the recognized and undisputed leader of the Chicago crime syndicate who had been at the meeting and was able to effect an escape when the authorities raided the meeting and that Sam Giancana took over control of the Chicago mob in 1957 immediately after a warning shot had been fired at Anthony J. Accardo, who then voluntarily stepped down as supreme boss of the Chicago mob. We didn't know then that this meeting was a "national meeting" of the leaders of organized crime, now referred to as the

"La Cosa Nostra," that a larger national meeting was reportedly held several weeks earlier at the estate of hoodlum Richie Boiardo at Livingston, New Jersey. Among the main topics discussed then were the recent assassination of New York mob boss Albert Anastasia (Murder Inc.) and the selection of Carlo Gambino to replace him. Also discussed was the recent assassination attempt of mob leader Frank Costello, who wisely stepped down to allow Vito Genovese to replace him. They also decided to temporarily close the membership books of the New York families, because Albert Anastasia had been reportedly selling mob memberships for $40,000 to $50,000, each and his family had greatly surpassed all the other New York mob families.

Needless to say, the FBI, the premier law enforcement agency in the world, was taken by surprise and was disappointed by the lack of criminal intelligence information available about the obvious existence of a National Organized Crime Syndicate as well as the lack of prior knowledge of this secret and sinister hoodlum gathering. One of the primary principles of FBI Director J. Edgar Hoover and the FBI had long been "don't embarrass the bureau," and the bureau found itself placed in a very embarrassing situation. FBI headquarters immediately dispatched a teletype communication to all of the field offices that covered the locality where each Apalachin attendee resided. They instructed each field office to immediately institute an investigation into the background and activities of those individuals in attendance or ten of the most prominent hoodlums in their respective division. The Chicago Division was instructed to assign ten FBI agents exclusively to investigate the ten top hoodlums in the Chicago area. Thus, the FBI's "Top Hoodlum Program" was created and launched as a top priority matter that was to be afforded immediate and continuous investigative attention. Never before had the FBI been involved exclusively in a criminal intelligence gathering type of investigation of organized crime members without allegations of a specific federal violation within the jurisdiction of the FBI.

In 1957, I had been assigned to Criminal Squad #1 in Chicago, commonly referred to as the C-1 squad, having transferred in from New York City where I handled Soviet Satellite matters. The Chicago Division had nine criminal squads, C-1 through C-9, and five security squads, S-1 through S-5. Each squad specialized in handling specific federal violations within the jurisdiction of the FBI. I was very fortunate and pleased with the types of criminal cases being handled by the C-1 squad such as bank robberies, extortion cases, kidnapping cases, fugitive matters, theft of government property cases, and other closely related criminal investigations. My mentor and partner at that time was Lenard Wolf, a fine agent who was known for his unusual prowess in locating and arresting hard-to-locate fugitives. I was truly enjoying my work on the C-1 squad. The supervisor of the C-1 squad was Roswell (Ross) Spencer, who had gained fame solving bank robbery cases in the Chicago Division. Spencer went on to retire from the FBI several years later to take the position of chief investigator for the Cook County, Illinois State's attorney's office.

Spencer was told by the special agent in charge (SAC) of the Chicago FBI Office that the Top Hoodlum Program was now the responsibility of the C-1 squad and to fully comply with and implement the bureau's directive. Ross Spencer called me into his office and told me that I had been selected to be one of the ten agents assigned exclusively to the new Top Hoodlum Program. I was somewhat surprised and also disappointed with the news because I was really enjoying the challenge of the criminal cases assigned to me. I then asked Ross Spencer why he had selected me for this type of assignment. He replied that he selected me because I was of Italian descent. Without trying to appear ungrateful or disrespectful, I asked him, "What does that have to do with me?" His reply was that I would be able to pronounce the Italian names, which made absolutely no sense to me, but I accepted his decision and was prepared to make the best of my new assignment. Little did I realize at that time that I would be assigned to wage war against the most powerfully entrenched Chicago crime syndicate since the days of Al Capone for the next nineteen years and that I would be in charge of the C-1 squad for the last thirteen years of my assignment in the Chicago office of the FBI.

ABOUT THE AUTHOR

By way of background, I was born and raised in the shadows of the North End of Boston, Massachusetts. My father, Gasparo Inserra, also known as Jasper Inserro, was born just outside the city of Palermo, Sicily. My mother, Theresa, nee DeGregorio, was born in the small town of Mirabella Eclano, located in the Province of Avellino, near Naples, Italy. I have always considered myself to be an American of Italian descent, a first-generation Italian who was, and still is, proud of my heritage. My parents arrived separately in America with their entire families at very young ages. It was back in the early twentieth century when millions of Italians and other Europeans came to the shores of the United States in search of a new life. They traveled in cramped steerage-class ocean liners and endured great hardship and privation, carrying with them what little possessions they had along with their family steamer trunks. What courageous and dauntless people they were to leave their homeland, not knowing the challenges they would be facing upon their arrival in a foreign country.

They settled in the vicinity of the North End of Boston, which was occupied exclusively by Italian immigrants and was commonly known as "Little Italy." They lived in four-story tenement housing that had no bathing facilities. You had to go to a public bathhouse to bathe. There was only one toilet located on each floor at the end of the hall, which was used by all of the occupants on that floor. You could see their laundry hanging on lines stretched between buildings in this tightly packed neighborhood. Today the North End of Boston has been completely renovated and is considered to be one of the trendiest and most desirable parts of Boston to reside. The Italians who live there reportedly are reluctant to sell to anyone unless they are Italian, but everything has its price. Parking remains difficult though because of the narrow streets and alleys.

When Mother and Dad got married in 1920, they moved to Roxbury, Massachusetts, a close suburb of Boston. I was the oldest child of a family of five, and on weekends, my dad would take me to the North End to visit his parents. My grandparents, Vincenzo and Concetta Inserra, spoke very little English; and I had a very difficult time communicating with them because my parents rarely spoke Italian in my presence. But it was always a pleasant experience, especially because my dad would always provide us with a delicious assortment of mouth-watering Italian pastry. My grandfather, after whom I was named, made his living as a street peddler. He used to push a heavy two-wheeler cart through the streets of the North End to sell his fresh crabs obtained from Boston Harbor along with ice water and a variety of vegetables. During the winter months, he rested. This was during the Prohibition era in the United States when you could smell the wine fermenting in most of the basements of the buildings. Wine was a commodity that Italians could not live without. It was part of their daily ritual, and they weren't about to be denied.

Mother and Dad had very little formal education but spoke good English. My dad was a barber at an early age and later became a hairdresser. He opened the first beauty salon in the Filene's Department store in downtown Boston and called it "Inserro's Beauty Salon." He used the name of "Inserro" because phonetically I guess he thought it sounded better. He was quite the entrepreneur. He worked seven days a week and would also give free haircuts and hair permanents to friends and family members on weekends. When he wasn't working, he was always grocery shopping for the family. Our family always ate well, especially on holidays. Since my parents had no living relatives in Italy, they had no desire to return to their native country for a visit. They were supremely happy in the United States with all of its opportunities and freedom. Our family included my brother Joseph (deceased) and sisters Jean, Terry, and Marie Elena; and they were all the focus of their life.

I attended public schools in Roxbury, Massachusetts, along with my Jewish and black neighbors. Roxbury is now a predominately black suburb of Boston. Upon graduating from high school, I decided to work for a year to raise some money so that I could continue with my education. My parents did not have the finances to send me to college. In 1941, I obtained a job at the Sears Roebuck mail-order store in Brookline, Massachusetts. The general manager of the store at the time was a large Texan by the name of Crowdus Baker, and we became good friends. Mr. Baker would eventually become president of Sears in Chicago, and we would meet up again later during an FBI transfer to Chicago.

WORLD WAR II: NAVY FIGHTER PILOT

T hen along came World War II, and it completely changed my life. I left Sears and took a job with the United States Army Quartermaster Corps in Boston because I wanted to do something to help out the war effort. This job was short-lived because I had a strong desire to join the navy and become a naval aviator. I wanted to select my branch of the service rather than wait around to be drafted in the army. I visited the Navy Recruiting Center in Boston and applied to be a navy pilot. I passed the written exams and was given an extensive physical exam. I passed all aspects of the physical exam except for the eye exam. I was told that my vision was so bad that I could never become a navy pilot. Pilots were not allowed to wear glasses. I explained to the examiner that I had a very bad head cold and that it was affecting my vision. I requested that I be allowed to be reexamined in several weeks after I got rid of my head cold. They refused my request and told me that my eyes were too bad for me to qualify as a navy flier.

I was devastated by being rejected by the navy. I told my parents the bad news, and then my dad had a suggestion. He had a female client whose husband was a high-ranking navy official, believed to be an admiral, and my dad made an appeal to his client to have her husband intercede so that I could have my eyes retested. The admiral agreed to do so because he felt that it was the patriotic thing to do at that time. It took several months for them to give me a reexamination. They reluctantly retested my vision and were absolutely astounded over the positive results. The eye charts, the depth perception tests, and all of the other related eye exams were utilized. They were still not convinced and felt that perhaps I had memorized the charts so they brought out a complete set of new eye exams. I had no problem with any of them, and they were bewildered and amazed over the fact that now my vision met all of the standards for the position of a navy pilot. All of these procedures delayed my entry into the US Navy as a V-5 cadet by about six months in 1942.

I was eventually sworn in as a naval cadet and for the next twelve months was subjected to long hours of study and training, strenuous periods of physical activity and conditioning, and countless hours of flying, both day and night. I received training at Williams College in Williamstown, Massachusetts; Lenoir Rhyne College in Hickory, North Carolina; the Naval Air Station, Millington, Tennessee; University of Georgia, Athens, Georgia. I finally earned my wings and graduated from the Naval Air Station at Pensacola, Florida, with the rank of ensign. I opted to be a carrier-based fighter pilot as opposed to a land-based pilot. For the remainder of the war, I primarily flew the Grumman Wildcat fighter plane, which was similar to the aircraft flown by the late Lieutenant Commander Edward "Butch" O'Hare, after whom Chicago O'Hare Airport was named in his memory. Lieutenant Commander O'Hare was the first US Navy ace and a Medal of Honor recipient. I flew from small escort carriers, which were about half the size of a regular aircraft carrier. I served on the USS *Guadalcanal,* CVE 60, and the USS *Takanis Bay,* CVE 89. The Wildcat was ideal for small escort carriers where its short takeoffs and landings allowed it to operate where larger planes would have difficulty. Landing on these small escort carriers during the daytime did not pose too much of a problem; however, night landings on pitching decks of carriers were more of a challenge than I cared to experience and at times darn right scary. I was assigned to Air Group 7 in the Pacific Theater during the balance of the war and was greatly relieved and overjoyed when the war came to an end in 1945, thanks to President Truman.

Vince Inserra in cockpit of the Grumman Wildcat fighter plane.

Vince Inserra (right) on board battleship USS Missouri after the official Japanese surrender documents were signed aboard the battleship on September 2, 1945

Along the way, a tragic accident occurred to my roommate Harry Kaufman that I will never forget. He was a fine young man, twenty-two years of age, from the Washington DC area, and was a good friend. He and I trained together as fighter pilots, and we had engaged in simulated "dogfights" together. He always seemed to have the advantage over me. He was a very daring and aggressive pilot who took considerable chances. One day during a bombing exercise, Kaufman was a little late in pulling out of his dive and flew into the side of a mountain. He was killed instantly. We previously signed up to look after each other in the event of a fatality, and little did we realize that it would become a reality. I had the painful responsibility of escorting his remains back to his home by train. It was truly a sad experience to deliver his body to his sister, Mrs. Lynn Goldenberg, and family in Washington DC. I attended the memorial service and then returned to my air group unit.

Photo of Harry "Sonny" Kaufman

I served almost four years as a naval aviator and was discharged in September 1946 and attained the rank of lieutenant. I remained in the naval reserve for eleven years and continued to fly on weekends at the Naval Air Station at Squantum, Massachusetts. I was assigned to a Naval Reserve Torpedo Squadron and primarily flew the Grumman TBM Torpedo Avenger. This plane was similar to the plane flown by George Bush Sr. when he was shot down in the Pacific. I also volunteered to ferry navy aircraft from the naval station at Norfolk, Virginia, to an aircraft reconditioning center on the West Coast whenever the need would arise. I would then fly back a recently rehabbed aircraft to Norfolk. This allowed me to earn a few dollars as I was preparing to enter Boston College in January of 1947 under the GI Bill. I attended Boston College and graduated with a degree in business administration.

While in the naval reserve, I had occasion to travel on weekends to the summer resort town of Hyannis in Cape Cod, Massachusetts. It was at this time that I met a very charming young lady by the name of Janet DesRosiers, who at that time was the secretary of Joseph Kennedy Sr., the former ambassador to the United Kingdom. Ms. DesRosiers would spend the summer months at Hyannis Port with the Kennedys and then spend the winter months with them at their compound in Palm Beach, Florida. On one occasion, I took a training flight in a Torpedo bomber to the Naval Air Station at Opa-Locka, Florida, rented a car, and called on Ms. DesRosiers at the Kennedy residence and took her out to dinner. Our relationship never got off the ground because she was geographically inaccessible. She worked for Joseph Kennedy Sr. for about nine years. She then served as a secretary to President-elect John F. Kennedy and later became known as Janet Fontaine. Our paths never crossed again. Little did I realize at that time that I would eventually become acquainted with Bobby Kennedy and his family during my career in the FBI.

FBI CAREER BEGINS

Following college, I was single and still looking for adventure. I then applied for a position with the FBI in Boston. Having passed my written and physical exams as well as my background investigation, I eventually received a letter signed by Director J. Edgar Hoover, granting me a probationary appointment as a special agent employee in the FBI at an annual salary of $5,000. I was ecstatic over the news. I was instructed to report to the old post office building in Washington DC on April 23, 1951. My training period would last for eight weeks, six days a week, at Washington DC and at the FBI Academy at Quantico, Virginia. Training throughout the eight weeks was intense. The physical requirements and conditioning were demanding and could be disqualifying. The firearm's training was challenging but enjoyable. Daily training classes required considerable study periods every night in an attempt to assimilate all of the detailed work required by the FBI. Our new agent's class consisted of about thirty-five members. Several of the new agents failed to make the grade. Upon graduation, there was a great sigh of relief, and it was time for a celebration. We all attended an informal graduation dinner along with our class counselors at the famous Benny Bortnick's Restaurant in Washington DC. Benny Bortnick was a famous boxer, wrestler, and restaurateur personality and was one of the most respected athletes in the DC area at that time. The following is a photograph taken of the new agent's graduation class #26 at the conclusion of our training period as we impatiently waited for the news of our new assignments to our respective field divisions as first office FBI agents.

New Agents Class #26 at Benny Bortnick's Restaurant

Seated in the second row, second from the left, was Agent Kenneth Bounds who was my roommate during the training session. Kenny and I became good friends. He was a large person with an incredible physique. He played basketball and football at the University of Missouri and was an outstanding athlete. I had the good fortune or misfortune of having Kenny as my defensive tactics partner, and there was no way that I was going to "dominate the situation" with Kenny as my opponent; still it was fun trying. He was truly a gentle giant when he had to be. Kenny Bounds was one of the agents selected to escort James Earl Ray, the convicted assassin of civil rights leader Dr. Martin Luther King Jr., back to the United States from London, England. Kenny ended his career as a physical training instructor at the new FBI Academy in Quantico, Virginia. Kenny Bounds passed away in 2010. He was one of the finest agents ever to be associated with the FBI during his twenty-three-year tenure.

CHICAGO ASSIGNMENT

The transfer orders arrived dated June 1, 1951, and I found myself being transferred to the Chicago Division of the FBI as a first office agent. I was somewhat disappointed to be assigned to Chicago because I was hoping for an assignment to a warmer climate or possibly return to the area of my home in Boston. Three other agents from my training class were also transferred to the Chicago office; and they were Thomas G. Forsythe III, John W. Miller, and Edward Charbonneau. Since we were all single agents, the four of us rented a two-bedroom apartment at the Ridgeview Hotel in Evanston, Illinois, so that our commute to Chicago would not be a long one; and our living expenses would be minimal. In 1951, the Chicago FBI office was located at 105 W. Adams Street. I was delighted to learn that I would be assigned to a major criminal squad supervised by Wayne Murphy. This criminal squad was the forerunner of the C-1 squad that I would eventually supervise some twelve years later. I was impressed with the huge amount of talent and experience on this squad and everyone's willingness to help out a newly assigned first office agent. My mentor and partner was Lenard Wolf, a highly respected and experienced agent who was a graduate of Purdue University. Agent Wolf taught me well, and my future progress in the FBI can be attributed to his patience and guidance.

One of the major cases that I recall participating in at that time was the theft of an interstate trailer load of 40,000 pounds of US prime beef taken from a Chicago truck terminal. The case agent was David Starner, an experienced and thorough investigator who was originally from Ohio. Investigation centered on several suspects known to have been involved in this type of hijacking activity in the past, and surveillances were instituted at various suspect farms in the western suburbs of Chicago. The trailer was ultimately located, and a search warrant was successful in recovering the entire load of beef. The owner of the farm, Silvio Blondi, was arrested for the possession of stolen property. It was interesting to learn that Silvio Blondi had been previously arrested during the horse meat scandal in Chicago in the early1950s. When he was taken before the judge to make bond, the judge set his bond at $100,000. Upon hearing the amount of the bond, Silvio cried out in a loud voice and said, "Judge, whaddya think I ground up War Admiral or something?" The judge, who apparently had a sense of humor, could not contain himself and immediately released Silvio on his own recognizance. I guess it pays to speak up.

My experience on this major criminal case squad was invaluable and prepared me well for my bureau career ahead. As I was nearing the end of my assignment in Chicago, I took my first vacation and returned to my home in Boston for a brief visit with my parents. While at my family home, I received an urgent call from the secretary of the SAC of the Boston FBI office. She told me that SAC Don Hostetter wanted to see me at his office as soon as possible on an urgent matter. She did not go into any detail, but I was burning with curiosity and overwhelmed by the nature of the call. What could be so important that could not wait until I returned to the Chicago office in a few days?

I reported to the Boston FBI office the following morning as instructed and met with SAC Hostetter in his office. He told me that a very serious situation had come up, and he needed to talk to me confidentially. I told him I would be happy to cooperate in any way possible. He told me that the FBI and local authorities recently arrested a gang of thieves who had stolen a large shipment of shoes. These thieves suspected that someone in their gang was an informant who was responsible for their arrest and the prompt recovery of the stolen shipment. One of the thieves told the gang that he had a cousin in the FBI and that he would contact his cousin and determine the identity of the informant. Because the informant was actually at this meeting, he was greatly concerned for his own safety and reported this information to the authorities and to the FBI. The name of the subject, who had a cousin in the FBI, was Joseph Puzzangara Jr. I immediately acknowledged that Joseph Puzzangara Jr. (currently deceased) was my cousin and that he was the son of my father's sister. I admitted that I saw Joe Jr. occasionally at family gatherings; however, I had absolutely no association or any personal dealings with him. I told the SAC that I was well aware that Joe Jr. had a criminal record and had served time in prison for a series of thefts. I reminded the SAC that I had no control over the behavior of any of my relatives. I assured SAC Hostetter that there was absolutely no chance that Joe Jr. would ever contact me in this matter because he knew that I did not approve of his lifestyle and I would never compromise my sacred oath of office. SAC Hostetter assured me that this situation would have no bearing on my career in the FBI and that the matter was closed. Needless to say, my cousin never attempted to contact me during my FBI career.

On a more pleasant note, it was during my first office in Chicago that I was about to meet my future wife with whom I would spend more than sixty years of wedded bliss.

On a Sunday morning, I attended the twelve o'clock Mass at St. Nicholas Catholic Church in Evanston, Illinois, which was only one block from my residence. As Mass began, a young lady attempted to enter my pew. At first I was somewhat annoyed because I did not feel there was sufficient room in the pew for anyone else; however, upon seeing this attractive young lady, I made sure there was enough room for her to sit next to me. After Mass, we left church together, and I found myself walking in the same direction behind her. Neither one of us had driven a car to church. I took note of the apartment building in which she entered. The following Sunday, I wondered if she would be attending the twelve o'clock Mass at St. Nicholas, and my curiosity was rewarded. Out of the apartment building, she came; and as she entered the church, Father Long was greeting the parishioners. He called out, "Good morning, Marilyn." I now knew the first name of this young lady and the address where she lived. By using a public reverse address directory, I was able to determine the name and phone number of the young lady in question whose name was Marilyn Traweek at that address. Of course, my intentions were strictly honorable.

The following week, I phoned her and identified myself as a newcomer in town and a good friend of Father Long from St. Nicholas Church. I added that Father Long had suggested that I call her. That pretext sounded a bit corny, but it was the best I could think of at that time. At first she found it hard to believe what I had just said, but when I told her she could call Father Long and verify the information, she eventually accepted my invitation to dinner. On our first date, we dined at Ivanhoe's, a unique restaurant with all of its catacombs, at 3000 N. Clark Street in Chicago. We had an enjoyable time, and Marilyn wanted to call Father Long and thank him for the referral, but I convinced her it was not necessary. I was greatly relieved that she did not follow through with Father Long. We continued to date for several months, and then it happened. Our relationship was temporarily interrupted when on April 17, 1952, I received notice of my FBI transfer from Chicago to the Savannah, Georgia, FBI office. We said our goodbyes and promised to keep in touch with each other, not knowing what the future had in store for us.

SAVANNAH ASSIGNMENT

The Savannah Division was completely different from my previous Chicago assignment. I stayed only one night in Savannah and was quickly dispatched the next day and transferred to their resident office in Aiken, South Carolina. I was assigned there primarily to handle a huge volume of applicant background checks on persons seeking employment at the Savannah River Site, a proposed nuclear facility, located in the vicinity of Aiken, South Carolina. Thousands of employee background applications had to be processed with short deadlines, and we did not have the benefit of any stenographers to take dictation. We had to type up our own investigative reports because Dictaphones were in short supply.

Aiken was also considered to be the polo grounds of the south where J. Strom Thurmond, former governor and later senator of South Carolina, resided nearby. Governor Thurmond was kind enough to allow the agents to use his permanent parking space on the polo grounds, when it was not in use on Sundays, to observe the polo matches in Aiken. About eight months later, I was transferred back to Savannah, which was much more enjoyable of an assignment. Savannah and all of its historical charm and beauty and sandy beaches was a pleasant change. I handled primarily road-trip cases in southern Georgia and southeastern South Carolina. Whenever I traveled to Claxton, Georgia, a small town west of Savannah, I would always be asked if I knew Cartha "Deke" De Loach, the third most senior man to Director Hoover in the FBI. Claxton was the birthplace of Mr. De Loach, and the entire populace was extremely proud of their local FBI hero. Also, Hilton Head, South Carolina, which was covered by the Savannah Division, was in its infancy. Access to the island at that time was primarily by ferry. The island was sparsely populated with indigent residents and shanties. The local postmaster told us that we should consider investing in property on the island because developers from up north were going to transform the island. And the postmaster was certainly right with his prediction. Today Hilton Head, South Carolina, is one of the finest island resort towns on the East Coast. Hilton Head had also been the residence of former FBI Deputy Director Cartha "Deke" De Loach (deceased) since his retirement from the FBI in 1970. Mr. De Loach had been one of the most respected and admired FBI officials ever to have served during Mr. Hoover's administration.

While in Savannah, I received a surprise visit from my Evanston, Illinois, girlfriend Marilyn Traweek. It appeared that our romance was waning because of our being separated for almost a year, and we needed to have an understanding about our relationship, especially because I was in a constant travel status. Following a serious discussion, we decided to get married and set our wedding date for May 23, 1953, in Evanston, Illinois. I flew back to Chicago several days before the wedding and stayed at the Ridgeview Hotel where I had resided as a new agent. It was a small but nice wedding, and of course, it took place at St. Nicholas Church where we originally encountered each other. The day after the wedding, we loaded Marilyn's small black 1946 Chevrolet with all of her belongings and drove to Sea Island, Georgia, for our honeymoon. We said our prayers before departing not only because of the uncertainty of our journey but also because of the questionable condition of Marilyn's car. We finally arrived safely at "The Cloister," a luxurious five-star resort hotel that catered to honeymoon couples in Sea Island, Georgia. Following a week of sumptuous accommodations and an incredible environment, we returned to Savannah to face the reality of our barren one-room efficiency apartment at the Drayton Arms, which had absolutely no furniture and very few furnishings. We used an ironing board for a table and suitcases for chairs and borrowed a cot to sleep on. We eventually were able to furnish this small apartment with all of our basic needs and to our complete satisfaction and comfort.

One man who made a lasting impression on me during my assignment in Savannah was Joseph D. Purvis, not to be confused with Melvin Purvis of John Dillinger fame. He had been the SAC in four field divisions, namely Norfolk, Richmond, Washington DC, and Savannah. He was transferred to his home in Savannah because of a personal family hardship. We became close friends, and Joe Purvis was always more than willing to help a younger agent with advice and guidance. He was an agent's agent, and I relied upon his sound judgment when difficult decisions had to be made. Joe Purvis was my inspiration in Savannah, and I will always cherish the memories of our friendship. Joe Purvis (now deceased) was a thirty-two-year veteran of the FBI with an incredible career.

About seven months later in December 1953, immediately following Christmas, I was again transferred to the FBI resident office in Augusta, Georgia, which was within the jurisdiction of the Savannah Division. Augusta was a very lovely town with which I was familiar because it was located only about fifteen miles from Aiken, South Carolina, where I was previously assigned. Of course, Augusta is world renowned as the home of the Augusta National Golf Club where the annual Masters Golf Tournament takes place. In 1954, I had the good fortune and distinct pleasure of having been assigned to an investigative matter at the Masters Golf Tournament. Having resolved the FBI investigative matter, I was able to catch a glimpse of the final golf match between golf greats Ben Hogan and Sam Snead. A sudden death playoff took place the following day, with Snead beating Hogan in an exciting finish. My assignment in Augusta was cut short because I received another transfer to New York City only eight months later.

New York City Assignment

My wife and I were disappointed to leave the Savannah area because we thoroughly enjoyed the people and the surroundings. She had enjoyed playing the role of being a "southern belle." My greatest concern, however, was that we were leaving a relatively inexpensive cost of living state and moving to New York City where living expenses and taxes were considerably higher. It was tantamount to taking a huge reduction in salary. At that time, the FBI did not allow for cost of living increases. We found a small apartment in Fort Lee, New Jersey, thanks to the assistance of SA William F. Beane, who later became SAC of the New York office. This location allowed me quick access to New York City via the George Washington Bridge and all of its toll charges.

I was assigned to a security squad that involved daily surveillances of Soviet Satellite Nationals, primarily the Yugoslavs, who were suspected of spying for their country while posing as delegates to the United Nations. The surveillances were 24/7, and it was tedious work trying to maintain coverage of these individuals who were frequently utilizing the crowded public subway systems in New York as well as driving throughout all of the congested boroughs of New York City. This type of work lasted for about two and a half years, and there was no end in sight. My daily surveillance partners were agents Hugh Hart and Dino Simonini, two fine agents. We were virtually joined at the hip in the same car on a daily basis for several years. It was called "the bucket squad."

I also tried out for the New York Office fast-pitch softball team, which was affiliated with the Banker's League in New York City, and I qualified to play the position of shortstop for two seasons. If needed, I would fill in occasionally as catcher. In 1956, the New York FBI team took first place in the league, and the following is a picture of the championship team in uniform. New York SAC Kelly later bestowed the winning trophy to team captain Bob Johnson.

Row 1, left to right: Dick Stromme, Bob Johnson, John Hawken.

Row 2: Reesie Timmons, Jim Dewhirst, Vince Inserra, Don Koman, Emil Hracek.

Row 3: Ed Bergholz, Courtney Gerrish, Frank Leonard, Shelby Smith, Tom Hanrahan.

Photo of NYO Championship Softball Team

It was during this period that our first daughter, Christine, was born in Teaneck, New Jersey. My work involved long hours at night and on weekends; and the commute from Fort Lee, New Jersey, to New York City and back, made for an even longer day. I found myself spending less time with my family, and the high cost of living began to weigh heavily upon me so that I began to consider leaving the FBI and the New York area. Routine transfers out of the New York office were unheard of, and it was rumored that an agent had to lose his credentials at least twice before he would receive a disciplinary transfer out of New York. I came very close to resigning from the FBI when all of a sudden my situation took an unexpected turn, and the unintended consequences came as a complete and pleasant surprise.

Apparently, the Yugoslav Delegation became aware of the 24/7 FBI surveillances and lodged a formal complaint with FBI headquarters. The New York Office (NYO) was asked to respond to the complaint, and the NYO reported that the Yugoslav complaint was unfounded. The Yugoslav officials then provided FBI headquarters with a list of NY license plate numbers of the cars allegedly involved in the surveillances. The bureau then asked the NYO if the license numbers were those of FBI vehicles. The NYO had to reverse their position and admit that those cars did in fact belong to the FBI. As expected, the bureau was placed in an embarrassing situation and immediately dispatched Inspector B. C. Brown and his staff of agents to the NYO to investigate the entire matter. Sworn statements were taken from all the agents and supervisory personnel involved in this matter. Disciplinary action followed where appropriate, and the inspection staff concluded that the NYO had a surplus of twenty-five agents and recommended they be transferred to the Chicago office, which was in need of additional personnel.

RETURN TO CHICAGO

As luck would have it, I was one of the agents who received a routine transfer on February 18, 1957, from New York City to the Chicago Division, which is where my career in the FBI began in 1951. Needless to say, my wife was simply overjoyed to return to her home and to all of her family and friends. The Chicago FBI office was now located at 212 W. Monroe Street. The SAC was Don Hostetter, whom I met in Boston during the time he interviewed me regarding my wayward cousin. He assigned me to the C-1 squad, which was the most desirable criminal squad in the Chicago Division, supervised by Ross Spencer. I finally found my niche in the FBI on the C-1 squad and was eventually assigned to the Top Hoodlum Program in 1957.

TOP HOODLUM PROGRAM TAKES FLIGHT

The ten C-1 agents assigned to the Top Hoodlum Program immediately began reviewing pertinent intelligence files in the Chicago Division to determine the ten most deserving Chicago hoodlums to be included in this program. The review included the General Intelligence Information File, which contained volumes of newspaper clippings of criminal activities in the Chicago area as well as the organized crime intelligence file known as the "Reactivation of the Capone Gang" (CAPGA). Both were dormant intelligence files, copies of which had been routinely disseminated to FBI headquarters in the past. This new venture by a handful of FBI agents into the unchartered waters of Chicago's most powerful empire of organized crime was an enormous undertaking in view of the absence of any specific federal violation that was within the jurisdiction of the FBI. The C-1 agents selected were actually pioneers in unfamiliar territory because organized crime, with all of its illegal gambling, murders, loan-sharking, narcotics, extortion, racketeering, corruption, and intimidation, were primarily at the time within the jurisdiction and responsibility of local and state authorities. The FBI had very little federal authority or federal statutes with which to investigate and prosecute members of organized crime.

The following ten top hoodlums were selected for investigation under the anti-racketeering statute because these hoodlums were presumed to be in violation of the Federal Hobbs Act extortion statute, which required criminal interference with interstate commerce. The agents listed below were assigned to these hoodlums as follows:

1. **Salvatore "Momo" Giancana,** a.k.a. Sam Giancana, was the undisputed boss of the Chicago mob and was originally assigned to SA James J. Files who was transferred a year later. The case was reassigned to SA Frank Mellott and then to SA Ralph Hill who had the case for several years until his transfer to FBI headquarters. The Giancana case was then assigned to SA Marshall Rutland, who along with SA Hill were the principal case agents throughout the turbulent days leading up to the prosecution of Giancana during the

1960s. Upon Rutland's transfer to the bureau, the case was reassigned to William F. Roemer Jr. Upon Roemer's departure from the C-1 squad, SA William Thurman was the case agent, assisted by SA James York, leading up to the time of Giancana's murder in 1975. SAs Ralph Hill, Marshall Rutland, and William F. Roemer Jr. are all deceased. Their accomplishments and contributions to this program were enormous and should never be overlooked or forgotten.

2. **Anthony J. Accardo,** a powerful former boss of the Chicago mob, was assigned to SA John W. Roberts who was the case agent throughout the entire period of the Top Hoodlum Program. SA Roberts was responsible for developing volumes of intelligence information which allowed the Chicago office to penetrate the criminal activities of Accardo and his Chicago mobsters.

3. **Ralph Pierce,** a Chicago south side gambling boss, was assigned to SA Raymond Stoelting. Following his transfer, the case was reassigned to SA William F. Roemer Jr.

4. **Gus Alex,** a Chicago loop boss, was assigned to SA Elliott Anderson who later left the bureau, at which time the case was reassigned to SA Roemer. SAs Robert Cook and John Parish also took over the Alex case at a later date.

5. **Murray "The Camel" Humphreys**, the mob's political fixer, was assigned to SA Lester Esarey, who was later transferred, and the case was reassigned to William F. Roemer Jr. Roemer was one of the agents who contributed to the overall success of the C-1 squad and was responsible for assisting in the development of some of our key electronic sources of information that led to the development of critical intelligence information against the Chicago mob.

6. **Fiore "Fifi" Buccieri**, a Chicago West Side boss and enforcer, was assigned to SA Lenard Wolf, who partnered throughout the Top Hoodlum Program with SAs Harold K. Johnson, Eugene Sather, and George Perkins. These agents were highly successful in penetrating and curtailing the activities of Buccieri and his mob associates.

Lenard Wolf was originally my mentor and partner as a new agent and was one of the senior members of the C-1 squad. He was the most prolific fugitive hunter in the Chicago Division, having participated in the arrest of four of the FBI's "Ten Most Wanted Fugitives," a program that began in the 1950s. Very few agents have been involved in a single arrest of a Top Ten fugitive let alone multiple captures under this program of bringing badly wanted fugitives to justice. Lenard Wolf's accomplishments in this program were unprecedented. He was a worthy and welcomed addition to the Top Hoodlum Program.

7. **Ross Prio,** true name Rosario Priolo, was a Chicago North Side boss and was assigned to SA Vincent L. Inserra.

8. **Leonard Patrick** was a Chicago North Side gambling boss and enforcer who was assigned to SA Roy Ragsdale, who was later transferred, and the case was reassigned to SA Vincent L. Inserra.

9. **Marshall Caifano** was the mob's Las Vegas representative and mob enforcer. He was assigned to SA Frank Matthys, one of the senior members of the Top Hoodlum Program, who was most familiar with the Chicago hoodlums and their activities. SA Matthys was always willing to assist the agents in this new venture. Matthys retired from the bureau a short time later and became chief special agent for the Elgin, Joliet, and Eastern Railroad. The case was then reassigned to SA Richard Cavanagh.

10. **Frank La Porte** was the Chicago far south-side gambling boss and was assigned to SA Kenneth Groeper in the Chicago Heights, Illinois, resident agency. This case was later reassigned to SA Thomas Parrish.

During the first year, C-1 agents wrote detailed background reports on these subjects and their past activities. They conducted periodic physical surveillances in an attempt to identify hoodlum contacts and meeting places that could potentially be a source of information regarding the current activities of their subject. This was about the time of the McClellan Senate Rackets Committee Hearings in Washington DC, inquiring into labor racketeering. Senator McClellan was the chairman, then Senator John F. Kennedy also participated, and Robert F. Kennedy was chief counsel along with others. The FBI was requested to serve subpoenas on various leading hoodlums in the United States, including Chicago. Once we began serving subpoenas, the mobsters became aware of these hearings, and they made themselves scarce to avoid being served. It gave the agents a good opportunity to familiarize themselves with these hoodlums, their hangouts, and their associates. As expected, all of the hoodlums who appeared before the Rackets Committee invoked the Fifth Amendment. It became abundantly clear that federal law at that time provided very few tools or legislation for the US government to combat organized crime on a national basis. These hearings would eventually result in the enactment of new federal laws designed to combat organized crime.

During the early stages of the program, FBI headquarters dispatched an urgent communication to the Chicago Division, entitled "The Mafia," and they wanted to know what steps the Chicago office was going to take to penetrate it. A new case was opened and assigned to me. I was somewhat baffled by this request because the Chicago FBI office had never used the term "Mafia" when referring to the Chicago mob or the Chicago crime syndicate. It did not apply to the Chicago mob, and I considered the use of the name inappropriate and misleading because it disparaged the Italian American community to refer to all mobsters as Mafia. The Chicago mob was more commonly referred to as "the Outfit" or "the Crime Syndicate." The term Mafia is a misnomer that dates back to the early twentieth century, when some black-hand extortionists from Sicily came to the shores of the United States. The name was perpetuated during the Prohibition era in Chicago and the United States. Then in 1963, Joe Valachi, a foot soldier from the ranks of the Vito Genovese family of organized crime in New York, testified before the McClellan Committee and documented the existence of the Italian organized crime families in New York as "La Cosa Nostra" (LCN), which literally translates into "Our Thing" or "Our Cause." Thus, the use of the name La Cosa Nostra became a household name for organized crime throughout the United States. Valachi at that time emphatically stated that the LCN was not known as the Mafia.

The Chicago mob, however, had many prominent members who were not Italian, let alone "Mafia." For example, Gus Alex, Gus Zapas, and George Bravos were Greek; Edward Vogel, Lenny Patrick, and Dave Yaras were Jewish; Ralph Pierce was English; Murray "The Camel" Humphreys was Scottish; Ken Eto was Japanese; and so on. It was recognized, however, that the control and the core of the Chicago mob had always been Italian. So my response to the request of FBI headquarters regarding "the Mafia" was brief and to the point. I told them that as soon as I established the existence of the Mafia operating in Chicago, then I would set forth my plans to penetrate this organization. I was stalling for time. This response seemed to satisfy them temporarily. I prefer calling it the Chicago mob, the Chicago outfit, or the Chicago Crime Syndicate, but certainly not "the Mafia", which is historically incorrect. The Chicago mob is referred to by its members as "the Outfit," and members who are "made" are referred to as "Outfit Men."

INTELLIGENCE UNIT OF THE CHICAGO POLICE DEPARTMENT

The C-1 squad had a need to establish contact with a trustworthy element of the Chicago Police Department because it was readily apparent that organized crime could not flourish without the support of widespread police and political corruption. Organized crime had its tentacles in all walks of life, including the police departments, the political arena, and in all levels of city, county, state, and federal government.

There was a small but effective Chicago police Intelligence Unit called Scotland Yard. The person in charge was Joseph Morris, and his number one assistant was Bill Duffy. Scotland Yard was temporarily disbanded when it was discovered that they had wiretapped a bookmaker in a Chicago loop hotel that had been used by the Democratic Party. Later when Joe Morris became deputy superintendent of the Chicago Police Department, the unit was reinstated and Bill Duffy became commander of the Intelligence Unit. Morris and Duffy had the reputation of being two of the most reputable and completely trustworthy men on the police force. Various politicians and police officials had often tried to neutralize or discredit Bill Duffy and his Intelligence Unit without too much success. Duffy and his men had the complete backing and support of the agents of C-1 squad. We worked very closely with the Intelligence Unit over the years and always came to their defense whenever possible. Unfortunately, on February 27, 1968, Superintendent James B. Conlisk, Chicago Police Department, transferred Captain William J. Duffy from the Intelligence Unit to the Albany Park District as watch commander. There was little that we could do about Captain Duffy, but we continued to work closely with the men of the Intelligence Unit. Because of the relatively large size of their Intelligence Unit, they had the manpower to cover numerous mob functions and were generous in cooperating and sharing their intelligence information with the FBI. We held many joint conferences and shared the findings of our investigations. It was like having a task force long before task forces became popular. We also used the Intelligence Unit to conduct local gambling raids over the years based on FBI affidavits in Chicago, which greatly disrupted the mob's gambling operation. Gambling was their number one source of income. We generally avoided contact with the officers of the Vice Control Division of the Chicago Police Department, who had primary jurisdiction over local gambling, vice, and prostitution. We found that there were some from that unit who were of questionable character and some who had direct links to organized crime.

Some of the Intelligence Unit officers that had worked for Commander Bill Duffy over the years that had the complete trust of the C-1 squad were Frank Nash, Robert Sheehan, Michael O'Donnell, Lee Gerhke, John Zitek, Don Herion, Don Lappe, Ed Berry, Joseph DeLopez, Wayne Johnson, Jerry Gladden, Lou Cantone, Matt Rodriguez, and many others too numerous to mention. Upon retirement from the Chicago Police Department, several of these officers became chiefs of police of neighboring communities. Matt Rodriguez served as superintendent of the Chicago Police Department from 1992 to 1997. All had contributed immeasurably in helping the FBI wage war against the Chicago mob and are deserving of our sincere gratitude and thanks.

ALBERT D. MEHEGAN, LEGENDARY FBI AGENT

D uring August of 1962, the following photograph was taken of the members of the Chicago office of the FBI after having completed a religious weekend retreat at the Villa Redeemer Facility in Glenview, Illinois.

Photo of Chicago Members of the FBI at the Villa Redeemer Facility

Row 1: (l to r) Jack McDonough, Dick Hosteny, Bill Berwanger, Jack Quinlan, and Albert D. Mehegan. Row 2: Paul Grieber, Joe Travers, Jack Matthews, and Hugh Hart. Row 3: Frank Kahl, Jim Broder, Maurie White, and Frank Matthys. Row 4: Ray Hogan, Gene Geis, Jack Whelan, Retreat Director Peter Sattler, and Vince Inserra.

The senior member of this group was Albert D. Mehegan, a legendary FBI agent who is pictured in the lower right-hand corner of the photo. Mr. Mehegan was the longest-serving agent in the history of the FBI, who predated the late and legendary FBI Director J. Edgar Hoover. Mr. Mehegan graduated from Purdue University and earned letters in baseball and football. He was one of the outstanding halfbacks in Purdue football history. He joined the FBI's predecessor agency, the Bureau of Investigation, in 1922 when Warren G. Harding was president. Special agents were not as yet permitted to carry firearms. In 1924, the agency became known as the Federal Bureau of Investigation when Mr. Hoover became director. Mr. Mehegan retired in 1975 with fifty-three years of active service. No one will ever exceed that record of service with the FBI. He began his career by tracking down bootleggers and cartage thieves, and while serving in the Chicago office for a period of forty-three years, his specialty was investigating interstate thefts from railroad and trucking lines. He was the ultimate authority in his field and served as the FBI liaison agent with trucking and railroad security police. Mr. Mehegan was a man of faith and integrity, who passed away in 1983 at the age of ninety-five. He will never be forgotten by his many admirers for his unprecedented dedication and devotion to the FBI as well as for his many contributions to the agents of the C-1 squad.

CELANO CUSTOM TAILOR SHOP: SURVEILLANCE ACTIVITY

In late1958, C-1 agents John Roberts, Bill Roemer, Ralph Hill, Marshall Rutland, and I participated in joint physical surveillances of several of the top leaders of the Chicago mob in an effort to determine their prime meeting places. These surveillances had to be discreet so that the subjects in question would not deviate from conducting their regular activities. It was at a time when the bureau was encouraging agents on the Top Hoodlum Program to consider the use of microphone surveillances at key meeting places so that vital intelligence information could be developed. Once a meeting location had been determined, authority from the SAC of the Chicago FBI office had to be obtained as well as approval from FBI headquarters who would in turn receive the approval of the US Department of Justice prior to the use of any eavesdropping devices. It was not a requirement at that time to obtain a court order for microphone coverage.

Surveillance of several key Chicago mobsters disclosed that they were occasionally entering the rear of a commercial building separately at 620 N. Michigan Avenue in Chicago. It was not known at that time which one of the many offices in the building they were frequenting, the identity of the person visited, or the purpose of the visit. An office lookout was established across the street so that a pattern of activity could be established without arousing suspicion. It became readily apparently that these prominent hoodlums were meeting on a regular basis in a private conference room on the second floor at the Celano Custom Tailor Shop. It was also determined that James Celano, the owner of the tailor shop, was a close associate of these hoodlums and would not likely cooperate with the FBI. Also, James Celano was the brother of Louis Celano, the business agent for Local 134 of the IBEW, who also had hoodlum affiliations.

This location appeared to be an excellent meeting place for microphone surveillance. Approval was granted to the Chicago Division by bureau headquarters to proceed with such coverage. This was a delicate operation, because C-1 agents had to gain access to the building and to the locked premises of the tailor shop surreptitiously during the late night and early morning hours, without the knowledge of the tenant(s) and the police. The building was located on Michigan Avenue in the highly visible and fashionable section of Chicago, known as the "Magnificent Mile," which required many police and security patrols during all hours of the night.

During one of our entries, we encountered one small unexpected problem that could have derailed our mission. One of our sound technicians, whose nickname was "Moose," while in the crawl space of the second floor, accidentally stepped through the ceiling tile of the first floor restaurant. Our project was placed on hold until repairs could be made to the ceiling tile without alerting the tenants, especially the tailor shop. The repairs were made without incident. The installation was finally completed after four or five covert entries. The next problem we encountered was that the microphone was placed too close to a radiator, which was drowning out the conversations with its hissing sound. This required an additional entry to relocate the microphone and correct the problem. The source became operational during the summer of 1959 and was given the code name of "Little Al," an oblique reference to the late Al Capone. The mobsters also had their own code name for this meeting place, and that was "Schneider," which in German means "tailor."

Our persistent efforts were immensely rewarded. What a wealth of criminal intelligence information was forthcoming from this confidential source, which remained in existence for a period of about six years. Leaders of the Chicago mob would meet at this location several times a week in the morning in this conference room and discuss the affairs of organized crime. It was virtually their unofficial headquarters. We struck pay dirt on our very first try. We had to be very circumspect with the information obtained so that our source would not be compromised as we monitored the daily pulse and activities of the Chicago mob. This information could not be used in a court of law for purposes of prosecution but was merely obtained for criminal intelligence purposes to keep abreast of the activities of organized crime.

Hoodlum leaders who were frequent visitors as well as occasional visitors to this source were Murray "The Camel" Humphreys, Gus Alex, Ross Prio, Anthony Accardo, Sam Giancana, Frank "Strongy" Ferraro, Ralph Pierce, Les Kruse, Frank LaPorte, politicians, and a host of others. This group included at least seven of our original ten top hoodlums who were targets under the Top Hoodlum Program. Thanks to this source, we were able to identify the Chicago hoodlum hierarchy, their lieutenants and underlings, their daily activities, their gamblers and gambling interests, their police and political contacts, their labor union affiliations, their Las Vegas investments and contacts, their travel plans, their financial and business dealings, their associates, and much more.

Probably the most significant piece of intelligence information that was received several months after the installation of this source had to do with the existence of "the Commission," a national ruling body, or board of directors, comprised of the most powerful bosses of the major crime families in the United States. This information was received in a conversation between Sam Giancana, boss of the Chicago crime family, and Anthony J. Accardo, who preceded Giancana as boss in Chicago. "The Commission," which varied in number from nine to twelve members, was identified as follows during this conference and included the five New York crime families:

Joseph Bonanno, New York
Carlo Gambino, New York
Joseph Profaci, New York
Vito Genovese, New York
Tommy Luchese, New York
Joseph Zerilli, Detroit
Raymond Patriaca, Boston
Steve Maggadino, Buffalo
John La Rocca, Pittsburgh
John Scalish, Cleveland
Sam Giancana, Chicago

When FBI headquarters was notified of the existence of a "National Commission" and its purpose of resolving disputes between crime families on a national basis, they did not believe us and requested a copy of the tape so that they could listen to the tape and decide for themselves. About two years later, they confirmed what we had told them, and similar information was received by the Philadelphia office as further confirmation. Then in 1962, Joseph Valachi, while serving time in a federal penitentiary for a narcotics conviction, learned that he was marked for death as an informer and decided to turn against his hoodlum confederates. In 1963, Joseph Valachi testified under oath and admitted to being a foot soldier in the Vito Genovese New York crime family. He gave further evidence and documentation of a National Crime Syndicate by referring to the Italian crime families in New York and elsewhere as being part of La Cosa Nostra (LCN). Valachi admitted to having been a member of the LCN since 1930 and confirmed my belief that it was not known as "the Mafia." Based on Valachi's significant revelations, the LCN name has been adopted by the FBI and other federal agencies as being synonymous with various Italian organized crime families on a national basis.

Some of the terminology dealing with the La Cosa Nostra, or LCN, may be expressed as follows in various parts of the country such as:

Capo—boss
Sottocapo—underboss or second in command
Caporegima—captain
Regima—group of more than ten LCN members

Decina—group of less than ten LCN members

Crew—a slang term referring to a regima or a decina

Compare—godfather or close friend

Consigliere—counselor or advisor

Don—term of respect

Omerta—code of silence

Soldier or Button Man—rank-and-file LCN member

Made—individual has been accepted as a member of the LCN

Also, in 1959, this confidential source provided us with information that former Chicago boss, Anthony Accardo, and his wife Clarice were taking an extended six-week European trip and that they would be accompanied on this trip by Anthony DeGrazio and his wife. DeGrazio was then a lieutenant on the Chicago Police Department. This information was confidentially provided to police department officials, and this unholy alliance was exposed and received extensive publicity in the Chicago press. It resulted in the termination of DeGrazio from the Chicago Police Department for his fraternization with mob boss Anthony Accardo. It also came to light that in 1934, DeGrazio and his wife accompanied the Accardos on their honeymoon when DeGrazio was a police sergeant.

On November 17, 1959, this confidential source revealed an unusual role performed by former Capone mobster Murray Humphreys. Apparently, Humphreys was acting as a benefits administrator for the widows and families of prominent hoodlums. Humphreys was in possession of a letter from Albert "Sonny" Capone, the son of the late and notorious Alphonse Capone, requesting the need for $25,000 for various expenses that would be in addition to his usual compensation. Humphreys canvassed some of the leaders of organized crime for their approval, such as Gus Alex, Frank Ferraro, and Sam Giancana. All were in favor of granting approval of the payment because they felt that Mrs. Mae Capone had been loyal to Al Capone all these years and that they owed it to her. Sam Giancana was opposed, and his vote vetoed the request. As a result, Humphreys dictated the following letter to Albert "Sonny" Capone in Florida:

> Dear Sonny:
>
> I am in receipt of your letter of October 30, 1959 showing a breakdown of your expenditures of $10,000 plus $5,000 for the doctor and others. This matter has been taken up with the interested parties and rejected. Give my best to your mother.
>
> > Yours as ever,
> > Murray

It was noted that in 1966, Albert Francis Capone, the only son of Al Capone, legally changed his name to Albert Francis.

On February 12, 1960, C-1 agents John W. Roberts, Ralph Hill, William F. Roemer, Marshall Rutland, and I received letters of commendation and cash awards from Director J. Edgar Hoover for the development of this highly confidential source of information, which was of vital importance to the organized crime field. Since this source of information required almost daily monitoring and evaluation of volumes of conversation, the above agents were primarily responsible for rotating the monitoring assignment over the six-year period.

Photo of the Celano Custom Tailor Shop

SAMUEL
GIANCANA

ANTHONY
ACCARDO

PAUL
DELUCIA

ROSS
PRIO

GUS
ALEX

MURRAY
HUMPHREYS

FRANK   FERRARO

Photo of Chicago Hoodlum Hierarchy, 1960

ANTHONY J. ACCARDO

In 1959, the US attorney general appointed a special task force in Chicago to investigate organized crime activities. It was headed by Richard B. Ogilvie, a special prosecutor for the US Department of Justice, who later became governor of the state of Illinois. The services of various government agencies were utilized, including the FBI, to assist Mr. Ogilvie in this matter. I was one of the agents assigned along with C-1 agent John W. Roberts, who was the case agent on Accardo, and other C-1 agents. Mr. Ogilvie had targeted Anthony J. Accardo, former boss of the Chicago mob, as the primary subject of this investigation, with emphasis on his alleged income.

Accardo, the "Beer Salesman"

Photo of Anthony Accardo

Over the years, Accardo amassed a fortune from illegal activities. He was acutely aware that for tax purposes, he had to report sufficient income to support his lifestyle. He did not want to find himself in the same predicament as Al Capone, who was convicted for tax evasion on a net-worth basis. From 1940 to 1955, he reported total income of over $1million, of which about $300,000 was received from the notorious Owl Club gambling casino in Calumet City, Illinois. He also reported income from several miscellaneous gambling sources. His average annual income during this sixteen-year period was about $73,000. On several occasions, the IRS requested Accardo to be more specific on his miscellaneous gambling sources. On one occasion, he was asked to explain a miscellaneous item of $20,000. Accardo claimed that he won the $20,000 by wagering on the horses. His tax attorney and adviser at the time was Eugene Bernstein, who used the same ploy with Paul "The Waiter" Ricca regarding the claiming of miscellaneous income from wagering on horse races. Accardo was warned by the IRS to be more specific in the future.

With the increased pressure from the IRS, it became apparent to Accardo that he needed to report a legitimate source of income on his tax returns to compensate for his illegal income and to support his lifestyle. The Chicago mobsters then came up with a solution to Accardo's taxable income problem, and that was for Accardo to report income as a top "beer salesman" for Premium Beer Sales in Chicago. In the mid-1950s, Fox Head Brewery of Waukesha, Wisconsin, merged with Fox Deluxe Beer Sales of Chicago. Principal investors of Fox Head at that time were Chicago mobster Murray "The Camel" Humphreys, who owned 2,200 shares, and mobster Jack Cerone, a lieutenant and chauffeur of Anthony Accardo, who also owned 2,200 shares. Cerone was also on the payroll of Fox Head as a salesman at a salary of $25,000 a year. In 1956, an important business meeting was held at the Armory Lounge in Forest Park, Illinois, a notorious hoodlum establishment, which included the officials of Fox Head and Fox Deluxe. The Chicago mobsters made a proposition to the brewery officials that Anthony Accardo be hired by Fox Head as a $65,000-a-year beer salesman. Naturally, the officials were strongly opposed at the thought of having Accardo on their payroll, especially for $65,000. After some arm-twisting persuasion, the brewery officials had little choice but to agree to the terms of the mobsters. It was decided that Anthony Accardo would be placed on the payroll of Premium Beer Sales, the sole distributor of Fox Head beer in Cook County, and that Fox Head would actually reimburse Premium Beer Sales for the $65,000 annual salary of Anthony Accardo. No sales quotas were discussed or required of Accardo, and his future career as a "beer salesman" appeared to be assured. It was interesting to note that Dominick Volpe, a close friend of Accardo, was president of Premium Beer Sales and leased its premises from the OK Motor Service, a company in which Accardo previously had claimed an interest. This seemed to be a foolproof arrangement to insulate Accardo from the IRS; however, this scheme would soon unravel and expose Accardo to federal prosecution.

The Task Force of Special Prosecutor Richard Ogilvie, which included agents of the C-1 squad, determined that for the three-year period of 1956, 1957, and 1958, Accardo claimed income on his tax returns as a beer salesman from Premium Beer Sales of $178,083. Accardo was receiving a weekly check of $1,250 from Premium Beer Sales, which was then charged back to Fox Head Brewery. Accardo also deducted travel expenses of $3,995 for his alleged use of his red Mercedes-Benz sports car as a beer salesman. Accardo avoided claiming any miscellaneous income from gambling sources on his tax returns. He felt certain that he cleverly complied with the IRS requirement by claiming a legitimate source of his income, which would support his expensive lifestyle. Little did Accardo realize that his career as a beer salesman was soon to be exposed as a complete sham.

C-1 agents including John Roberts and myself canvassed practically every tavern, lounge, retail liquor store, and restaurant in greater Cook County that carried Fox Head Beer; and photos of Anthony Accardo and Jack Cerone were displayed to each owner. No one could identify Accardo or Cerone as ever having been a salesman of Fox Head Beer at these establishments during the years in question. All officials and employees of the brewery were interviewed in depth with the same result. No one had ever seen Accardo, who was an obvious phantom beer salesman.

In April 1960, a federal grand jury returned an indictment charging Anthony Accardo with filing false income tax returns for 1956, 1957, and 1958. Also, the car expenses of $3,995 deducted by Accardo for the alleged use of his red Mercedes-Benz Coupe as a salesman for Premium Beer Sales were false. The indictment claimed that Accardo did not perform any duties as a beer salesman and that his total salary of $178,083 was simply a pretext to conceal the true source of his illegal income.

The trial began in September 1960 before US District Court Judge Julius J. Hoffman. The government produced numerous witnesses that clearly established the fact that Accardo was a beer salesman in name only. Officials of the brewery, including the president, vice presidents, board of directors, salesmen, delivery men, bookkeepers, and many others, all testified that they never encountered Accardo in the role of a beer salesman. Also, there was absolutely no record of any beer sales ever submitted by Accardo. The defense attorney for Accardo was a Maurice J. Walsh, a well-known and experienced hoodlum defense attorney. He produced many witnesses, all of whom claimed that Accardo sold them Fox Head beer at their establishments. On cross-examination, most of the witnesses were found to be former bootleggers, ex-convicts, gamblers, friends, and associates of mobsters. One such witness was Ben Fillichio, then co-owner of Austin Liquors in the Chicago area. When asked by Mr. Ogilvie if he was the Ben Fillichio who had been convicted of a bootlegging crime in the past, he hesitated to respond and then claimed that he could not remember. That destroyed Fillichio as a credible witness. Ben Fillichio had been listed as one of the licensed owners of Austin Liquors, which would indicate that he may have falsified his state liquor license application regarding a past conviction. His name suddenly disappeared from the state liquor license records as co-owner of the Austin Liquors chain.

Two witnesses who came to the defense of Accardo were a Joseph Nicoletti, a Chicago tavern owner, and a Tom Letchos, the owner of a Melrose Park Steak House, who both claimed they purchased Fox Head beer from Accardo. On November 1, 1960, I was called to testify as a rebuttal witness to Joseph Nicoletti. I remember the day very well because that was the day my wife Marilyn was about to give birth to our second son. I was having difficulty keeping my mind on the trial, not knowing the status or the condition of my wife. I testified that I had interviewed Joseph Nicoletti in 1959, and he had denied ever having bought beer from Accardo or Jack Cerone. Nicoletti even denied knowing Accardo or Cerone after having been shown photographs of them. Tom Letchos also had a bad memory. He had been previously interviewed by agents and made similar denials about Accardo and Cerone. Both Nicoletti and Letchos were subsequently indicted and convicted for perjury and sentenced to prison, so much for Accardo's credible witnesses.

In the meantime, just prior to the start of the Accardo trial in September 1960, we received some very disturbing news from our confidential source at the Celano Custom Tailor Shop. In a conversation among mobsters Murray Humphreys, Gus Alex, and Frank Ferraro, it was learned that they had acquired a jury panel list of about 150 prospective jurors from which twelve jury members would be selected. They were studying the list by name, town, and neighborhood to determine who would be most susceptible to a contact and be sympathetic to their cause and vote for an acquittal. One lady juror was selected from Lyons, Illinois. She was contacted on a Sunday afternoon on September 18, 1960, by a neighbor friend named Hoffman also of Lyons, Illinois, who asked to speak to her about a confidential matter. He asked her if she was on the Anthony Accardo jury. She replied yes. Hoffman then said, "I have known Tony Accardo, and regardless of what people say about him, he's a nice guy. Accardo did me a couple of favors, and I never had a chance to repay him. I wouldn't want you to do anything that would go against your feelings, but I would like you to assure me that you won't vote him guilty, unless you are absolutely sure." Hoffman implied that if she found Accardo not guilty, she would get something out of it. The juror voluntarily reported the incident to Judge Julius Hoffman, who decided that no jury tampering had occurred, and the trial was allowed to continue. The Chicago FBI office did not report the incident to the court because that information could have tainted the outcome of the trial and/or placed our confidential source in jeopardy.

In November 1960, the federal jury in Chicago found Anthony Accardo guilty on each of the three counts of the indictment. Judge Hoffman then sentenced Anthony Accardo to serve six years in a federal penitentiary and fined him $15,000. Judge Hoffman referred to Accardo as a "purveyor of degradation and violence." Accardo was released on a $25,000 bond pending an appeal. This was a great victory for the federal government and especially for Richard Ogilvie, a Republican who went on to be the sheriff of Cook County and president of the Cook County Board of Commissioners before being elected as governor of the state of Illinois. As a result of the Accardo case, Richard Ogilvie and I were soon to become close personal friends.

Unfortunately, in January 1961, the US Court of Appeals Seventh Circuit reversed the lower court decision of Judge Julius Hoffman on a 2-to-1 vote, citing newspaper publicity as being prejudicial to the case. It was noted that Judge Hoffman specifically instructed the jury to disregard any newspaper publicity in this case as it was not uncommon at that time for any prominent mobster who was being prosecuted in Chicago to receive similar attention from the local press and media. In addition, the Appellate Court claimed that the admission of Accardo's earlier income tax returns was said to contribute to prejudicial error. Justice Elmer Schnackenberg, who entered a strong dissenting opinion, insisted that no prejudicial error took place. Even Chief Judge William J. Campbell strongly criticized the Appellate Court decision on the aspect of prejudicial error.

In October 1962, Anthony Accardo was retried in federal court and was acquitted of the charges based primarily on the absence of his prior tax returns, which previously provided the government with a motive for Accardo's actions in this case. Once again, Accardo was able to thwart the government's continuing efforts to prosecute him.

Background: Anthony J. Accardo was born in Chicago on April 28, 1906. His parents arrived in the United States from Palermo, Sicily, in 1905. He was the second of six children. His father was a self-employed shoemaker on Chicago's near-West Side in an area known as "the Patch," occupied primarily by Italian immigrants. Accardo was expelled from school at the age of fourteen and as a teenager had several minor arrests. He came from a neighborhood that spawned many members of the Capone gang with whom he became acquainted. On June 11, 1934, Accardo married Clarice Porter in Crown Point, Indiana. They had four children, Anthony, Joseph, Marie, and Linda Lee.

The Rise in Power of Tony Accardo: Accardo was a suspect in the infamous St. Valentine's Day massacre on February 14, 1929, when members of the Capone gang dressed as policemen entered a warehouse at 2122 N. Clark Street in Chicago, which was the headquarters of the rival gang of George "Bugs" Moran. Seven rival members were lined up against the wall, and while pretending to be placing them under arrest, the Capone mobsters mowed them down with machine-gun fire. At the time, Accardo was known to his intimate friends as "Joe Batters" because he was quite adept on using a baseball bat on his victims.

In 1930 and again in 1931, Accardo was arrested with several members of the Capone gang and was charged with illegal possession of a weapon. On each occasion, the charges were dismissed. His attorney in the 1930 gun case was Roland V. Libonati, then an Illinois state legislator and later a US congressman. Libonati had been photographed sitting next to Al Capone at a Cubs game at Wrigley

Field. In 1931, the Chicago Crime Commission published a "Public Enemy" list of twenty-eight prominent underworld figures. Anthony Accardo was included at the age of twenty-five.

Accardo had been arrested a total of twenty-three times as a suspect in murders, kidnappings, illegal gambling, and various other criminal violations and served only one night in jail. On Lincoln's birthday, February 14, 1945, Accardo spent his first and only night in jail; and it was purely by accident. While traveling in Chicago on this holiday, he was arrested as a gambling suspect. Since the courts were closed for the holiday, he had to spend the night in jail. On the following day, he appeared in court and was released on bond.

In 1944, Accardo was indicted on gambling charges. The charges were dismissed when his attorney told the court that Accardo was going to be inducted into the US Army during World War II and that he was eager to join the service. Accardo was rejected by the army for being morally unfit to serve.

Browne-Bioff Multimillion-Dollar Motion Picture Extortion Case

During the 1930s, Willie Bioff, a labor racketeer, and George Browne, a business agent of a local motion picture operator's union, began to shake down theater owners by threatening to close them down if they did not kick-back to them. They were so successful that they came to the attention of Capone mobsters Frank Nitti, Paul "The Waiter" Ricca, Louis "Little New York" Campagna, Phil D'Andrea, Frank Maritote, Charles Gioe, John Roselli, Nick Circella, and others. George Browne, with the help of the Capone mobsters, was elected president of the International Theater and Stage employees and Motion Picture Operator's Union. The mobsters muscled in as partners and the motion picture extortion operation expanded to Hollywood and took in millions of dollars. The movie industry victims complained and took their grievances to the FBI.

Following an FBI investigation, Willie Bioff, George Browne, and Nick Circella entered a guilty plea in 1942 to charges of anti-racketeering; and each was sentenced to eight years in prison. On March 18, 1943, indictments were returned against Nitti, Ricca, Campagna, D'Andrea, Maritote, Gioe, and Roselli. On the very day of the indictment, Frank Nitti, then Chicago hoodlum boss, committed suicide. Following a lengthy trial in that year, all subjects were found guilty, and each was sentenced to serve ten years in prison and fined $10,000. The entire top leadership of the Chicago mob had been decimated and imprisoned as a result of the FBI investigation. The convictions of the mob hierarchy, along with the death of Frank Nitti, left a huge power vacuum in the leadership of the Chicago mob. It was a great opportunity for Anthony Accardo to step up as interim mob boss and display his leadership qualities.

Ricca, Campagna, and D'Andrea were sent to the federal prison in Atlanta, Georgia; and the other Capone defendants were incarcerated in Leavenworth,

Kansas. Ricca and the others wanted to be united with their fellow mobsters in Leavenworth, and they let it be known to Accardo. Through powerful political connections, Accardo was able to affect their transfer notwithstanding the strenuous objections of US prison officials. This was an incredible display of power and authority by Accardo. He then made numerous trips to Leavenworth to visit and converse with Ricca and others to carry on the day-to-day affairs of the Chicago mob without interruption. He gained access to the prison by falsely claiming to be a Chicago attorney named Joseph I. Bulger. Regulations at Leavenworth at that time prohibited visitors unless they were relatives or attorneys of the prisoners. Accardo used the name of attorney Joseph I. Bulger, when visiting his hoodlum associates in prison because Bulger had represented the Capone mobsters in the past. Bulger, whose true name was Joseph Imburgio, had been a prominent crime syndicate lawyer for decades. His brother Lawrence was a partner of Accardo in the operation of the notorious Owl Club gambling casino in Calumet City, Illinois.

Accardo was not finished. This time, he tried for the impossible by skillfully manipulating the early release and parole of Ricca, Gioe, Campagna, and D'Andrea after they had served only three years of a ten-year sentence. This was a long shot, especially for Capone mobsters. The objections and the outcry would be virtually impossible to overcome. Accardo, assisted by his Chicago tax attorney Eugene Bernstein, had anticipated all of the obstacles; and the Capone mobsters were granted an early release and parole. The entire incident caused a public uproar and a congressional investigation. Accardo and Attorney Eugene Bernstein were subsequently indicted by a federal grand jury in Chicago for conspiring to use false identities while visiting the Capone mobsters in Leavenworth. Both were later acquitted. Accardo clearly demonstrated his leadership capabilities, and his performance again solidified his claim as the undisputed leader of the Chicago mob.

River Forest, Illinois, Residences

Now that Anthony Accardo no longer had a legitimate source of income to support his extravagant lifestyle, he had a compelling need to sell his mansion at 915 Franklin Avenue in River Forest, Illinois, and move into a home that was less ostentatious. He and his family had moved into the twenty-two-room mansion at Franklin Avenue in 1951 for a reported bargain price of $125,000. It had been built in 1930 at a cost of $500,000 by a former millionaire radio manufacturer. It was fenced with wrought-iron pickets. It had six master bedrooms and six master baths. One bathtub was cut out of a solid block of Mexican onyx at a cost of $10,000. Bathroom fixtures were gold-plated. It had two bowling alleys, a billiard room, a pipe organ, an indoor swimming pool, and an open air garden on its roof. It was at this residence that Accardo held his lavish Fourth of July lawn parties and entertained the entire mob hierarchy along with his powerfully influential political friends. These parties were a confirmation of the power and wealth of Anthony Accardo, the boss of one of the most powerful organized crime organizations in America.

Accardo sold the Franklin Avenue home in 1963 for a reported price of about $200,000. He then constructed a new home at 1407 N. Ashland Avenue in River Forest at an approximate cost of $110,000. This new home was a sixteen-room ranch and was less pretentious than his previous mansion. Thus, Accardo was successful in downsizing his style of living and made a substantial cash profit on the transaction.

In December of 1977, the home of Anthony Accardo at 1407 N. Ashland Avenue in River Forest was burglarized by six thieves while the Accardo family was out of town on vacation in Palm Springs, California. Accardo maintained a walk-in vault in the basement of his home, which allegedly contained stolen jewelry worth several hundred thousand dollars. The leader of the burglary crew claimed that he was merely trying to recover what he believed was originally stolen from him. What a disastrous mistake.

Accardo was angered over the fact that he, of all people, would be the victim of a crime. Rather than report the matter to the police, he issued orders to his enforcers that the burglary crew in question be identified and eliminated. Several weeks later, on January 16, 1978, the leader of the burglary crew, John Mendell, who said he was merely trying to reclaim his stolen jewelry from the Accardo residence, was lured to his death by a fellow burglar. His body was beaten and tortured unmercifully, and his throat was slashed. Convicted for the killing of Mendel was Frank Calabrese, a Chicago mob leader and hit man who died in prison in December of 2012 while serving a life sentence for thirteen murders resulting from the FBI's famous "Operation Family Secrets" investigation. A short time later, five other burglars met a similar fate. Accardo's retaliation was a classic example of how the mob maintains discipline among those who live a life of crime. Accardo's brand of justice was swift and final.

In 1978, Dominic "Butch" Blasi, former bodyguard chauffeur of the late Sam Giancana, was called before a federal grand jury in Chicago investigating the gangland slayings of the five Chicago area burglars. Blasi refused to testify and after a grant of immunity was jailed for eighteen months for contempt of court. Blasi remained true to the code of silence and followed the same path taken by his former boss Sam Giancana who was jailed in 1965 for refusing to testify. Anthony Accardo died of natural causes in 1992 at the age of eighty-six. Without a doubt, Accardo was the most powerful, most capable, and most effective leader of the Chicago Crime Syndicate since the days of Al Capone.

Pictures of Anthony Accardo and Sam Giancana as Hunters

Anthony Accardo and Sam Giancana, the great white hunters, photographed during happier times and enjoying a period of relaxation after bagging a grizzly bear on a hunting trip to the north woods in 1956. Other mobsters who were part of the hunting party were Joe "Black Joe" Amato, a northwest suburban gambling boss; Marshall Caifano, mob enforcer and Las Vegas representative; and Dominic DiBella, a Chicago North Side gambling boss.

TOP HOODLUM PROGRAM RE-ENERGIZED

In 1960, the Top Hoodlum Program was languishing and losing a bit of its luster. The original ten agents on the program were reduced to five, and demands were being made upon the C-1 squad to help out other criminal squads who had pressing and high-profile cases with deadlines. FBI headquarters, however, continued to maintain the pressure on the Top Hoodlum Program for more positive results, which allowed the program to get its second wind and additional manpower. Also contributing to the intensification of the program was the election of President John F. Kennedy in 1960 and the appointment of his brother Robert F. Kennedy as the US attorney general, a staunch opponent of organized crime. Hoover knew that Bobby Kennedy would demand a greater effort on the part of the FBI to obtain more results against organized crime figures, and Hoover would gladly oblige.

Upon Ross Spencer's retirement, Agent Harold D. Sell, an attorney from Nebraska, replaced him as supervisor of the C-1 squad. Sell was a great agent and had a good grasp of the organized crime problem in the Chicago area. A short time later, he appointed me as his relief supervisor. Other agents who were added to the C-1 squad were John Bassett, formerly of Vermont and New Jersey. He had been a professional light heavyweight prize fighter and fought under the name of "Irish Johnny Burns" using his mother's maiden name. When asked why he gave up fighting, John Bassett calmly responded, "I can't stand violence." He was truly a gentle giant who performed well.

Also, Brad Riggs became the C-1 organized crime representative in the Rockford, Illinois office. Riggs took on the Rockford crime family of Anthony Musso and did a superb job in neutralizing the activities of that criminal group. Joseph Zammuto took over the leadership from Musso as boss of the Rockford crime family consisting of about fourteen members. His underboss was Frank Buscemi. The consigliore of the group was Joseph Zito, the brother of Frank Zito, who was in attendance at the infamous Apalachin meeting in 1957. Brad Riggs was assisted in Rockford by SA Jim Sacia, who upon retirement became a member of the Illinois House of Representatives. Upon retirement, SA Riggs became a judge for the Seventeenth Circuit Court in Rockford, Illinois. In addition, Bill Meincke, who later became an assistant director of the FBI, had partnered with Joseph Shea; and they did a great job as members of the C-1 squad. Herb Briick, an experienced investigator and polygraph operator, also joined the C-1 squad. SA Richard Cavanagh, an attorney from Buffalo, New York, and a police instructor was added to the squad and performed admirably. John Dallman, formerly from Wisconsin, and assisted by a Peter Kotsos, did an exceptionally fine job in obtaining convictions against major Chicago hoodlums. Dallman had the difficult assignment of handling the cases involving hoodlum boss Sam Battaglia and a number of his prominent henchmen. Dallman also obtained convictions against a number of corrupt Chicago police officers who were shaking down business establishments in the Austin Police District. August "Gus" Kempff, a former Buffalo, New York, police officer, also joined the C-1 team. Kempff was one of the first agents to shave his head long before it became popular, and he could project an image of intimidation when necessary. Also, Dennis Shanahan, an outstanding investigator, was added to the C-1 squad. He would eventually become my gambling supervisor followed by Curtis Hester, a former track star from the University of Notre Dame. We had quite the all-American team. The number of agents assigned to the C-1 squad continued to expand, and the members of organized crime and their contacts continued to be identified and targeted for investigation and prosecution.

It was noted that Dennis Shanahan's father, Edwin C. Shanahan, was the first FBI agent killed in the line of duty on October 11, 1925, by Martin Durkin, a fugitive car thief. Durkin was eventually apprehended the following year and was sentenced to thirty-five years for the murder of SA Shanahan plus an additional fifteen years on stolen motor vehicle charges.

Giancana'sHeartthrob, Phyllis McGuire

Phyllis McGuire and her sisters Christine and Dorothy were part of the famous singing trio known as the McGuire sisters. Phyllis was the lead singer, and they were often compared in style with the Andrews sisters. In August 1959, while the McGuire sisters were performing at the Desert Inn Casino in Las Vegas, Phyllis was introduced to Chicago mobster leader Sam Giancana by Frank Sinatra. It was reported at that time that Phyllis had run up a gambling debt of about $16,000 at the gaming tables, and between performances, she would occasionally fill in as a card dealer at the blackjack table to work off her gambling debt. Because of her debts, gambling operators had standing instructions not to allow her to gamble at this casino. Sam appeared at the table where Phyllis was dealing, and Giancana reportedly lost about $10,000. They later had a drink together and commiserated over their mutual losses. Giancana then took Phyllis over to the crap tables, and as partners, they reportedly won about $100,000. Since she met Giancana, she was no longer concerned about the need for money.

From that moment on, Phyllis McGuire aggressively pursued Sam Giancana, who overwhelmed her, with large amounts of money, expensive gifts, and jewelry, reportedly valued at about $300,000. Over the years, there were rumors that they were either contemplating marriage or were actually married. Giancana reportedly offered Phyllis McGuire half a million dollars in cash, a home, a car, and a chauffeur if she was to marry him; but she turned him down. In June of 1961, Giancana rented a home for a month at Green Gables Ranch, Paradise Valley in Las Vegas, Nevada, during the current engagement of the McGuire sisters at the Desert Inn Motel, where he and Phyllis resided. He reportedly purchased a new white 1961 Cadillac Convertible for Ms. McGuire. This was the beginning of a long and highly publicized relationship, which eventually would be harmful to both of their careers. They continued to spend considerable time together and were constant travel companions throughout the United States and Mexico. The McGuire sisters, Christine and Dorothy, were very distressed that Phyllis was dating a top underworld character. Even though Giancana was devoting most of his time with his newfound love, he still found time to have romantic interludes with his former favorite mistress Marilyn Miller, a young twenty-three-year-old beautiful brunette, who was a former chorus girl at the Chez Paree nightclub in Chicago. Giancana met Ms. Miller while at a party with Frank Sinatra, and since that time, Giancana had showered her with money and expensive gifts. Giancana, as boss of the Chicago mob, was obviously neglecting the affairs of organized crime by running around with Ms. McGuire and others; and his hoodlum associates were becoming very unhappy with his flamboyant style of leadership.

Phyllis McGuire and Sam Giancana, 1960

It was apparent that Giancana was conducting his illegal business while in the company of Phyllis McGuire so it was decided to put some pressure on this relationship and attempt to disrupt and exploit their activities. In July 1961, Sam and Phyllis traveled to Phoenix, Arizona, where they stayed at a motel. Information was received that they were planning to depart Phoenix on July 12,1961 on American Airlines Flight 66 for New York City with a brief stop in Chicago at 7:00 p.m. Sam would be traveling under an alias, which by today's standards would be virtually impossible to do. We obtained a federal grand jury subpoena for Phyllis McGuire from a Chicago Strike Force attorney who was conducting an investigation into an organized crime matter. She was scheduled to appear before the grand jury on the following morning for testimony. We felt that this would be a good opportunity to place Phyllis under oath and have her testify about Giancana's activities from the time their relationship had begun about a year ago. It was decided that Agents Bill

Roemer and Ralph Hill would escort Giancana to a remote location of the airport for an interview, and John Bassett and I would accompany Ms. McGuire to a private American Airlines office to be interviewed separately. C-1 Supervisor Harold Sell and SA Gus Kempff would tag along to oversee the situation.

The flight arrived on time at O'Hare Airport. Giancana was observed exiting the aircraft from the front door of the plane and was greeted by SAs Roemer and Hill. Phyllis McGuire was seen leaving from the rear door of the plane and was met by Bassett and me. It was obvious that they did not want to be seen together at the Chicago airport. Ms. McGuire was escorted to a private office, and we identified ourselves as agents of the FBI and that we wanted to speak with her regarding her traveling companion, Sam Giancana. Before another word could be uttered, Ms. McGuire went into a tirade and began to rant and rave and used such foul language that actually shocked Bassett and me. It was inconceivable to me how such an attractive-appearing lady would be capable of such foul language. Her neck veins protruded as if they were about to burst. She was obviously putting on a performance to intimidate us. She claimed that her brother-in-law was the executive director of the Damon Runyon Cancer Fund and a bosom buddy of J. Edgar Hoover, and that Hoover was going to hear about this matter. She again asked me for my name, and I repeated it; and as she was writing it down, I told her to make sure that she spelled my name correctly. Her diatribe was directed at me and not at John Bassett, who was smiling and listening intently while playing the role of the nice guy. At a point when she hesitated talking for a moment, I interrupted her and told her very calmly that as far as I was concerned, there was nothing more to be said and that this interview was over because it was obvious that she had no intention to cooperate with the FBI. I advised her that I had a subpoena for her in my pocket, requiring her to appear before a federal grand jury in Chicago the following morning at ten o'clock. As I took the subpoena out my pocket, Ms. McGuire was stunned and shocked and quietly began to weep. She apologized for her outburst and said that she was not like Sam and she would help us if she could. She became gentle and friendly and was now conversing in a civil tone.

She claimed that she had known Giancana for only the past two years. Regarding the 1961 Cadillac convertible, she said that it was not a gift from Sam Giancana. She purchased the car from the Emil Denemark Cadillac Agency in Chicago for $5,200. Also, Ms. McGuire claimed that she had received only three gifts from Giancana; the total value was less than $5,000, all of which had been returned to him. It was obvious that Ms. McGuire was not being truthful. Ms. McGuire inquired as to whether or not her continued association with Giancana could jeopardize her career in the entertainment field and possibly expose her to unfavorable publicity. She was told that any continued association with Sam Giancana would have to be of her own choice and that the FBI could not advise her in this regard.

With respect to the 1961 Cadillac Convertible, it should be noted that the Denemark Agency was Chicago's oldest Cadillac dealer. Emil Denemark Sr. had received a telephone call from Giancana regarding the purchase of the 1961 Cadillac vehicle for Phyllis McGuire. Denemark had admitted in the past that he sold cars to Al Capone and to some of his gang members' years ago. Also, he was well acquainted with Sam Giancana and his late wife Angeline who had passed away about seven years prior. The Cadillac was driven to Las Vegas by Denemark's brother Marty, who delivered the car to Ms. McGuire at the Desert Inn Motel in Las Vegas.

Because Ms. McGuire's final destination was NYC, I saw no need to detain her any further, and the subpoena was withdrawn. She was told that we would save the subpoena for a later date for her to appear before the grand jury and testify under oath. She agreed to cooperate further at that time. We escorted her back to the terminal area where Sam Giancana and the other agents were located.

Bill Roemer and Sam Giancana were locked in a heated and boisterous exchange of words. It became so unruly that passengers in the terminal had gathered around the group to see what was going on. Every other word out of Giancana's mouth was vulgar, crude, and offensive. It appeared that the two of them were about to become involved in a brawl. It was fortunate that a fight did not break out because it would have been disastrous for Giancana, because Bill Roemer was a former Notre Dame boxing champion. Roemer returned the dialogue with loud demeaning comments about Giancana's bald head and his diminutive physical appearance and belittled him about being the boss of organized crime in Chicago. Giancana, in a loud voice, said, "You can tell your superboss that you spoke to Sam Giancana and tell him to (obscene obscene)." When asked who he was referring to as the superboss, he said, "You know who I mean, Kennedy," an obvious reference to Bobby Kennedy, the US attorney general. Giancana continued to fume and was out of control until we appeared on the scene with Phyllis McGuire. It was obvious that the situation with Giancana got out of hand at the airport, and Supervisor Harold Sell was not too pleased with all the attention it had attracted. This was not one of Bill Roemer's finer moments. When Ms. McGuire rejoined Giancana, he said in a very sarcastically loud voice to her, "Why didn't you tell them to go to hell like I did?" As Giancana was about to leave with Ms. McGuire, he brushed by Agent Kempff and said to him, "How much do you charge to haunt houses?" Kempff wisely ignored the comment. Giancana then turned to Roemer, and as he was leaving, he pointed a menacing finger at him and said, "I'm going to build a fire under you." As he began to depart with Ms. McGuire, she said, "I wish to apologize for Mr. Giancana's conduct and hope that you will disregard it. He told me that I should not have talked to you, but I told him that I could not be like him because I'm a lady." They departed Chicago for New York City, where Ms. McGuire maintained a Park Avenue residence. This was just the beginning of one of the many encounters that we would experience with Sam Giancana.

From August through December 1961, Sam Giancana continued to pursue Phyllis McGuire. Wherever the McGuire sisters were scheduled to perform, faithful "Momo" could be counted on to appear. He followed her from Valley Forge,

Pennsylvania, to Owings Mills, Maryland, and to a five-week engagement at the Talk of the Town nightclub in London, England. Upon departing from London, they toured Europe and traveled to Rome, Madrid, San Juan, and back to Chicago. They continued to conceal their intimate relationship from everyone except their immediate families. Rumors had been rampart that Giancana and Ms. McGuire may have been married during their recent trip abroad; however, no such evidence existed. On one occasion in London with Phyllis McGuire, he was observed wearing a wedding ring.

Sam Giancana and Phyllis McGuire deplaning separately, attempting to give the impression that they were not traveling together.

GIANCANA'S "COMMAND POST": THE ARMORY LOUNGE

Photo of the Armory Lounge

In 1960, it became apparent to the agents of C-1 squad that the Armory Lounge, located at 7427 W. Roosevelt Road, Forest Park, Illinois, was a prime meeting place of Sam Giancana and his henchmen. During the 1950s, the armory was known to be a hoodlum gambling site. It was now reportedly owned by Sam Giancana and managed by Tarquin "Queenie" Simonelli, reported to be a brother-in-law of Anthony Accardo. Because the local police department had been less than vigilant when the Armory Lounge was operating as a gambling location several years prior, we decided to avoid any contact with the chief of police or the police officers in Forest Park, Illinois. It was concluded that the Armory Lounge would be an excellent location for our next microphone surveillance that would give us daily coverage of Sam Giancana and his hoodlum associates and their activities. Giancana resided at 1147 South Wenonah in Oak Park, Illinois, which was located just a few blocks away from the Armory Lounge.

Approval for microphone coverage of the Armory Lounge was granted by FBI headquarters as well as the US Department of Justice. To assist us with our installation, we obtained a lookout post across the street at the naval armory ordnance facility so that we could observe the activity at the Armory Lounge during the late hours. This would enable us to determine when the best time would be for our covert penetration and microphone installation. We observed that a janitor employee of the Armory Lounge would be the last one to leave late at night and was responsible for locking the main door of the armory, which faced the busy thoroughfare of Roosevelt Road. We devised a plan that would help us obtain a copy of the master key to the Armory Lounge. One evening following the departure of the night employee, we waited until he had driven his car several miles away from the armory. He was pulled over and told that he resembled someone that the FBI was seeking and if he would please accompany us to our office to resolve the matter. He voluntarily agreed, and while he was being fingerprinted, a copy of the key to the Armory Lounge was made. We thanked him for his cooperation and told him he was not identical to the person we were looking for and that we would not say anything to his employer about this matter. He was relieved and thought that was a very good idea. He insisted that his boss not know anything about the incident.

Obtaining coverage at the armory was no easy task. Roosevelt Road was a heavily traveled road, and the large front window of the armory allowed anyone to look in and observe activity inside the lounge. It took at least four covert entries to resolve the problems we encountered. Also, during a period of remodeling at the armory, we had to enter several more times and make adjustments to the location of our coverage. Our main concern, however, was that Sam Giancana, who lived just a few short blocks away, would occasionally drive by the armory late at night and peer inside the large front window to see if anything was going on. Fortunately for Giancana and the FBI, he did not choose to enter the lounge because if he had, that could have posed huge problems for all concerned.

The information received from the Armory Lounge source was extremely productive. The code name for the source was "Mo," as a reference to Giancana's middle name Momo, and this coverage exceeded our expectations. It complemented and expanded the information that we were receiving from Celano's; in addition, it gave us continuous coverage on the daily activities, travel, and whereabouts of Sam Giancana. It provided the identity of close associates and contacts of Giancana as well as those seeking counsel and those who reported there on the orders of Giancana.

It disclosed income from various business ventures and mob operations, including Giancana's share of revenue, totaling in excess of $106,000 for an unspecified time, from the coin-operated machines boss Edward Vogel, owner of Apex Amusement Company, Niles, Illinois. It revealed the details of proposed and actual gangland slayings and the hoodlums involved. It identified the relative standing of persons within the organized criminal element. It disclosed Giancana's hidden interest in the Cal-Neva Lodge, located at Lake Tahoe, Las Vegas, and other Las Vegas gambling casinos and hotels. It provided information and activities of other Chicago top hoodlums, namely Charles English, Jack Cerone, Anthony Accardo, and Dominic "Butch" Blasi, Giancana's chauffeur and bodyguard, and many others.

GANGLAND SLAYINGS

Regarding the discussions of gangland slayings, in January 1962, a very interesting conversation took place at the Armory Lounge between Giancana and Jack Cerone, a prominent hoodlum and bodyguard chauffeur for former Chicago boss Anthony Accardo. Apparently, Giancana had assigned Cerone the contract to arrange for the killing of an individual known only as "Frankie," who was vacationing at the time at his home in Hollywood, Florida. The reason for the proposed killing was not known. Cerone was aware of Frank's location in Florida and had planned to rent a place in close proximity to the intended victim. Cerone provided our source with the address of his rental place and was lining up the hoodlum muscle to perform the killing. He had selected Fiore Buccieri, a Chicago West Side boss and enforcer, and his number one lieutenant James "Turk" Torello and Vincent Inserro, a mob enforcer. Dave Yaras, a former Chicago hit man and partner of Chicago North Side gambling boss Lenny Patrick, now residing in Miami, was also recruited. Frank "Skippy" Cerone, cousin of Jack Cerone, was also to participate. This situation posed an unusual and immediate problem for the C-1 agents because the identity of the victim was unknown and time was of the essence to prevent a gangland murder in Florida.

FBI headquarters and the Miami office were placed on notice. Miami requested assistance from Chicago, preferably agents who were acquainted with the hoodlums in question and their activity. The bureau approved sending two Chicago agents and two NYO agents to assist in this case. Chicago C-1 agents John Roberts and Ralph Hill were dispatched, and the NYO sent agents Warren Donovan and Pat Moynihan. Donovan was an outstanding agent who had been in my New Agents Class in 1951. The agents arrived in Miami before the hoodlums took possession of their rental location, and the Miami agents were able to install a microphone in the rental home to monitor the mob conversations. The intended murder victim was identified as Frank Esposito, a Chicago labor union leader who was a constant companion of John D'Arco, alderman of the First Ward of Chicago, who was also in Florida. At one point, it was decided that if necessary, D'Arco would be abducted along with Esposito and killed. The hoodlums were planning to abduct Frank Esposito away from his residence and take him for a boat ride to a designated location along the Florida Keys, where he would be killed and dismembered; and his body parts would be dumped into the ocean. With the assistance of the Dade County, Florida police,

FBI agents were able to maintain close surveillance of the Chicago hoodlums and the intended victim, which would ultimately hinder and thwart the mobsters from carrying out their attempt to murder Esposito. They became so frustrated primarily because we could anticipate their every move that they eventually called off their murder attempt. The intended victim was Frank Esposito, a Chicago official of the County Municipal Workers and Laborers International Union of North America. Esposito was known to be associated with hoodlum Alfred Pilotto, president of Local 5 of the laborer's union in Chicago Heights, Illinois. We had no idea why Giancana and the Chicago mob wanted to kill Frank Esposito. It would appear that the mob may have been attempting to infiltrate or control Esposito's union, and he was resisting their overtures. This killing would have sent a chilling message to other union members to cooperate with the mob or suffer the consequences.

Upon Frank Esposito's return to the Chicago area, an attempt was made to interview him regarding the mob's attempt to eliminate him. We attempted to gain his cooperation, but he declined to be interviewed in person and claimed that he knew of no reason why the Chicago mob would want to harm him. Esposito even denied knowing the hoodlums in question, which we knew was not truthful. He was assured that his life had been in danger while in Florida, and if he felt threatened in Chicago at any time in the future, he should notify the police immediately. Esposito did not appear grateful in any way for the information or the efforts of the FBI to save him from being brutally murdered; however, it would appear that Esposito sought a personal interview with Giancana and apparently resolved any differences between him and the mob. The C-1 agents had fulfilled their responsibility in this highly sensitive and delicate matter. Mr. Esposito died of a heart attack at his Chicago residence on January 12, 1969. We may never know the reason why the Chicago mob wanted to assassinate this high-ranking labor union official.

While in Miami, Jack Cerone, Fifi Buccieri, and Dave Yaras talked freely about some of their gangland hits and attempted hits in Chicago. The conversations confirmed their reputation as Chicago enforcers and hit men. It was not known at the time that Cerone was such a prolific hit man because he had been primarily a confidant and chauffeur for Anthony Accardo. Cerone spoke of his shooting "Big Jim" Martin and thought that he had killed him with double 00 buckshot, but Martin survived and fled the country. Cerone claimed that the shells he used were probably too old and didn't have the proper impact. This was an obvious reference to the attempted slaying of James "Big Jim" Martin, who in 1950 survived a shooting and was a major black policy wheel operator at that time. After the shooting, Martin left the United States for South America, and the Chicago mob took over the operation of his policy wheels.

This confidential source also advised that Sam Giancana issued a contract to mob enforcer Fiore Buccieri to kill John Hennigan, age forty-three, who was suspected of being an informer for the Cook County State's attorney's office in connection with several raids conducted at Cicero and Melrose Park, Illinois, syndicate gambling joints. Hennigan was shotgunned to death at close range across the street from his Chicago residence on November 16, 1961. Police found on Hennigan's person the telephone numbers and addresses of three of the mob's gambling locations.

In a later conversation at the Armory Lounge, the same individuals, namely Jack Cerone, Fiore Buccieri, and James "Turk" Torello, and others took delight in discussing the torture slaying of "Action" Jackson, a 300-pound juice loan collector for West Side hoodlum loan shark Sam DeStefano. This discussion was an obvious reference to William "Action" Jackson whose nude body had been found on August 11, 1961, stuffed in the trunk of his green 1957 Cadillac, which was abandoned on the lower level of Wacker Drive by the Chicago Police Department. Rope marks were found on Jackson's waist and ankles, which indicated that he had been tied, tortured, and beaten to death.

They described in detail the various torture methods used on Jackson whom they suspected was an FBI informant. Jackson was never an informant for the FBI. He may have been seen talking to an FBI agent in the past on another matter and apparently failed to notify the mob of such a contact. Jackson was grabbed at gunpoint by the mobsters and taken to a hoodlum meat-rendering plant on Chicago's near southwest side. His huge body was tied and impaled on a large meat hook through the anus and suspended from an overhead beam. He was tortured mercilessly as they questioned him about his relationship with the FBI. His repeated denials only caused more torture, which included the use of a blow torch to his face, an ice pick to parts of his body, and a bullet to his kneecap. They used an electrified cattle prod on his genitals and poured water on the cattle prod to increase the shock and pain and left him hanging on the meat hook for three days until he expired. They laughed throughout the entire ordeal because they found this brutally horrific murder to be amusing. In 1952, Virgil W. Peterson, operating director of the Chicago Crime Commission, wrote a book on Chicago crime and politics entitled *Barbarians in Our Midst*. That title was a perfect description of these uncivilized creatures.

VILLA VENICE, WHEELING, ILLINOIS

The Villa Venice supper club on Milwaukee Avenue in unincorporated Wheeling, Illinois, was originally built before World War II by Papa Bouche, a well-known restaurateur, and was known as Papa Bouche's Villa Venice. It was an expensive supper club that had big name entertainment where Venetian lights and Italian-style gondolas with singing gondoliers toured along the Des Plaines River. In October of 1956, Papa Bouche was bought out by the Meo brothers, Albert (Chuck) and James, who were the owners of Meo's Norwood House in Norridge, Illinois, a prime meeting place for Chicago hoodlums. James Meo had been the band leader at the Villa Venice during Papa Bouche's ownership. According to this confidential source, the Villa Venice became a hoodlum enterprise that came under the control of Sam Giancana in the late 1950s. In April of 1960, Leo Olsen aka Leonard Olsen, a former head waiter at the Fireside Restaurant in Lincolnwood, Illinois, reportedly purchased the Villa Venice from the Meos by assuming the supper club's obligations with no cash exchanged. Extensive remodeling was performed by Richard Bernas of Skokie, Illinois, who was a building contractor and neighbor of Les Kruse, a hoodlum gambling associate of Sam Giancana. Bernas was also known to convert private dwellings into gambling casinos for the Chicago mob. The supper club was closed during renovation. Richard Bernas was listed as a director of Villa Venice Inc. and was the liquor licensee of the corporation. Bernas was also reported to be a close associate of Matthew Capone, brother of Al Capone. Leonard Olsen was listed as president. It was noted that Bernas was the building contractor who performed the construction of a Lake Worth, Florida, residence allegedly owned by Sam Giancana and occupied by hoodlum Les Kruse. The Villa Venice also utilized the concession services of Attendant Service Corporation and the Zenith Vending Corporation to furnish car hikers, hat check girls, and vending machine services. Chicago hoodlum leader Ross Prio was on the payroll of these companies.

When Giancana appeared at the Villa Venice, it became obvious to all that he was in charge, and everyone was subservient to him including the Meos and the new owner Leo Olsen. The Chicago mob also used the private conference rooms for their confidential meetings. Whenever closed-door meetings were held, several guards were posted at strategic points on the grounds to challenge anyone not known to them. They also operated the mob's huge floating gambling casino located in close proximity to the Villa Venice that was housed in a large Quonset hut facility with a false business store front with displays of motor oil products. Alongside of the Quonset hut was the Flamingo Motel, which was controlled by Rocco Potenzo, a gambling lieutenant of Sam Giancana. High rollers from the Villa Venice often were shuttled by bus or limousine to the gambling facility. Les "Killer Kane" Kruse, the Lake County, Illinois, gambling boss, would assist Rocco Potenzo with the supervision of this gambling operation.

In April of 1960, the daughter of hoodlum leader Sam "Teets" Battaglia was married, and the wedding reception was held at the Villa Venice. Automobiles belonging to Anthony Accardo and other hoodlum dignitaries were also observed in attendance. On February 11, 1961, the daughter of Chicago North Side gambling boss Ross Prio was married at Our Lady of Perpetual Help Church in Glenview. An elaborate wedding reception followed at the Villa Venice. Many of the Chicago hoodlum hierarchy and associates were in attendance. On April 27, 1961, the hoodlum social event of the year took place at the Villa Venice when Anthony Accardo's daughter, Linda Lee, married Michael Palermo, the nephew of Nicholas Palermo, a Melrose Park hoodlum plumbing contractor. Accardo held a lavish wedding reception there and invited all of his hoodlum associates and political friends. This set the example for the mob to support one of their enterprises. Also, on June 10, 1964, when Accardo's son Anthony R. Accardo was married, their wedding reception was also held at the Villa Venice. The Chicago police and the Chicago press were out in full force, taking down license numbers of the cars and limousines of the guests in attendance. In addition, Paul "The Waiter" Ricca (true name DeLucia), the elder statesman of the Chicago mob, held the wedding reception of his son Paul DeLucia at the Villa Venice. The reception included the uninvited guests of the police and the press who were interested in the identity of the attendees. On September 17, 1966, the wedding reception of the daughter of James "Tar Baby" Cerone, cousin of hoodlum leader Jack Cerone, was held at the Villa Venice. Close to five hundred guests were invited and included the hierarchy of the Chicago hoodlum element.

During the summer months and early fall, the Villa Venice underwent extensive remodeling, and the club was scheduled to reopen on November 9, 1962. Giancana spent many hours overseeing the remodeling operation of the Villa Venice. Our confidential source at the Armory Lounge advised that Sam Giancana was attempting to contact Frank Sinatra and Dean Martin for the purpose of having them appear for an opening night performance at the Villa Venice. Giancana wanted them to perform for a ten-day period. Sinatra and Martin were not responding to Giancana's request, which angered him. Giancana issued an ultimatum through a Las Vegas Stardust Hotel casino contact for Sinatra and Martin to appear in Chicago or else. Giancana even spoke about taking action against Sinatra if he did not comply, but that was probably more out of frustration and bluster. Frank Sinatra eventually consented to assist Giancana with providing the necessary talent for the grand reopening of the Villa Venice. The featured entertainer for the opening date of November 9, 1962, was Eddie Fisher, who performed for eight days. He was followed by Sammy Davis Jr. for five days and then by Frank Sinatra, Dean Martin, and Sammy Davis Jr. for eight days through December 4, 1962. They were a huge attraction with standing-room-only crowds. It was an enormous financial success, especially because Giancana received their services for union wages, which was far below their usual compensation. Practically all of the Chicago mobsters were in attendance for the Sinatra performances that week, including Sam Giancana and his close associates and confidants.

In November 1962, information was confidentially received that the Chicago mob's large floating gambling operation was preparing to resume operations in the large Quonset hut immediately north of the Flamingo Motel at the intersection of US 45 and Milwaukee Avenue, in an area between Wheeling and Northbrook, Illinois, a short distance from the Villa Venice. This operation was under the control of Rocco Potenzo, a gambling boss and close associate of Sam Giancana. Operating the big game for Potenzo in the Quonset hut was Sam "Slicker Sam" Rosa, a well-known Cicero gambler and a frequent golfing partner of Sam Giancana. The Quonset hut was located in back of a gas station, behind which was a large well-constructed furnished room used for the large-scale gambling operation. Potenzo and his underlings had been contacting their gambling clients and offered them free reservations at the Villa Venice for the feature attractions of Frank Sinatra, Dean Martin, Sammy Davis Jr., and Eddie Fisher. The high rollers from the Villa Venice were taken by limousine to the Quonset hut gambling establishment location just around the corner. Parking for this operation by patrons was at the rear of the Flamingo Motel, after which a short walk was necessary to the rear of the Quonset hut. The service station attendant on whose property the Quonset hut was located served as a lookout and had radio communications with persons in the motel and the Quonset hut. This was a large and profitable gambling operation that depended on Villa Venice clientele.

Surveillance by C-1 agents was conducted at the Villa Venice on November 22, 1962. It revealed that Frank Sinatra and Dean Martin were accompanied into the club immediately preceding the second show by Joseph Fischetti, a prominent Miami area hoodlum. On November 27, 1962, Thomas Potenzo, brother of Rocco Potenzo, and Slicker Sam Rosa were observed at the Flamingo Motel, steering customers from the Flamingo to the Quonset hut wherein the gambling was located. Sam Rosa later met with Sam Giancana and hoodlum leader William Daddano at the Villa Venice.

According to our source, during the night of December 2 and early morning of December 3, 1962, Sam Giancana and his close associates were reportedly guests at a private party held in Frank Sinatra's suite at the Ambassador East Hotel in Chicago.

Immediately following their performance, Sammy Davis Jr. and Eddie Fisher were interviewed by the FBI and were either unable or unwilling to furnish any information of value. Information had been received that Eddie Fisher originally had an engagement at the Desert Inn in Las Vegas for substantially more money; however, because Sinatra had done Fisher a big favor in the past, Fisher agreed to cancel his Desert Inn performance and accepted the engagement at the Villa Venice for substantially less money. Fisher would not discuss the matter. Davis claimed that he was booked into the Villa Venice by the William Morris Agency, after which he learned that Frank Sinatra was to follow him; and as a favor to Sinatra, he agreed to stay over for the week of November 26, 1962, with Sinatra and Dean Martin. Sammy Davis Jr. was very cordial during the interview and said that he would like to cooperate further. However, he stated, "I have one good eye, and I want to keep it." That said it all. Both Fisher and Davis suggested that Frank Sinatra be contacted for further details.

In January 1963, Frank Sinatra was interviewed by the FBI in the presence of his attorney and financial advisor Milton Rudin in Los Angeles, California. Sinatra was very friendly and had no objection to being interviewed to answer any questions that the FBI would ask of him. He did say he was getting tired of having to answer questions about the many rumors that had been circulating about him. Among some of the topics discussed was the Cal Neva Lodge. Sinatra claimed to have no knowledge of any undisclosed hoodlum financial interests in the Cal Neva Lodge, Lake Tahoe, Nevada, or any other gambling casinos in Nevada. His current expansion plans for the Cal Neva Lodge would involve about $4,000,000 in additional capital and hoped to obtain a loan with sufficient collateral. He was hopeful that eventually he would be the sole owner of the Cal Neva Lodge. Regarding the appearance of himself, Dean Martin, Eddie Fisher, and Sammy Davis Jr. at the Villa Venice Supper Club in the Chicago area during November, 1962, Sinatra claimed that his old friend Leo Olsen approached him and asked him to help promote his Villa Venice Club and that he agreed to help Olsen purely as a favor to Olsen. He was responsible for bringing in the other entertainers of his group. They all received their regular rates for their appearance and were paid by check by Olsen. Sinatra also claimed that he knew Giancana because in his business he meets all kinds of people and he had not in the past, or in the future, plan on having financial dealings with anyone other than those on his financial records. Furthermore, Sinatra claimed that Giancana had nothing to do with his appearance at the Villa Venice. It was apparent that Sinatra was not being truthful about his relationship with Giancana. Sinatra also claimed to have no knowledge about the gambling operation that existed in a nearby Quonset hut that catered to Villa Venice clients until he read about it in a Chicago newspaper.

Regarding the mob's large-scale floating gambling casino located in the Quonset hut, a crime reporter for the *Chicago Daily News* exposed this operation in an article on November 30, 1962. Considerable publicity was given to the Rocco Potenzo gambling operation, linking it to Sam Giancana and the Villa Venice, and it shut down immediately. The mob then scrambled to move all of their equipment from their location and had to abandon the Quonset hut building, which was eventually demolished. Cook County State's Attorney Daniel Ward said that his police were preparing to raid the Quonset hut gambling den just before it closed down. Giancana eventually was forced to sell his investment in the Villa Venice because of the reputation of this establishment and because of the lack of the monetary benefit from the gambling casino. On March 4, 1967, an oven exploded in the kitchen of the Villa Venice, which caused extensive fire damage to the supper club. There was no indication of any arson. The Villa Venice had long been regarded as a fire trap with its satin ceilings, and this information had been disseminated to the local fire marshal's office by the Chicago FBI, which caused the club to undergo many inspections until they complied with local fire ordinances. The fire insurance was handled by Anco Insurance Company, which was controlled by the First Ward Organization of Alderman John D'Arco. Villa Venice ceased to be the prime social gathering place for the mob, and Giancana divested himself from this investment.

Sam Giancana seemed to have an attraction toward well-known entertainers and celebrities. In December of 1963, Sam Giancana and Phyllis McGuire traveled to Honolulu, Hawaii, and checked into the new Kahala Hilton Hotel and registered as Mr. and Mrs. John Flood, New York City. On December 31, 1963, Sam Giancana and his golfing partner and well-known operator of the mobs' large-scale gambling operation, Sam "Slicker Sam" Rosa, played a round of golf at the private Waialea Country Club in Honolulu along with legendary baseball figure Joe DiMaggio and his golf partner. Giancana played golf daily with Sam Rosa and hoodlum Johnny "Haircuts" Campanelli. Also, Giancana was in telephone contact on several occasions with DiMaggio during his stay in Honolulu. On January 15, 1964, Joe DiMaggio was interviewed in Beverly Hills, California, by the FBI regarding his reported association with Sam Giancana. DiMaggio said that he traveled to Honolulu with his friend George from New York during the latter part of December 1963. They stayed at the Hilton Hotel before going on to Maui, where they remained until January 1964 when they returned to the mainland. On one occasion on December 31, 1963, he played golf with Sam Giancana and his friend named Sam (Rosa). The golf game was not prearranged, and he intended to play as a twosome with his friend. Giancana invited them to play with him and Sam (Rosa). The entire conversation during the game had to do with golf. He has known Sam Giancana for several years, having first met him in New York when he was playing baseball. He knew absolutely nothing about Giancana's activities other than what had been reported in the press. During the evening of the golf game, he was invited to have a drink in the hotel lounge with Giancana and some of his associates whose names he did not recall. He also saw Phyllis McGuire at the hotel and presumed she was with Giancana. He had known Ms. McGuire for several years. He had no further contact with Giancana or any of his associates.

In the fall of 1964, while attending the performance of the well-known Italian singer Enzo Stuarti at Manny Skar's Sahara Inn Motel in Schiller Park, Illinois, Giancana became very friendly with Stuarti who then became a rather constant golfing companion of his during the golfing season. On several occasions, when Giancana was the host of large groups at the Sahara Inn Motel, Enzo Stuarti focused his floor show to a large degree on Giancana and his entourage and would make comments on some of the events that took place during their golf game at the Fresh Meadow Golf Course in Hillside, Illinois.

In February 1969, Dale Robertson, the famous TV and western movie star, was contacted at his home by the FBI in the Los Angeles, California, area regarding his reported association with Sam Giancana. Mr. Robertson was very friendly and cooperative and said that he first met Giancana about twenty years ago at a golf course in Banff, in the province of Alberta, Canada. Since that time, he had maintained a friendly relationship with him. When he first met Giancana, he had no idea who he was, and Giancana told him that he was a car salesman from Chicago. It was not until sometime later that he actually learned the true background about Giancana. He was not very proud of his association with Giancana and was very disappointed to hear about his reputation. Giancana had been very pleasant to him and always acted as a gentleman. He had not seen Giancana recently, however, believed that he was out of the country and living in Mexico. Giancana had introduced him to some of his associates over the years such as Rocco Potenzo, Milwaukee Phil Alderisio, and Sam Battaglia. Several years ago, he received two Doberman pinscher dogs as a gift from Sam Giancana that was personally delivered to him by Rocco Potenzo. Also during the latter part of 1968, while he was in Chicago, he had dinner with Rocco Potenzo at a restaurant called "That Steak Joynt" in the Old Town section of Chicago. Robertson claimed he never had any business dealings with Sam Giancana or his associates. In late 1969, according to a confidential source, Giancana reportedly contacted Dale Robertson and told him that if anyone inquired about his income, to tell them that Giancana borrowed one million dollars from Dale Robertson. No money was ever transacted, and it would have been a paper transaction only. In this manner, Giancana would be able to live beyond his means on money allegedly borrowed from Robertson. This allegation was received after the interview of Mr. Robertson; therefore, he was never asked to comment on the veracity of this information.

FIRST WARD REGULAR DEMOCRATICORGANIZATION

In 1962, the First Ward Headquarters was located at 100 N. LaSalle Street in Chicago, across the street from the city hall. It encompassed the entire lucrative loop area, which included the Magnificent Mile of Michigan Avenue and some sections of the south and southwest side of Chicago. The alderman and First Ward committeeman was John D'Arco, and his executive secretary was Pat Marcy, who was later determined to be the real power behind D'Arco and the First Ward, and was the master fixer and the conduit through which Giancana and the mob would operate. Not to be overlooked was Benjamin "Buddy" Jacobson, a former associate of Capone mobsters who had been a longtime member of the First Ward. By his own admission to agents, Jacobson's primary responsibility had been "fixing judges and political figures for years" as well as being a messenger for the First Ward. D'Arco's brother-in-law was Louis Briatta, the gambling boss of the First Ward who reported to hoodlum leader Gus Alex. From our source at Celano's, where John D'Arco and Pat Marcy were occasional visitors, and from the conversations heard at the Armory Lounge, there was absolutely no doubt in our minds that Chicago's First Ward was owned lock, stock, and barrel by the Chicago mob and that Sam Giancana was the absolute authority in directing their activities.

It was noted that when Sam Giancana returned to the United States from Mexico on June 15,1959, he was carrying a piece of paper with about fifteen names of major hoodlums in the city of Chicago, along with the names of John D'Arco and Buddy Jacobson. On July 21, 1959, C-1 agents John Roberts and William Roemer Jr. contacted John D'Arco at his office at 100 North LaSalle Street in Chicago. He was informed about his name being on a paper list belonging to Sam Giancana and that the agents had come to him as a man in a position of public trust to determine the purpose and significance of this list. D'Arco said he had no idea about the meaning of the list nor could he speculate as to the meaning of this list. He claimed that he knew Giancana in his youth because they grew up in the same neighborhood and had not seen him for a long time. He refused to comment when informed that information had been received that he was a close associate of Chicago hoodlum leader Gus Alex. D'Arco was obviously not telling the truth and did not intend to cooperate.

D'Arco then made this statement, "You guys can't embarrass me in this town. I'm a big man, and if my constituents are satisfied with the way I represent them, then I don't have to worry about nobody else." Our confidential source advised that John D'Arco during December 1961 was in contact with Sam Giancana and presented Giancana with approximately $33,000, the purpose for which was not known.

It was decided that the First Ward Headquarters would be an ideal location to expand our FBI microphone coverage. Upon presenting the matter to FBI headquarters, they were at first somewhat reluctant to approve our request because of possible political ramifications; however, we convinced them that the First Ward was at the very heart of political corruption in Chicago and was under the complete domination of Sam Giancana. Permission was granted. Our next hurdle was gaining access to their office without alerting the tenants, building security, or police. The downtown location was in the heart of the financial district of Chicago with large banks and heavy traffic, with many police patrols and private security guards. After several successful covert entries, we finally accomplished our goal. We now had three highly productive sources that would allow us to be fully informed on the criminal activities of the Chicago mob and their police and political connections. We were well aware that organized crime could not continue to flourish without political and police corruption.

Some of the highlights of information confirmed by this source were as follows:

- It provided the connection between organized crime in Chicago and Chicago politicians, the most significant being the influence and the control of Sam Giancana over the political organization of the First Ward of Chicago.
- It was the sole decision of Sam Giancana to remove John D'Arco as alderman of the First Ward. Also, as a result of action taken by C-1 agents, the First Ward was left without an alderman for two years. John D'Arco, during the latter part of November 1962, met with Sam Giancana personally to make a last plea effort to restore his position as alderman of Chicago's First Ward.
- Source confirmed payoffs to local police in the 1st Central Police District for protection of vice and gambling dens operating within the confines of Chicago's First Ward. In February 1963, the monthly payoff to the 1st Police District was $4,200 a month. As a barometer of the effectiveness of gambling raids based on FBI secured warrants and other pressures, in September of 1964, these monthly payments were reduced to $600 per month. Pat Marcy said to the bag man to "tell them that this year has been a very, very bad year." In addition, in December of 1962, the monthly payoffs to the 10th Marquette Police District were reduced from $3,000 a month to $1,000 a month in December 19, 1963. The bag man for the 10th District was Irv Gordon, who had to scale back the payments to the commander, three watch captains, four lieutenants, and twelve sergeants.

- It was confirmed that Pat Marcy, executive secretary of the First Ward, was the direct representative of Sam Giancana and executed the orders of Giancana with regard to the local police, the judiciary, and politicians.
- Source furnished information on the identities of local judges and the degree of control and dominance of the First Ward politicians over their rulings and opinions.
- Chinese gambling games operating within the First Ward produced approximately $6,000 in income per month for the Chicago crime syndicate.

Also, the First Ward was in complete control over the construction of establishments and the need for building permits for renovations within their ward. It was common practice for Pat Marcy to withhold or delay the required construction with work stoppage by union workers until the owners would agree to buy insurance from Anco Insurance, controlled by the First Ward. Other service suppliers, such as laundry, valet parking, etc., were also solicited if they wanted to do business in the First Ward.

As a further confirmation of this practice, a prominent Chicago businessman had previously advised in strict confidence that during the process of building a motel on Michigan Avenue, work suddenly came to a halt by the building trade unions. He then received a call from Pat Marcy who advised him that he could not build a motel in his ward without taking insurance from Anco and other service providers. Once they agreed to the terms of Marcy, the construction of the motel was allowed to continue. The businessman would not go on the record for fear that the First Ward would retaliate in some way and that he would be driven out of business. This matter was not pursued out of deference to the businessman's request and concerns.

Richard J. Daley was mayor of Chicago for twenty-one years. During that time, he was basically a good mayor. He was well aware of the hoodlum influence in the First Ward but chose not to interfere as long as it did not affect him. As long as they supported him, they could coexist. As time went on, Daley became stronger and tried to distance himself from their influence. He survived the Summerdale Police Burglary scandal, when in 1959, a babbling burglar by the name of Richard Morrison, who was being protected by numerous police officers during burglaries in that district, was caught and immersed the police department in corruption practices. Mayor Daley had insisted that the Chicago Police were the finest in the nation. This brought about the appointment of Orlando W. Wilson as the new superintendent of the Chicago Police Department. The mayor also survived the brutal riots that occurred at the Democratic National Convention in August of 1968 when police were accused of overreacting to the unprecedented rioting and damage caused by left wing radicals. Mayor Daley lost his composure at the convention and hurled obscenities at some of his Democratic colleagues.

THE KILLING OF JOHN A. KILPATRICK, LABORLEADER

John A. Kilpatrick, president of Local 300, United Industrial Workers of America (UIWA) was found dead in his car parked in an alley in Chicago with a gunshot wound to his head on October 20, 1961. Two sticks of unexploded dynamite were taped to the steering column and wired to the ignition of the car. It was not known why the dynamite failed to explode. Kilpatrick, at the time prior to his death, was involved in a power struggle with Angelo Inciso, president of Local 286, United Auto Workers Union, who formerly held Kilpatrick's position in the UIWA. Inciso was a Capone mobster associate of Anthony Accardo and recently had been sentenced to serve ten years in prison on a Taft Hartley labor violation, which he blamed on Kilpatrick. Inciso began serving his ten-year prison sentence on December 1, 1961. Because this murder was a local violation, no investigation was conducted by the Chicago FBI until the Chicago office received a phone call from the new US Attorney General Bobby Kennedy. Bobby requested that the Chicago FBI office initiate an investigation of the Kilpatrick murder to determine whether or not there was a violation of federal law. This was an unusual request from the attorney general on a local murder case, and we complied. The C-1 squad was assigned the responsibility of investigating the Kilpatrick murder. We created a task force of about forty agents, which included agents from other squads, and we handled this case as a special priority matter. Investigation centered on Angelo Inciso and Ralph Eugene Polk, a labor goon and close associate of Inciso, who were early suspects in the murder case. Polk had been interviewed by C-1 agents but denied any involvement. William Triplett, then incarcerated at Detroit, Michigan, on armed robbery charges, was questioned about the murder but denied any involvement. He was subsequently interviewed by Chicago FBI agents and on December 28, 1961, confessed to his involvement in Kilpatrick's murder. Triplett disclosed that his uncle, Dana Horton Nash, an ex-convict, who was also in jail in Detroit as a parole violator, had shot and killed Kilpatrick. According to Triplett, they were hired for $500 by Ralph Eugene Polk, the union thug and business agent for Angelo Inciso, to inflict a beating upon John Kilpatrick but not to kill him. Triplett was to receive $250 for his role. Nash got carried away and shot Kilpatrick once in the back of the head. Triplett disposed of the murder weapon in the flush tank of a toilet at a nearby lounge. The weapon was later recovered by the Chicago police. Because there was no apparent federal violation, the local murder case was handled by the Chicago Police Department and prosecuted in Cook County Court in Chicago, where Triplett turned state's witness. Nash was found guilty and received a sentence of 99 to150 years. Triplett was found guilty and received a fourteen-year sentence. The fact that Triplett was a cooperative witness was taken into consideration by the sentencing judge. Angelo Inciso and Ralph Eugene Polk were never charged in this murder. The Chicago news media described the case as the first gangland slaying solved by a confession in thirty years in Chicago. In a separate local case, on September 13, 1962, Ralph Eugene Polk, Inciso's union thug, and his accomplice, Coleman Polo, were each sentenced to serve one year in the county jail for the baseball bat beating of a victim on August 14, 1961.

Angelo Inciso et al.

We were not quite through with Angelo Inciso and Ralph Eugene Polk. On March 2, 1965, subjects Ralph Eugene Polk, Benjamin Tarsitano, and John Barkowski entered guilty pleas to conspiracy to embezzle funds from Local Union 286 and to making false records in violation of the Labor Management Relations Act. Angelo Incisco also pleaded guilty to making false records. On May 13, 1965, Ralph Euene Polk received a three-year sentence and fined $5,000, Tarsitano received a two-year sentence and fined $2,000, and Angelo Incisco received a one-year sentence and fined $2,000. On August 16, 1965, Barkowski was sentenced to two years and fined $2,000.

BOBBY KENNEDY'S VISITS TO CHICAGO

Robert F. Kennedy, more commonly referred to as Bobby, was appointed US attorney general by his brother President John F. Kennedy in 1961. Bobby had an intense dislike for hoodlums and organized crime, and he let it be known to the FBI and other federal agencies that this was one area that was going to receive his close personal attention. Director J. Edgar Hoover needed no prodding because our Top Hoodlum Program had changed its name to the Criminal Intelligence Program (CIP) and had gradually increased the number of men on the C-1 squad to about sixty to seventy agents to handle our additional responsibilities. In 1961, Congress passed additional laws designed to help combat organized crime, which came under the investigative jurisdiction of the FBI and the C-1 squad. These were the antigambling statutes referred to as interstate racketeering (ITAR), interstate transportation of wagering information (ITWI), and interstate transportation of wagering paraphernalia (ITWP). In 1964, Congress enacted the federal sports bribery statute, and in May of 1968, the extortionate credit transactions (ECT) law was passed and designed to combat hoodlum loan sharks who charged their victims exorbitant interest rates.

The case load as well as the manpower on the C-1 squad increased dramatically over the next several years. Agents Joseph Doyle, Bob Malone, Jim Annes, Dane Hill, Bobby Gillham, James York, Peter Wacks, Phil Heil, Jim Bonner, Francis Henwood, James Dewhirst, John Osborne, Robert Long, James Gerblick, Robert Tompkins, and William Bailey, who later became an assistant director at FBI headquarters, were added to the squad. Jim Abbott, Charlie Brown, George Benigni, Paul Neumann, Bill Dougherty, John Riordan, Joseph Cucci, David B. Kelly, Burt Jensen, George Perkins, James Reilly, Peter Bussone, Merle Hamre, Frank Ford, John Oitzinger, and Paul Frankfurt were also added to the C-1 squad. Supervisor Harold Sell left the FBI and accepted a position with the Chicago Crime Commission as operating director. I was appointed in 1963 to replace Sell as the supervisor of the C-1 squad.

In 1962, we were notified that Bobby Kennedy was going to make an inspection visit to the Chicago FBI office. The SAC at the time was Marlin W. Johnson who was very supportive of our program. We were instructed to prepare our individual presentations and accomplishments for Bobby on various phases of organized crime in Chicago. Bobby arrived with his press secretary Ed Guthman and FBI Assistant Director Courtney Evans. Following a brief introductory period, Marlin Johnson began reading from a prepared statement when he was interrupted by Bobby who said, "Let's hear from the agents." He exchanged seats with SAC Johnson; and each agent, about six of us, gave detailed reports on particular targets as well as organized crime in general and police and political corruption in Chicago. Bobby was told about several of our highly confidential microphone sources; and at his request, several tapes were played for him, which detailed the extent of this corruption. Bobby was impressed by the nature and scope of the information developed. He suggested that the information on police corruption be disseminated to Police Superintendent Orlando W. Wilson. Because his request was a suggestion, we hesitated to furnish this highly confidential information to the Chicago Police Department at this time for fear that it could jeopardize our sources. At the conclusion of the conference, SAC Johnson invited Bobby and his group to join him for lunch in the executive conference room. Bobby accepted and told SAC Johnson to include the six agents who were present at the conference. Food and beverage were provided for everyone in attendance, thanks to Bobby Kennedy.

In 1963, Bobby Kennedy had a chance meeting with Superintendent Orlando Wilson and informed him about the police corruption information that the Chicago FBI Division had developed on various police officials of the Chicago Police Department. Superintendent Wilson subsequently made a request of Bobby Kennedy for more details regarding police corruption on his force. The C-1 squad was instructed to provide this information to Wilson. I was given the responsibility of preparing such a report. It had to be prepared very carefully so that our confidential sources would not be exposed or compromised. It was entitled "Alleged Police Tie-ups with Organized Crime in the Chicago Area." It was an eighteen-page document and listed twenty-nine police officers reportedly on the payroll of the Chicago mob. It was a blockbuster and included the names of some high-ranking police officers and their subordinates. The report was forwarded to the personal and confidential attention of Superintendent Wilson, who responded and asked for more evidence to support the allegations. He was told that we did not have any additional documentation; however, it was pointed out that the sources that provided the information had furnished reliable information in the past and that this report was to be used for their confidential administrative guidance. Superintendent Wilson provided a copy of the report to Mayor Richard J. Daley who publicly ridiculed the report as "gossip, rumor, and innuendoes" and described it as "a pretty vicious document." Unfortunately, we could not identify the sources of our information, which we considered at the time to be unimpeachable. As far as we could determine, no corrective action or follow-up was ever taken by Internal Affairs regarding the police officers mentioned in the report. We had complied with the instructions of Attorney General Bobby Kennedy and were careful to avoid confiding in those police officers who were listed in the report.

Bobby Kennedy, accompanied by his press secretary Ed Guthman, would make occasional business trips to Chicago to give speeches and attend various political functions. In each instance, he would call ahead and request an FBI escort for his visit. The C-1 agents who were assigned to this responsibility were John Bassett, Marshall Rutland, Bill Roemer, and me. As a result, Bobby Kennedy and Ed Guthman became good friends with the C-1 agents. On one occasion, John Bassett and I attended a late-night banquet with Bobby. When we returned to the Hilton Hotel, Bobby advised that they had other plans for the evening and would not be using the presidential suite. He told us that we could stay in their hotel room overnight if we so desired. Because it was late at night, we accepted the offer. That was the first time that I experienced sleeping in a bed with satin sheets.

On another occasion, Bobby called and asked if we could meet a late flight at O'Hare airport and give escort to his brother Senator Ted Kennedy and his wife Joan, who were arriving in Chicago from a skiing trip. Bobby was very security conscious about the travel of the members of his family and wanted to make sure that his brother and his wife arrived safely at their hotel. He was assured that the matter would be taken care of, and Marshall Rutland and I took over the assignment and complied with his request.

On another occasion, Bobby arrived with his wife Ethel and their daughter Kathleen, the eldest child of the Kennedys, who at the time was about thirteen years of age. Bobby was met by Mayor Richard J. Daley and his entourage, and I took over the escort responsibilities of Mrs. Kennedy and Kathleen, who had a different agenda than Bobby. Ethel visited the Holy Name Cathedral in Chicago and borrowed a few dollars for the purchase of some religious articles. She requested a brief tour of Chicago for her daughter, especially the Merchandise Mart, which had been long associated with the Kennedy family. Her younger brother Christopher Kennedy eventually would become president of the Merchandise Mart Properties from 2000 to 2012. After some brief shopping, they finally checked into the Ambassador East Hotel. Kathleen Kennedy Townsend went on to become the lieutenant governor of the state of Maryland in 1995. She ran unsuccessfully for governor of Maryland in 2002.

In December of 1963, I received the following Christmas card from Robert and Ethel Kennedy, which depicts Kathleen Kennedy, seated and holding her five-month-old brother Christopher Kennedy, who is now the Chairman of the Board of Trustees, at the University of Illinois:

Kerry   Courtney   Joe   Bobby   David   Michael
Kathleen   Christopher

"Hark The Herald Angels Sing
Glory To The New Born King"

Robert and Ethel Kennedy

1963 Christmas Card From Robert and Ethel Kennedy

THE KILLING OF PRESIDENT JOHN F. KENNEDY

With the assassination of President John F. Kennedy on November 22, 1963, that shocked the world, the FBI initiated an immediate and intense nationwide investigation of this killing. Lee Harvey Oswald, a former high school dropout who was discharged from the US Marine Corps and was an expert marksman, was subsequently arrested two days after the slaying of President Kennedy at a movie theater in Dallas, Texas. Then in a bizarre sequence of events, while being filmed on national TV, and in the presence of numerous journalists and police officers, Oswald was shot to death by Jack Ruby, as he was being transferred from the Dallas jail to the county jail. Jack Ruby was the owner and operator of the Carousel Club, a sleazy strip joint in downtown Dallas. Ruby apparently was devastated by the assassination of the president and reacted irrationally. Ruby was arrested for the murder of Oswald and, while on trial for murder, died about three years later of cancer. It was a common theory at that time that the slaying of President Kennedy, and the killing of Lee Harvey Oswald, was a conspiracy and possibly the work of organized crime. C-1 agents in Chicago were dispatched to the Dallas office to assist in the investigation of the killing of President Kennedy. Because Jack Ruby was originally from the Chicago area, C-1 agents conducted an exhaustive background investigation on Ruby. While in Chicago in the mid-1940s, Ruby was a small-time operator of a strip joint for a brief period of time. No further contact could be established by anyone with Ruby since he left Chicago. The allegation at that time was that the Chicago mob hired Ruby to find someone, namely Lee Harvey Oswald, to kill Kennedy and then silenced Oswald so that there would be no witnesses. That theory could not be farther from the truth. What possible motive would the Chicago mob have for wanting to kill President Kennedy? Sam Giancana was the undisputed leader of organized crime in Chicago, and any decision to kill Kennedy by the Chicago mob would require his personal approval. Granted, Bobby Kennedy, as attorney general, was waging war against organized crime; and the Chicago crime syndicate was not pleased about it, but the FBI had been relentlessly pursuing the Chicago mob since 1957, which was well before Bobby Kennedy became attorney general. It was more of the same and nothing new. In the early 1960s, Giancana was recruited by the

CIA to assist in the assassination of Fidel Castro, so he was friendly with that branch of the government. Giancana was well aware that Frank Sinatra was a good friend and longtime supporter of President Kennedy, and Giancana would not interfere with that relationship. As the person in charge of the FBI's Organized Crime unit in Chicago, we had the responsibility of investigating all of the Chicago aspects of this case. We conducted an extensive investigation into all of these allegations and concluded that there was not one single shred, not one scintilla of evidence, linking Jack Ruby to anyone in the Chicago mob or any link to a conspiracy of any kind since Ruby left Chicago almost twenty years earlier.

In addition, regarding the allegation that there was more than one shooter involved in the assassination of President Kennedy other than Lee Harvey Oswald, no such credible evidence could be found that would substantiate this theory or any of the many other theories that have been proposed. Oswald was known to be a loner. He didn't have a friend in the world. He had renounced America and defected to Russia, where he joined the Socialists Worker's Party. Unhappy in Russia, he returned to America and was trying to flee to Cuba but was unable to do so. He was virtually penniless and was not living with his wife or family. He was an avowed Communist who despised the perceived injustices of the capitalist system. He was able to find a menial job at the Texas School Book Depository in Dallas, which was strategically located along the route of President Kennedy's motorcade visit to Dallas. As a former US Marine, he was an expert sharpshooter and had purchased an Italian war surplus rifle for $19 that had a high-powered telescopic sight. He was able to position himself on the sixth floor of the Texas School Book Depository building and from this excellent vantage point was able to fire three shots in nine seconds at the presidential limousine, the first of which struck the president in the neck and another in the head. After a year of investigation by the FBI and the appointment and scrutiny of the Warren Commission that reviewed the results of the investigation, the Warren Commission also concluded that Lee Harvey Oswald acted alone in the killing of President Kennedy as well as the wounding of Texas Governor John Connally. Also, Jack Ruby acted alone when he killed Lee Harvey Oswald on November 24, 1963. There was no credible evidence of a conspiracy, even though much controversy still exists today among many self-described experts and theorists, but absolutely none can be supported by any facts.

Further and more importantly, had there even been the slightest hint of an organized crime connection or a conspiracy in the slaying of President Kennedy, Bobby Kennedy, as attorney general of the United States, and the highest-ranking law enforcement officer in the nation, with his intense dislike for the members of organized crime, would have initiated an all-out federal grand jury probe into this matter. This was not done or even considered. He was still the attorney general for almost a year following the death of his brother. In addition, at that time, C-1 agents of the Chicago FBI Division had numerous unimpeachable microphone sources available that were monitoring the pulse and the daily activities of the top leaders of the Chicago mob, and there was absolutely not one whisper of information that was forthcoming that organized crime was involved in any way with the assassination of President Kennedy.

Expressions of sympathy were sent to Robert and Ethel Kennedy over the tragic loss of President John F. Kennedy, and the following response cards were received from Robert and Ethel Kennedy in 1963:

We are deeply touched by your thoughtfulness in letting us know that you share in our sorrow.

We are consoled by the knowledge that the love he gave is returned in full measure.

Robert and Ethel Kennedy

**Memorial Card of President Kennedy and Acknowledgment Card
from Robert and Ethel Kennedy**

In 1968, Bobby Kennedy was now a US senator from the state of New York and a front-running presidential candidate for the Democratic Party. He won the important California presidential primary race; and as he was leaving the ballroom of the Ambassador Hotel in Los Angeles, he decided to take a shortcut through the kitchen, despite being advised against it by his close friend and bodyguard Bob Barry, a former FBI agent. In the narrow kitchen corridor, he was accosted by Sirhan Sirhan, a Palestinian who shot him three times in the head with a .22 caliber gun. Robert Kennedy died on June 6, 1968. What a tragic loss of a good friend and a fine attorney general, who had a promising future as president of this great country.

ELECTRONIC SURVEILLANCES (ELSURs) OF CHICAGO HOODLUMS

W ith the success in establishing electronic surveillances (ELSURs) on three of the Chicago mob's prime locations as previously reported, C-1 agents continued to expand their microphone surveillances on additional hoodlums in the Chicago area. The following are a few additional locations that were deemed appropriate for coverage, all of which had the approval of FBI headquarters as well as the US Department of Justice:

Law Offices of Bieber and Brodkin, 188 W. Randolph Street, Chicago, Illinois

This was a highly productive source located in the offices of Michael Brodkin and George Bieber, two of the most unethical and unscrupulous practitioners of law in the city of Chicago. They were well-known mob attorneys and political fixers. Brodkin was a frequent visitor to the Celano Custom Tailor Shop along with John D'Arco and Pat Marcy. Brodkin was in daily contact with many of the leading hoodlums and always carried out their instructions. Bieber and Brodkin were also reportedly involved in assisting the Chicago mob transporting skimmed money from Las Vegas gambling casinos to Chicago and elsewhere. Milwaukee Phil Alderisio, a mob leader and enforcer, was practically a daily visitor to the office of Bieber and Brodkin. Their office was also used as a prime meeting place and a key message center for the members of the Chicago hoodlum hierarchy. On occasion, they were known to assist in attempting to tamper with jury panels in cases involving Chicago hoodlums. They were actively involved in lining up political support to oppose various anticrime legislation bills in the state of Illinois on behalf of organized crime, especially those related to loan sharking, granting of immunity, gambling, wiretapping, and searches and seizure. This source provided the identity of numerous professional and judicial contacts used by the Chicago mob. Also, this source revealed many of the investments of hoodlums and associates along with their daily travels, whereabouts, and activities. There was no question that Bieber and Brodkin were under the complete control of the Chicago hoodlum hierarchy. In 1968, a series of bitter disagreements between Bieber and Brodkin threatened to rupture the partnership of these two hoodlum attorneys. The hoodlum group was very concerned about their breakup because they were an essential part of their organization with their political contacts especially in the local judiciary. Hoodlum leader Gus Alex did everything possible to patch up their differences and to discourage their break up, but to no avail. In early 1969, Bieber and Brodkin dissolved their law partnership and went their separate ways, much to the chagrin of the hoodlum hierarchy.

Sunshine Restaurant, Niles, Illinois

Sunshine Restaurant was located at the corner of Milwaukee Avenue and Harlem Avenue in Niles, Illinois, and was a prime meeting location for Ross Prio, Chicago's North Side boss and his hoodlum associates. Source provided us with Prio's daily activities and the identity of many of his associates. Ross Prio, while residing at 1721 N. Sunset Ridge Road in Glenview, Illinois, would be picked up in the morning by Vincent Solano, his bodyguard chauffeur, and would be taken to the restaurant. He would meet with his associates such as Jimmy Allegretti; the three Doms, namely, Dominic DiBella, Dominic Nuccio, and Dominic Brancato; as well as Joseph DiVarco, Rocco Potenzo, and others. Source provided us with the identity of his bodyguard chauffeur, Vincent Solano, the president of Local 1 of the Laborer's International Union in Chicago, a position held by Solano for twenty-five years. Prio claimed to be a salesman for Kenneth Leonard, owner of Attendant Service Corporation, at a salary of $10,000 a year. This company controlled the valet parking in the Rush Street nightclub area. When Prio passed away in December of 1972, Dominic DiBella replaced Prio. Upon the demise of DiBella in 1976, Vincent Solano took over Prio's Chicago North Side responsibilities.

It is interesting to note that in 1983, an attempt was made to kill Chicago North Side gambling figure Ken Eto by mobsters Jasper Jay Campise and Johnny Gattuso, a Cook County deputy sheriff. Eto was shot in the head several times and miraculously survived the attempt because the ammunition used was old and defective. Ken Eto identified his boss as Vincent Solano, who had ordered his assassination. In July of 1983, the decomposed bodies of Gattuso and Campise were found in the trunk of a car, apparently murdered for botching the killing of Ken Eto.

Apex Amusement Company, Niles, Illinois

In 1962, this source advised that Apex Amusement Company, 7730 N. Milwaukee Avenue, Niles, Illinois, was a distributor of jukeboxes and cigarette vending machines owned by hoodlum boss Edward Vogel. These machines were located primarily in mob-controlled restaurants and bars. The Vogel family previously had been a distributor of slot machines. Hoodlum leader Gus Alex was on the payroll of this company and had a controlling influence of Apex. Source provided "skimming" information from this coin machine operation of approximately $250,000 per year to avoid federal income taxes. Proceeds received from the "skimming" was split between Vogel and Sam Giancana. In addition, source was able to furnish the identity of contacts of Vogel, Alex, and Apex, as well as other hoodlum associates, business interests, and their travel plans.

On March 7, 1969, Kenneth Groeper, a former FBI agent, then an investigator for the Fraud Unit of the Illinois Department of Revenue, advised that his unit, together with the Illinois State Police, made a series of raids on that day and confiscated coin-operated amusement devices for failure to pay state license taxes, based primarily on information provided by the Chicago FBI office. Four simultaneous raids were conducted with one each in Calumet City, Melrose Park, Cicero, and Chicago. Approximately sixty pinball and/or jukeboxes were confiscated. Preliminary investigation indicated that about a quarter of a million dollars per year was being evaded in state taxes by the machine operators. Primary companies involved were Apex Amusement Company, Niles, Illinois, in which Edward Vogel and Gus Alex were connected, and Cooperative Music Company in Chicago Heights, Illinois, in which hoodlums Frank LaPorte and James Catuara held an interest.

Gus Alex and Murray Humphreys' Residences

In 1962, Gus Alex resided at 1150 N. Lake Shore Drive, Chicago, Illinois. Source provided the identity of contacts and associates of Alex and his whereabouts and travel plans on a daily basis. In addition, it identified his business ventures and legitimate enterprises dominated by the hoodlum element.

In 1963, Murray Humphreys resided in Marina City, 300 N. State Street, Chicago, Illinois. Source identified his bodyguard chauffeur as Hy Godfrey, who relayed messages to and from Humphreys' associates. Source provided the identity of Humphreys' associates, meeting places, travel plans, and wide range of influence in union and political affairs.

COMMERCIAL PHONOGRAPHSURVEYINC.

In 1964, Commercial Phonograph Survey Inc. (CPS) was located at 25 E. Chestnut in Chicago, Illinois. Source identified this company as a front for hoodlum activities operated by Joseph "Gags" Gagliano, a Chicago loan shark boss, and his mob associates. Source identified employees of this company as Albert Sarno and Chris Cardi, both former Chicago police officers, and Willie Messino, all loan shark collectors. This company reportedly functioned as a "public relations" association for jukebox operators; however, no such public relations service was ever known to have been rendered. They allegedly would "investigate" new member applicants in the association, and the results would be furnished to Recorded Music Service (RMS). RMS was operated by Earl Kies, the general manager of Apex Amusement Company. When complaints would arise among its members, they would refer them to RMS who would turn them over to CPS for an "investigation." An association fee of $1.25 per month was paid by each jukebox operator for each machine they operated in Chicago. This money went to CPS and RMS, which were operated by members of the Chicago outfit. There were approximately eight thousand jukeboxes licensed in the city of Chicago, and the projected breakdown of income for each month amounted to 0.90 cent per machine to CPS, which would be about $86,400 per year. The RMS association would charge 0.35 cent per machine and received a total of about $33,600 per year. CPS was operated by Joseph Gagliano and his loan shark collectors, Sarno, Cardi, and Messino, would furnish the necessary muscle.

Inasmuch as practically no tavern or restaurant owner or other businessman was permitted to own or lease his own jukebox, other than association members of CPS and RMS, the above jukebox situation appeared to be a violation of the restraint of trade provision of the federal anti-trust statute. These facts were presented to the US Justice Department, and they declined to take any action based on the facts. In February of 1970, this information was subsequently disseminated to the Illinois State Attorney General's Office who showed great interest in this matter. On February 11, 1970, the state attorney general's office filed an anti-trust suit in the Circuit Court of Cook County against CPS and RMS from further actions in restraint of trade and demanded $50,000 fines of CPS and RMS, as well as Apex

Amusement and twenty-eight other jukebox distributors in the state. Apex was one of the largest jukebox distributors in the state under control of hoodlums Edward Vogel and Gus Alex. The attorney general acted under a new civil law passed in 1969 by the Illinois legislature, giving the attorney general broad powers to act against monopolies, especially those controlled by organized crime.

On January 11, 1971, Bernard Carey, newly appointed chief of the Organized Crime Division in the attorney general's office, advised that a consent decree was obtained ending eleven months of litigation charging CPS and RMS with violation of Illinois's anti-trust laws. As a result of the consent decree, the jukebox industry was now free from restraint of trade and could freely solicit individual businesses for the placement of their jukeboxes. Carey termed the decree a huge victory for the state of Illinois and free trade, and expressed his appreciation to the FBI for its cooperation. The above action constituted a serious impairment to the control of organized crime over the Chicago jukebox industry and a drastic reduction of income previously obtained from this industry. The C-1 agents that contributed to making this accomplishment possible were William F. Roemer, William L. Bailey, Harold Johnson, and Lenard Wolf. It should also be noted that CPS loan shark collector Willie Messino was sentenced locally to serve ten to thirty years in prison for kidnapping and torturing a juice loan victim. Also, enforcer Chris Cardi, upon his release from jail, was killed in gangland fashion; and Joseph Gagliano died of a heart attack in 1971 at the age of fifty-six.

JAMES ALLEGRETTI ET AL.

James "The Monk" Allegretti was the hoodlum overseer of the mob-controlled nightclubs and establishments in the Rush Street area of Chicago under the control of Chicago North Side boss Ross Prio. In the early 1960s, there was a hijacking of a large truckload of liquor shipped in interstate commerce from Louisville, Kentucky, to Chicago, Illinois. Chicago agents, assisted by C-1 agents Merle Hamre, Frank Ford, and Gus Kempff, were able to trace most of the stolen liquor into various hoodlum Rush Street clubs under the control of Allegretti. In 1962, a federal grand jury indicted James Allegretti and three of his henchmen, namely, Dave Falzone, a nightclub proprietor; hoodlum Louis Darlak; and Frank "Hot Dog" Lisciandrello, an enforcer of Allegretti.

On June 26, 1962, in US District Court in Peoria, Illinois, Allegretti, Falzone, Darlak, and Lisciandrello were convicted for interstate theft; and each was sentenced to seven years in prison and fined $3,000. All subjects appealed their convictions, but all were upheld in 1965 on appeal. Allegretti tried to avoid prison by claiming poor health and being at death's door with diabetes. Three doctors testified on behalf of Allegretti's poor health condition. C-1 agents, forewarned of this situation through informant coverage, had prepared a special report for the US attorney in which information was set forth concerning Allegretti's nightlife activities and mode of living, which did not conform to the testimony of the physicians. The federal judge in Peoria ruled that Allegretti would get better care in prison in view of the probation report indicating Allegretti overindulged at his nightclubs on Rush Street. Allegretti was released from prison in 1970 and died of a heart attack while en route to Chicago from the penitentiary. Dave Falzone died of a heart attack on April 10, 1965, just prior to serving his seven-year sentence.

JOSEPH A. RISO

J oseph I. Riso was a hoodlum enforcer associated with James Allegretti and North Side hoodlum boss Ross Prio. Based on information provided by a C-1 confidential source, Joseph Riso was arrested by FBI agents on January 25, 1967, as he placed a stolen painting valued at $350,000 in the trunk of his car. Riso was charged with Interstate Transportation of Stolen Property and was released on bond. The painting was identified as the "Virgin and Child with St. Nicholas of Bari and Donor" by Giovanni Bellini, a sixteenth-century Italian masterpiece that had been stolen on October 31, 1965, by burglars from St. Joseph's College, Rensselaer, Indiana. The painting was donated to the college in 1961 by a Chicago art patron. The Chicago mob was reportedly attempting to dispose of the painting through international sources because the painting was "too hot" to sell in this country. A Chicago C-1 source also implicated Riso in a local assault and robbery of a Dallas, Texas, businessman in Rosemont, Illinois. The matter was referred to Undersheriff Bernard Carey, a former FBI agent. Riso was subsequently identified by the victim in a lineup, and Riso was arrested by the Cook County sheriff's police on local charges. He was released on a $10,000 bond.

On June 23, 1967, a federal grand jury in Chicago indicted Joseph Riso for receiving a stolen painting, knowing that it was stolen in interstate commerce. On February 1, 1968, the trial began with AUSA Michael Nash capably handling the prosecution. Chicago agents testified as well as the curator of the J. Paul Getty Museum, Malibu, California, regarding the unchallenged valuation of the painting. On February 5, 1968, the jury returned a verdict of guilty. Riso's bond was increased to $15,000, and he was remanded to the custody of the US Marshal in lieu of bond. On March 20, 1968, Joseph Riso was sentenced by Judge Edwin Robson to serve eight years in prison. Also contributing to the successful outcome of this case were C-1 agent Edward F. Bloom and case agent Robert L. Baker.

Sports Bribery Statute (Leo Casale and Joseph Polito)

In 1964, the sports bribery statute was enacted to give the FBI an additional weapon in combating organized crime. Any scheme in interstate commerce designed to influence the outcome of a sporting event through bribery would be a federal violation. This would include not only to fix a game but to "shave points" in sporting events. Leo Casale and Joseph Polito were gambling associates of the Chicago mob. On February 1, 1965, information was received from a Chicago informant that Casale and Polito were attempting to fix a collegiate basketball game by shaving points. They reportedly were in contact with three Seattle University basketball players to shave points in specific games. The first game involved Seattle University and the University of Idaho in January of 1965. Seattle University was the favorite, and the betting line for the underdog was twenty points. Casale, the Chicago gambler, knew several Seattle players having entertained them at his Action A-Go-Go lounge in Chicago in the past. He traveled to Seattle using stolen identification papers of a Wakefield, Massachusetts, individual. He met with several of the key players of the Seattle team and reportedly got them to agree to win but not by more than nineteen points. Each player was promised $250. The Chicago gamblers bet heavily on the game taking the underdog and twenty points. Since betting was heavy, it drove the betting line from twenty to seventeen points. Seattle won by seventeen, which was exactly the closing betting line. Those who were in on the early betting line made considerable money. It was claimed that the Seattle team was not their usual aggressive selves, and they picked up the pace of the game when the score got close.

Now these two teams were scheduled to play again in February of 1965 at Moscow, Idaho, the home court of the University of Idaho. Based on past performance between these two teams plus the fact that they were playing on the home court of the underdog, the betting line opened up at fifteen points for Idaho. The scheme now was to have Seattle, the favorite team, win by more than fifteen points. Gamblers bet heavily on Seattle University, and Seattle won by twenty-one points. They set a torrid pace, tenacious defense, hit 60 percent of their shots, and the score would have been greater were it not for free substitution. The players denied that they were shaving points, but two players were eventually expelled from the varsity team for failure to report the bribery attempt. One Seattle player, Peller Phillips, was their highest scorer, top play maker, and an all-American candidate. The other player reportedly involved was the team captain. It was one of the city's worst sports scandals and prevented Seattle University from qualifying for the NCAA tournament that year. Leo Casale and Joseph Polito were convicted of sports bribery conspiracy. Casale was convicted by a jury and sentenced to six months in prison and three years on probation. Polito pleaded guilty and receive three months in prison plus three years on probation. These convictions were the very first ever obtained by the FBI under the newly enacted sports bribery statute. I handled this case personally because the information was provided by one of my confidential sources. On March 7, 1967, Joseph Polito, while still on probation, was shotgunned to death in gangland fashion while walking down a street in Chicago.

ERNEST "ROCKY" INFELICE ET AL.

In May 1966, Ernest "Rocky" Infelice, a hoodlum enforcer and West Side boss, was convicted in federal court in Chicago along with Americo DiPietto, James "Cowboy" Mirro, Frank Santucci, all prominent members of organized crime, along with hoodlum attorney Robert J. McDonnell. Subjects were charged in a conspiracy to pass about $15,000 of forged money orders, which had been stolen in Illinois and transported in interstate commerce in violation of a federal statute. Infelice, DiPietto, Mirro, and Santucci were each sentenced to serve five years in prison; and McDonnell received a sentence of two years in prison. David Schippers, chief of the Strike Force, handled the prosecution of this case. Contributing to the success of this case were C-1 agents Merle Hamre, Robert Malone, and Frank Ford. Shortly before the subjects were to begin their sentence, I received a phone call at the FBI office from James "Cowboy" Mirro. I had met him on one previous occasion. He invited me to his farewell party at Gino's East Restaurant in Chicago, which of course I politely declined. At least he still maintained his sense of humor as he faced the reality of going to jail for five years. I wished him well. Shortly after Mirro's incarceration, Anthony Silvestri, a former Cook County probation officer and former associate chauffeur of Mirro, was convicted on March 22, 1967, of one count of interstate conspiracy involving altered American Express Company money orders. On April 25, 1967, Judge Hubert Will sentenced Silvestri to six months in jail and three and one-half years on probation.

MARSHALL CAIFANO

Marshall Caifano had been a prominent hoodlum leader and enforcer for the Chicago Crime Syndicate, who later became the mobs representative in Las Vegas, where he changed his name to John Marshall. He was suspected of having committed a number of murders during his brutal life of crime. His brother Lennie Caifano was killed in 1951, while trying to kidnap Teddy Roe, in an attempt to take over Roe's illegal gambling empire on Chicago's South Side. According to our confidential source, Roe was shotgunned to death in 1952 on orders of Sam Giancana.

The big problem for Caifano as the mob's representative in Las Vegas was that he was one of the so-called underworld figures listed in the "Black Book" issued by the Nevada Gaming Control Board, banning undesirables in Las Vegas casinos. Caifano filed a civil suit in federal court against the Gaming Control Board, and a decision was handed down in 1964, which upheld the Nevada authorities' decision to bar notorious individuals from gaming casinos. Caifano admitted to six prior convictions and had an unsavory reputation of violence and intimidation.

In 1963, Marshall Caifano was arrested by the FBI in Los Angeles for conspiring to extort $60,000 from multimillionaire Ray Ryan, an oil tycoon and high-stake gambler, in violation of the interstate extortion statute. On February 7, 1964, Marshall Caifano together with Charles Tourine Jr. were found guilty in federal court, and Caifano was sentenced to ten years in prison. Tourine Jr. received a five-year prison sentence. The convictions were appealed, and both subjects were released on bond. Although Chicago was not the office of origin in this case, C-1 agent Richard Cavanagh materially contributed to this case as the primary auxiliary office. In 1977, Ray Ryan was subsequently killed in Evansville, Indiana, as a result of a car bomb.

Caifano, while on appeal from his ten-year jail sentence, continued to involve himself in fraudulent activities. On July 28, 1966, an indictment was returned in US District Court in Chicago, charging Marshall Caifano, Anthony Gallos, Dominick Donato, and John Fannon with using counterfeit stock certificates purportedly worth $250,000 as collateral on a loan from an Indiana bank in violation of the fraud by wire statute.

On October 12, 1966, C-1 agents arrested Marshall Caifano in Chicago on a warrant from Los Angeles after the US Supreme Court refused to hear Caifano's appeal on his ten-year extortion conviction. During the fraudulent stock certificate trial on June 23, 1967, Marshall Caifano entered a plea of guilty and was sentenced to serve twelve years in prison to run concurrently with the ten years he was serving for extortion. C-1 agent Richard Cavanagh was the case agent and did an outstanding job in this matter. Upon Caifano's release from prison, Marshall Caifano was again convicted of possessing shares of stolen Westinghouse stock certificates worth about $2,000,000, stolen from O'Hare airport in 1968. He was sentenced to serve twenty years in prison. As the mob's Las Vegas representative, Marshall Caifano was anything but a success. He was soon to be replaced by hoodlum leader and enforcer Anthony Spilotro. In April of 1971, when Anthony Spilotro was preparing to move to Las Vegas for his new assignment, this information was disseminated by C-1 agents to the IRS. When Spilotro attempted to move, six IRS agents seized his loaded furniture van to satisfy a $20,000 tax lien.

GIANCANA SURVEILLANCE 24/7

On March 6, 1963, a telephone call was placed from the telephone listed to Phyllis McGuire in New York City to one Porfirio Rubirosa in France. In May of 1963, we learned that Sam Giancana was considering investing in a gambling operation in the Dominican Republic. On May 23, 1963, Giancana traveled to Santo Domingo, Dominican Republic, where he remained for several days. He was joined by Les Kruse and others who were interested in this gambling venture. Kruse was Giancana's point man and was the gambling overseer for Giancana in Lake County, Illinois. Kruse continued to make biweekly trips to the Dominican Republic; however, no final decision had been made at that time. Giancana was making arrangements to meet with Porfirio Rubirosa, the former Dominican Republic ambassador to the United States with whom Giancana had an acquaintance. Giancana was contemplating a trip to Paris, France, to meet with Rubirosa in June 1963 to further negotiate gambling interests in the Dominican Republic. Based on this information, as supervisor of the C-1 squad, I approved an around-the-clock surveillance of Sam Giancana in an effort to deter the Chicago mob from establishing a foothold in that country, which would have reaped substantial illegal gambling profits for the mob. This called for a large commitment of manpower to institute such an undertaking. We knew in advance that a 24/7 surveillance coverage would be obvious to Giancana but felt that it would be worth the effort to disrupt Giancana's intended plan. Little did I realize at the time the legal furor that would be created by Sam Giancana with his civil suit against the FBI as a result of our surveillance.

The surveillance began upon Giancana's arrival in Chicago from Honolulu, Hawaii, where he had been in the company of Frank Sinatra. Upon his return to Chicago at O'Hare Airport, he was met by his bodyguard chauffeur Butch Blasi and was taken to his residence at 1147 S. Wenonah, Oak Park, Illinois. The agents were told not to engage Giancana in conversation, especially because of the previous volatile confrontation with Giancana at the airport in 1961, but to stay with him at all times wherever he went. Apparently, SA Roemer found it difficult to remain silent to some of Giancana's verbal abuse. As the surveillance became obvious to Giancana, he began to get frustrated and would constantly shout and hurl obscenities at the agents. We were aware that Giancana was an avid golfer and played regularly at the Fresh Meadow Golf Club in Hillside, Illinois. Agents anticipated his playing golf and had their golf clubs available for this assignment. The agent golfers were Bill Roemer, Marshall Rutland, Dennis Shanahan, and John Roberts, all physically large-appearing agents who were good golfers. They would arrange to have a tee time directly behind Sam Giancana and his hoodlum foursome. Some of the golfers with Giancana were Chuck English, Butch Blasi, Slicker Sam Rosa, Johnny "Haircuts" Campanelli, and Sam Pardee, a hoodlum gambler and associate of Anthony Accardo. The presence of the agents teeing off directly behind Gianana and the occasional yelling of "fore" between shots appeared to disturb Gianana, who seemed to spend most of his time hitting his ball from out of the ruff. Of course, the golf fees for the agents that I had to approve were increasing in cost but accepted by the FBI without too much of a challenge from the front office. I certainly thought that these expenses would at least be questioned.

Following about three weeks of constant FBI surveillance, Giancana's tactics and demeanor changed dramatically. He seemed to be more tolerant of the surveillance and was even attending church on Sunday morning and welcoming the agents to join him. As a matter of fact, the FBI agents were now being followed and photographed by the Chicago mobsters. Apparently, Giancana had hired a private investigative agency by the name of John T. Lynch Detective Agency to follow and record the activity of the FBI. The agency assigned Don Ricker to record the FBI surveillance. It was interesting to note that the founder of the John T. Lynch Agency was a former FBI agent, who apparently had no hesitation about investigating the FBI on behalf of Chicago mob leader Sam Giancana. The person behind this strategy was Anthony Tisci, an attorney and son-in-law of Giancana who was married to Giancana's daughter Bonnie. We were well aware that Anthony Tisci was a courier to the Chicago First Ward and was the administrative assistant to US Congressman Roland V. Libonati, a prominent hoodlum politician and former associate of Al Capone and Anthony Accardo. It was Anthony Tisci who reportedly convinced Giancana that his civil rights were being violated and that they should hire a civil rights attorney. They decided on George N. Leighton, a civil rights advocate who later became a Cook County Circuit Court judge. They presented the case to Leighton who agreed to represent Sam Giancana in a civil suit against the FBI and the federal government. It was a most unusual move by the boss of the Chicago underworld. The two former bosses of the Chicago mob, Anthony Accardo and Paul Ricca, were less than enthusiastic and unhappy about this strategy and the unwarranted publicity it would bring. They were more inclined to remain low key and stay out of the limelight.

George Leighton subsequently filed a petition in US District Court in Chicago in which he sought an injunction against the FBI for violating the civil rights of Sam Giancana by placing him under constant surveillance. The injunction named FBI Director J. Edgar Hoover, SAC Marlin W. Johnson, and the FBI. Naturally, FBI headquarters was not too pleased about the civil suit; however, they had been fully informed at the outset and throughout our 24/7 surveillance and our plans to prevent the Chicago mob from gaining a gambling foothold in the Dominican Republic. Apparently, we were being successful in accomplishing our goal; however, it appeared that Sam Giancana had the upper hand for the moment.

The case was heard by US District Court Judge Richard B. Austin who had not been very friendly to the FBI in the past. Attorney Leighton paraded his hoodlum witnesses in federal court. His key witness was Charles "Chuck" English, a lieutenant of Sam Giancana. English had taken some of the pictures of the FBI surveillances. They also played motion pictures of the surveillances as further documentation. I happened to be seated in the court room when Chuck English sat next to me and did not recognize me as being with the FBI. He kept nudging me each time he was on film and saying to me, "That's me. There I am." He was proud of the role he played in helping his boss in this case. Chuck English apparently had forgotten about our previous chance meeting and conversation at the Armory Lounge in the early 1960s.

Even Sam Giancana took the stand and narrated the sequence of events as played on the screen. What a wonderful opportunity the government had to question Giancana about his activities and his role in the mob. He certainly would not have been able to invoke the Fifth Amendment because he was the petitioner in this case. The US attorney at the time was Frank McDonald, who was not well versed about the affairs of organized crime. The assistant US attorney (AUSA) was not prepared for such a witness because he had received his orders from Attorney General Bobby Kennedy on how to proceed.

SAC Marlin W. Johnson was called to the witness stand by Giancana's attorney George Leighton and declined to answer all questions about the FBI agents and the purpose of the Giancana surveillance. After each question, Mr. Johnson read from a prepared statement issued by Attorney General Bobby Kennedy and said, "I respectfully decline to answer the questions based on instructions of the US attorney general." It was unpleasant to listen to the SAC of the Chicago FBI Office invoke the government's version of the Fifth Amendment in a case brought by Sam Giancana. To add insult to injury, on July 23, 1963, Judge Austin held SAC Johnson in contempt of court and fined him $500 for his refusal to answer questions. Mr. Johnson was fingerprinted, fined, and released. As supervisor of the C-1 squad, I had the dubious distinction of having recorded our first organized crime conviction, and that happened to be the SAC of the Chicago FBI Office. I took my lumps on this case from the front office. FBI headquarters was primarily focused on the outcome of the legal aspects of the case in the appellate and supreme courts. This matter did not deter us from continuing to proceed aggressively against Giancana and the Chicago mob.

Judge Austin then issued a preliminary injunction that ordered the FBI to keep an intervening foursome on the golf course between Sam Giancana and the FBI. Also, the FBI could use only one car for surveillance, which should be maintained at least one block away from the Giancana residence. Our contention was that the FBI was not violating the civil rights of Giancana, and we would continue to perform our official duties and conduct our investigation as necessary to discharge our responsibilities. Under our constitution, we have three branches of government, the executive, the legislative, and the judicial. Because there is a separation of powers, there is nothing in our constitution that gives one branch jurisdiction over the other, such as the judiciary over the executive. The preliminary injunction was promptly appealed; and on July 26, 1963, just three days later, the US Court of Appeals Seventh circuit ruled that the defendants, namely the FBI, are part of the executive branch of the government and are not subject to the supervision or direction of the judicial branch as to how they perform their duties. The preliminary injunction of Judge Austin was stayed pending further review. Giancana's attorney subsequently appealed to the US Supreme Court, which refused to review it. That ruling was a huge vindication for Attorney General Bobby Kennedy and the FBI. Sam Giancana was the big loser. He created unwarranted publicity and expense upon himself, and the Chicago mob was becoming more concerned about his flamboyant style of leadership. His control of the mob was in jeopardy. In the meantime, Richard B. Ogilvie, who was now the Cook County, Illinois sheriff, picked up where the FBI left off by having his deputies resume the surveillance of Sam Giancana at his Oak Park residence. All of Giancana's efforts to avoid scrutiny were wasted and ineffectual, and Giancana was prevented from meeting with Rubirosa regarding the mob's gambling interests in the Dominican Republic. Giancana continued in his attempt to gain a gambling foothold in the Dominican Republic. In May 1965, they contacted an individual in Miami, believed to be Hyman "Red" Larner, a hoodlum associate of Eddie Vogel. Larner was to be the contact man between the Chicago mob and the persons who were presently involved with the overthrow of the government. It was assumed that a new government would take control of the country and would allow the Chicago group to open their gambling operations. Giancana had some misgivings as to which group would take over. Our confidential source advised that two Chicago individuals had been in the Dominican Republic for some time on behalf of the Chicago mob; and they were Albert Meo, owner of Meo's Norwood House, Norridge, Illinois, a prime meeting place for Anthony Accardo and others. Meo's picture appeared in the local papers as one of the first Americans evacuated from Santo Domingo at the outbreak of hostilities. According to our source, Meo claimed that he did not bargain for being involved in a shooting war and decided to leave. The second individual to be evacuated was Carmen Peter Bastone, a known hoodlum associate of Chicago hoodlum Les Kruse, who had been involved previously with Giancana in the attempt to set up a gambling operation there. Kruse reportedly had stored a large quantity of slot machines in Florida in 1964 in anticipation of a shipment to the Dominican Republic. It appeared that the revolution resulted in the forced evacuation of Carmen P. Bastone, and the gambling arrangements of the Chicago mob failed to materialize. All gambling was shut down in April 1965 after the revolution broke out.

During all this excitement, Anthony Tisci, who was responsible for assisting Giancana in the civil suit against the FBI, was not finished. As administrative assistant to US Congressman Roland V. Libonati, Tisci assisted Libonati in introducing a bill in Congress to make it a violation of federal law for federal agents to violate a person's civil rights by placing him under surveillance. This bill provided a penalty of ten years and a fine of $5,000 or both. This bill was an obvious attempt designed to aid and assist Giancana but was never implemented. In January 1964, Libonati resigned his position citing family health and was replaced by Frank Annunzio, who had the approval of Sam Giancana. Annunzio was the former Illinois director of Labor and was the First Ward Democratic Committeeman prior to John D'Arco. Tisci retained his position as administrative assistant under Annunzio.

George N. Leighton, the attorney who represented Sam Giancana in his civil rights suit against the FBI, was elected judge of the Cook County, Illinois Circuit Court on November 4, 1964. Just a few months later on March 5, 1965, Judge Leighton rendered a decision that was found to be most disturbing to law enforcement officials. It involved a person, who was trying to cut people with a broken beer bottle. Two off-duty plainclothes police officers who were on their way home responded to the scene. They drew their guns, identified themselves, and ordered the person to drop the jagged beer bottle. The subject cursed at the officers and said, "Come and get it." As they attempted to disarm the subject, he slashed the face of one of the police officers, which required twenty-eight stitches and hospital confinement. In local court, Judge Leighton released the two men accused of this crime and made the following statement, "The right to resist unlawful arrest is a phase of self-defense. What is a citizen to do when he is approached by two officers with a gun?" Judge Leighton considered the actions of the police officers as an illegal arrest.

Two patrolmen associations had called for the removal of Judge Leighton from the Criminal Courts and State's Attorney Daniel Ward and Police Superintendent Orlando W. Wilson called the ruling a miscarriage of Justice. On December 19, 1975, President Gerald Ford appointed George N. Leighton to the federal bench in US District Court in Chicago.

As a result of the furor and national publicity caused by the Giancana civil suit against the FBI, Giancana's woes began to mount. He issued instructions to all of his political associates to discontinue the practice of attending weddings and funerals of hoodlum associates because of the adverse publicity attendant to these affairs. Giancana left Chicago to be with his girlfriend, Phyllis McGuire, who was performing with her sisters at the Cal Neva Lodge, Lake Tahoe, Nevada. It was this romance that received nationwide attention during the Giancana trial. Giancana, while with Phyllis McGuire in her chalet at the lodge, got into an argument with her road manager Victor Collins. Mr. Collins shoved Ms. McGuire toward a chair, which she missed and fell on her pride. Giancana came to her rescue, and a fight followed between Giancana and Collins, with Collins getting the upper hand. Frank Sinatra who was in a nearby chalet heard the commotion; entered Ms. McGuire's chalet along with Edward King, the maître d'; and broke up the fight. It did not take long for the Nevada State Gaming Control Board to learn about the presence of Giancana at the lodge and the highly questionable relationship that existed between Frank Sinatra and Sam Giancana, who was listed in their "Black Book" as an undesirable with a notorious reputation of arrests and convictions. Giancana's presence was not to be tolerated in licensed gambling establishments in Nevada. Because Frank Sinatra was the principal stockholder and licensee of Park Lake Enterprises, which owned the Cal Neva Lodge, he was interviewed on August 8, 1963, by the Nevada Gaming Board about his relationship with Sam Giancana. Sinatra denied the presence of Sam Giancana at the lodge and denied information about the fight with Vic Collins. Sinatra claimed that Giancana was a "decent man" and verbally abused Edward Olsen, the chairman of the Nevada Gaming Control Board, during these hearings. Sinatra had his gaming license revoked, and the Cal Neva Lodge was forced to close. Sinatra also had to give up his interest in the Sands Hotel. That was a huge price to pay for his continuing unsavory relationship with Giancana. Also, a rift had occurred between the McGuire sisters. Dorothy McGuire reportedly had issued an ultimatum to her sister Phyllis to discontinue her association with Giancana, or Dorothy would refuse to sing with the sisters.

1963 Picture of Frank Sinatra's Jet Used by Giancana and Ms. McGuire

This is a picture of Frank Sinatra's jet airplane in 1963, which was made available to Sam Giancana and Phyllis McGuire. N711S was identified as a Gulfstream II jet named *The Sunbird.* Mr. Sinatra's longtime experienced pilot was called "Johnnie."

GIANCANA'S GRANT
OF IMMUNITY

David P. Schippers arrived on the scene as chief of the Strike Force of the US Department of Justice. As a young federal prosecutor, he began his career as an assistant US attorney. In 1963, he joined a branch of the US Department of Justice's Organized Crime Strike Force and on January 1, 1965, was appointed chief of that unit. Dave Schippers was an extremely dedicated, capable, and aggressive attorney. His primary assistant was Samuel J. Betar. Schippers was like a breath of fresh air in the US attorney's office, and the agents of the C-1 squad were about to have a close and highly productive working relationship with him in our war against organized crime.

In 1964, C-1 agents held several discussions with the Strike Force about the best way to proceed against the Chicago mob. Since Sam Giancana had brought suit against the FBI in 1963, we felt it was time for the FBI to return the favor and bring suit against Giancana and his hoodlum associates and corrupt political officials. Normally, the government would consider a grant of immunity to a hoodlum underling to implicate his superior; however, we decided to grant immunity to Sam Giancana, the boss of the Chicago mob, for the purpose of exposing his hoodlum organization and his corrupt contacts. It had never been done before. The concern was that if Giancana was granted general immunity and was able to spin the government's questions, he would be free from all of the crimes of the past and would not be subject to prosecution. We had developed a huge amount of vital intelligence information from which we compiled hundreds of questions. We also put together about nine criminal situations that we felt Giancana could not answer truthfully, and if he lied about them, we were reasonably certain we could prove perjury and he would go to jail. If he told the truth, he would expose the Chicago mob and his corrupt politicians to prosecution. If he refused to answer the questions, he could be held in contempt of court and go to jail for the duration of the grand jury, which usually was for a period of eighteen months. It was a long shot. Of course, the US Department of Justice would have to approve of such a bold plan, because all of the federal agencies were trying to make a case against Giancana, and to grant him immunity could interfere with their investigative plans.

A conference was held with Dave Schippers and his assistant Sam Betar of the Chicago Strike Force. The immunity plan was presented to them. They thought that it was a great idea, but it had to be approved initially by the US Attorney Edward V. Hanrahan before it was presented to the Department of Justice. Schippers was a very bright attorney and was very knowledgeable about organized crime in Chicago, having been born and raised in the Chicago area. Schippers was able to obtain Hanrahan's permission to proceed, but Hanrahan had his reservations about doing so. Schippers and Hanrahan made several trips to Washington to present the matter to their superiors. They met with William Hundley, head of the Organized Crime and Racketeering Section of the US Department of Justice. Hundley then obtained the approval from Attorney General Nicholas Katzenbach, an appointee of President Lyndon B. Johnson. We were all set to embark on a new strategy, with all eyes focused on Chicago. We were about to take on the powerfully entrenched Chicago mob with our focus on its leader, Sam Giancana. It was payback time, and we could hardly wait.

We prepared a long list of hoodlum leaders and their associates as well as their political contacts to be subpoenaed. Of course, we started out with Giancana, who was served on May 9, 1965, while in a phone booth near the Armory Lounge. His heartthrob Phyllis McGuire agreed to appear before the grand jury in Chicago through her attorney, Edward Bennett Williams. We would give Phyllis a second opportunity to tell us about Giancana, because she declined to do so during our initial meeting at O'Hare Airport in 1961. Victor Collins, Phyllis McGuire's road manager, was also summoned. Also included was Bergit Clark, who was Giancana's paramour when Phyllis was not available. It was felt that Bergit might prove to be a psychological weapon on Ms. McGuire, who was known to be extremely jealous of Giancana's other feminine interests. It was noted that Giancana had showered Bergit Clark and Phyllis McGuire with lavish gifts over the years, including expensive jewelry, some of which had been reportedly stolen.

We included the First Ward Organization of John D'Arco, Pat Marcy, and Buddy Jacobson. Also included was the hoodlum hierarchy of Anthony Accardo, Paul Ricca, Gus Alex, Edward Vogel, Ralph Pierce, Jack Cerone, Fiore Buccieri, Lester Kruse, and Sam "Teetz" Battaglia, who would probably succeed Giancana in the event he had to step down as boss. Battaglia was finally subpoenaed after having reached speeds of one hundred miles per hour in his Cadillac while en route to his horse breeding farm near Pingree Grove, Illinois. Others included Leo Manfredi, a gambling figure; Manny Skar, who was later killed in gangland fashion; Hyman Godfrey, courier for Murray Humphreys; Ernest "Rocky" Infelice, hoodlum enforcer; Guido DeChiaro, a jukebox distributor; and Stephen Anselmo, an attorney who was reported to be "Giancana's man."

In addition, we included Giancana's close personal friends, his son-in-law Anthony Tisci, his bodyguard Dominic "Butch" Blasi, Richard Cain, former chief investigator for Sheriff Richard Ogilvie, and Chuck English, who had gloated over taking photos of FBI agents during the 24/7 surveillance of Giancana earlier in 1963. The subject of Frank Sinatra was raised, but it was decided that we would not subpoena Sinatra. We did, however, include many questions for Giancana regarding his questionable alliance with Sinatra, who had reportedly invested in several Las Vegas establishments for Giancana. The subpoenas were issued and served by C-1 agents. The stage was set, Giancana was our target, and the greatest show on earth was about to begin.

C-1 Agent Marshall Rutland was designated as an agent of the federal grand jury. He was the first one to testify and detailed the background of Sam Giancana and his relationship to Phyllis McGuire and others. Based on a suggestion of Dave Schippers, the next witness called was an incarcerated Chicago hoodlum named Americo DiPietto, who had been convicted the previous year of operating a $10 million narcotics ring. He was subpoenaed from Leavenworth penitentiary where he was serving a twenty-year sentence. In May of 1965, DiPietto appeared as the next witness. It was Schippers's strategy to keep DiPietto on the stand for a while so that the other witnesses might think that DiPietto may be a cooperative witness. One by one, the hoodlum witnesses appeared before the federal grand jury in Chicago, and all refused to testify by invoking the Fifth Amendment against self-incrimination, except for their names and addresses. Murray Humphreys refused to state his name and address and was dismissed immediately and held over for the following week. Anthony Tisci also took the Fifth Amendment and was highly embarrassed by the degrading questions asked for such a person in a highly placed government position. Phyllis McGuire stole the show. She looked as glamorous as ever and was the center of attraction. She did testify about certain telephone calls made from her credit card; however, she took the Fifth Amendment about her calls to Sam Giancana and his associates. She answered some questions about her travels with Giancana and admitted associations with certain subjects who were appearing before the grand jury. Ms. McGuire was held over for a second day. It was felt that each additional witness would further ensure Giancana's continued refusal to answer questions. Victor Collins, Ms. McGuire's road manager, testified as to the use of McGuire's credit cards by Giancana, placing of calls to Giancana, the use of aliases by Giancana, and the details of the fight that took place at the Cal Neva Lodge in 1963.

Sam Giancana was called to appear on May 14 and again on May 20, 1965, at which time he took the Fifth Amendment to a constant barrage of highly penetrating questions. On May 27, 1965, Giancana again appeared before the grand jury and again refused to testify invoking the Fifth Amendment. He was taken before Chief Judge William J. Campbell, at which time Judge Campbell offered Giancana complete, broad, and absolute immunity from prosecution and explained that this immunity applies to all crimes, state or federal, that may arise from his testimony. He ordered Giancana to return to the grand jury and answer the questions truthfully. Giancana did not anticipate this procedure. He had always invoked the Fifth Amendment numerous times in the past based on the advice of his attorney and was able to walk away without any problem. His attorney Tom Wadden was not allowed to be with him during the grand jury proceedings. Sam, at this time, was before the grand jury and was completely on his own.

June 1, 1965, was decision day for Giancana. No one knew what Giancana planned to do. Was he going to lie and subject himself to perjury, was he going to tell the truth and expose himself to the wrath of the Chicago mob, or was he going to remain silent and be held in contempt of court? His choices were not too promising. Giancana informed the court that he was going to testify. That statement reverberated throughout the halls of the federal court house. US Attorney Edward V. Hanrahan called me and said in a very frantic tone that Giancana was going to testify and that it was up to us to prove perjury. I calmly assured Hanrahan that Giancana could not possibly testify truthfully, and if he did testify, we would prove perjury. Our reputation was on the line, and we felt confident of our position.

Giancana then went before the grand jury for the fourth time and furnished his name and address only. He again refused to answer any further questions. He was taken to the courtroom of Chief Judge Campbell and admitted to the judge that he refused to testify. Judge Campbell told Giancana that he was in direct and continuing contempt of the court, at which time he was turned over to the custody of the US Marshal. Judge Campbell reminded Giancana, "You have the key to your own cell. When you decide to obey the order of this court, notify the US Marshal, and he will return you to the grand jury." Our strategy worked. It was a great victory for Dave Schippers, the Department of Justice Strike Force, the US Attorney Edward Hanrahan, and for the C-1 agents of the FBI. All of our efforts were rewarded. Hanrahan and Schippers publically expressed their sincere appreciation for the tremendous job done by agents of the FBI, who laid the groundwork of evidence that was furnished to the federal grand jury.

Sam Giancana, the boss of one of the most powerful crime syndicates in the nation, had been jailed and humiliated. The jailing of Giancana caused great discontent and disruption to the Chicago mob. The duration of the grand jury term had one year remaining before it expired, which meant that Giancana would be in jail for at least one year unless and until he agreed to testify.

Giancana's attorneys were busy filing appeals, seeking his release; however, the US Court of Appeals denied Giancana's request for release on bond. Edward Bennett Williams, Giancana's attorney from Washington DC, filed a petition asking the US Supreme Court to review the case; however, they refused to do so. The end result was that the contempt of court citation was not subject to a bond or to an appeal. Sam Giancana was in control of his own destiny and was now incarcerated in cell block Tier C-1 of the Cook County jail, as a constant reminder of the C-1 agents who put him there.

In June 1965, Strike Force Chief Dave Schippers notified the FBI that he was in receipt of phone calls from three Chicago attorneys, advising him that rumors were prevalent among Chicago attorneys that there was an outstanding offer of

$100,000 to any attorney who was able to come up with a legal maneuver to free Giancana from his contempt of court sentence, under which he must remain in jail for the next year. According to Schippers, the offer was nationwide in scope. A story appeared in the *Chicago Tribune*, indicating the same information. This would indicate that various Chicago attorneys were at least giving thought to freeing Giancana, but none had been successful to date. Our confidential source advised that over $100,000 has been expended by Chicago hoodlums in their efforts to free Giancana.

Regarding Anthony Tisci, son-in-law of Sam Giancana, who took the Fifth Amendment before the federal grand jury, US Congressman Frank Annunzio issued a statement in July 1965 indicating his complete confidence in his administrative assistant Anthony Tisci. He announced that he had no intention of requesting his resignation from his position as Congressional assistant because of the adverse publicity resulting from recent grand jury appearances. This statement apparently was to set the stage for a letter furnished to the local papers by Tisci to Annunzio, thanking him for his confidence, but said that for health reasons and upon the advice of his personal physician, he was tendering his resignation "for the more sedentary role of a practicing attorney." Tisci added that recent publicity in no way influenced his decision to resign at that time.

Shortly after the jailing of Giancana, information was received that Sam was receiving preferential treatment from the prison guards. They were providing him with Cuban cigars, steaks, wine, and other amenities. This information was provided to Sheriff Richard B. Ogilvie, who had Warden Jack Johnson initiate an investigation. As a result, it was determined that two guards, who were friendly with Giancana, were responsible for catering to Giancana's desires and were subsequently fired. Giancana was no longer receiving special treatment and was now enduring the usual hardships of being confined along with the other inmates. Giancana was visited on practically a daily basis by hoodlum attorney and associate, Anthony V. Champagne. It was apparent that Champagne was acting as courier between Giancana and the Chicago mob.

In August 1965, the Intelligence Unit of the St. Louis, Missouri Police Department received information that a meeting of hoodlums from the Chicago and Kansas City areas was to occur in St. Louis in the near future. They alerted the security men at various hotels to be alert for such activity. On August 20, 1965, they were notified that a group of four individuals from Illinois had arrived in a chauffeur-driven limousine and had checked into the presidential suite at the Chase-Park Plaza Hotel. The room had been signed for by Anthony Esposito. The four individuals arrived and were confronted by the Intelligence Unit of the St Louis Police Department and were interviewed. They each furnished basically the same story for being in St. Louis. They claimed they traveled to Springfield, Illinois, to attend the Governor's Day ceremonies at the Illinois State Fair and continued on to St. Louis. In the evening, they dined in the Frontier Room with an individual named Steve Gorman, the owner of a brick-laying business in St. Louis. It was noted that Gorman was a close associate of Frank "Buster" Wortman, the hoodlum leader in the St. Louis and downstate Illinois areas. The hotel bill was paid in full by Steve Gorman. The four persons identified themselves as follows:

- Charles Nicosia, employed as a security evaluator for the Illinois attorney general's office and worked out of Judge Thaddeus Adesko's Cook County Court
- Pat Marcy, former secretary to the alderman of the First Ward of Chicago, then employed with Anco Insurance in Chicago
- Anthony Tisci, a practicing attorney in Chicago
- Anthony Esposito, the recording secretary of Local 1001 of the County and Municipal Employees Union in Chicago

All denied knowing Steve Gorman except Esposito. All four individuals denied knowing any members of the crime syndicate in Chicago. It was noted that Local 1001 of the County and Municipal Employees Union was under the control of Vincent Solano, the president of the union. Solano was the bodyguard chauffeur for Ross Prio, a Chicago North Side boss. Also, Anthony Esposito was reported to be the brother of Frank Esposito, the powerful labor union official who was slated for a gangland slaying by Giancana in 1962. Nicosia, Marcy, and Tisci were apparently representing Sam Giancana's interests.

MURRAY "THE CAMEL" HUMPHREYS

With Giancana safely tucked away in a Cook County jail, our attention turned to Murray "The Camel" Humphreys, one of the most elusive and influential members of the Chicago mob dating back to the Capone era. It had been reported that Murray Humphreys was in ill health; however, that was all a ploy to divert attention away from his activities. Dave Schippers, chief of the Strike Force, was eager to bring Murray Humphreys before the federal grand jury again and issued a subpoena for his appearance. Bill Roemer was given the assignment to serve the subpoena and went to Humphreys' apartment on the fifty-first floor of the East Tower of Marina City in Chicago. His brother Ernest, also known as Jack Wright, a former bookmaker, answered the door and claimed that Murray Humphreys was not at home. It was readily apparent that Humphreys was home and now was aware that there was a subpoena outstanding for him. He fled to Norman, Oklahoma, to avoid the subpoena and to conveniently visit his first wife. The subpoena was sent to the FBI at Norman, Oklahoma, where agents were able to serve him for his appearance before the federal grand jury in Chicago. Because Humphreys had obviously fled Chicago to avoid the subpoena, Dave Schippers felt that Humphreys' actions constituted a contempt of court violation and issued a warrant for his arrest. Humphreys was arrested by the FBI and lodged in the county jail in Oklahoma City until June 28, 1965, when he was returned to Chicago by the US Marshal's office. He was released on a $100,000 bond.

On August 10, 1965, Murray Humphreys appeared before the federal grand jury. After sparring with the grand jury, he was taken before Chief Judge William J. Campbell and ordered to cooperate. When asked about the reasons for avoiding the recent subpoena by fleeing to Oklahoma as well as his avoidance of the subpoena for his recent appearance in the Sam Giancana grand jury, Humphreys' responses were contradictory and untruthful and led to his indictment on November 23, 1965, for perjury.

Immediately following the perjury indictment of Murray Humphreys, an arrest warrant was issued. Bill Roemer, the case agent on Humphreys, was reluctant to participate in the arrest of Humphreys. Roemer felt that because he admired

Humphreys whom he considered to be a worthy adversary, he did not want to be one of the arresting agents. I did not agree with Roemer's reasoning for not participating in the arrest of his subject; however, I did not make it an issue. Four agents were designated to execute the arrest warrant at the fifty-first floor Marina City apartment of Humphreys; and they were Marshall Rutland, Thomas Parrish, Dennis Shanahan, and John Bassett, all large athletic-appearing agents. They proceeded to Humphreys' apartment, knocked on the door, and announced their presence as being with the FBI in a loud and clear voice and that they had a warrant for his arrest. Humphreys had a peephole in the door so that he could see the agents. There was no response after four attempts. The agents demanded entry and began to use force to break down the door. Humphreys opened the door and appeared with a .38 caliber snub-nose revolver in his right hand pointed at the agents. The agents could have shot Humphreys right then and there, because they were threatened with a gun after having identified themselves as FBI agents; however, the agents pointed their weapons toward him and used unusual restraint to disarm him while placing him under arrest. Humphreys said, "If you guys had been cops, I would have killed you." The agents conducted a search of the apartment incidental to the arrest, which further infuriated Humphreys. He tried to break away from Agent Tom Parrish and drew blood by biting Parrish on the hand. His last words were "You don't have anything on me. You would have to be Houdini to get anything on me. I've covered my tracks all the time." Humphreys may have been highly regarded as a legal advisor to the mob, but as his own counsel, he was completely lacking in sound judgment at this time. Humphreys refused to cooperate during the search and was abusively resistant. The agents found a key in Humphreys' pocket, which led them to a closet safe where agents seized a second .38 caliber revolver and confiscated $25,000 in cash as well as some personal papers that were of intelligence value. He was allowed to call his attorney George Callahan, who appeared at the apartment as the search was in progress. He was taken to the FBI office for processing and was later delivered to the US Marshal's lockup. Defense Attorney Maurice Walsh also appeared on the scene and joined attorney George Callahan. They both arranged for Humphreys' release that evening after posting a $4,500 bond on his perjury charge. Because of Humphreys' role in organized crime, the Chicago news coverage of his arrest was considerable, including front-page headlines.

At about 9:00 p.m. on November 23, 1965, only about six hours after his arrest, his brother Ernest visited the Humphreys' apartment and found him lying face down on the floor of the apartment. He summoned a house doctor to examine Humphreys, and he concluded that Humphreys died of a heart attack. The assets that had been confiscated at the time of the arrest of Humphreys were subsequently turned over to his estate. Unfortunately, upon a recount of the cash, which had been previously seized and recorded as $25,000, we found that there was a shortage of several hundred dollars. The agent who inventoried the cash was John Bassett, our former light heavyweight boxing contender, who obviously made an honest mistake.

We resolved the shortage by having the agents involved in the case, as well as myself, pay the difference out of our own pockets. Strike Force Attorney Dave Schippers helped us in returning the money to the Humphreys' estate. Of course, when we inventory cash, it should have been counted by at least two agents. We learned the hard way, but it was worth it to take down an elder statesman of the Chicago mob and a former associate of Al Capone. He had been invaluable to organized crime because of his ability to corrupt public and judicial officials on all levels and thereby obtain all kinds of favorable treatment for his hoodlum associates. With the passing of Humphreys, the mob lost access to scores of his contacts who thereafter declined to grant favors to organized crime.

ELECTRONICSURVEILLANCES (ELSURs) DISCONTINUED

In 1965, there was considerable controversy between FBI headquarters and the US Department of Justice over the use of electronic surveillances (ELSURs) without the benefit of a court order. FBI headquarters' contention was that ELSURs had always been approved in advance by the US Department of Justice. Bobby Kennedy, as US attorney general, claimed that he was unaware that the FBI had ELSURs in operation. Since Bobby Kennedy had been in Chicago in1963 and had listened to ELSUR tape recordings in person, he had to be aware of the use of ELSURs by the FBI. The C-1 agents, who were present during the playing of these tapes for Bobby Kennedy, were asked to submit affidavits to that effect. These statements were forwarded to FBI headquarters to support of our position. In any event, President Lyndon B. Johnson, a civil rights advocate, signed an executive order in July of 1965 that effectively made the use of ELSURs, without a court order, a violation of civil rights. At this time, the Chicago office had about twenty ELSURs in operation. We immediately discontinued the use of our ELSURs that provided the Chicago FBI office with vital intelligence information on the activities of major organized crime hoodlums in the Chicago area on practically a daily basis for the past six years. FBI headquarters requested that all of the FBI equipment used in these ELSURs be removed from their locations. That was a monumental task because it required covert entries into all of the sensitive locations and greatly increased our exposure. This was accomplished over the next several months without incident. From a practical standpoint, I was somewhat relieved over the discontinuance of ELSURs because the daily monitoring of these taped conversations and the transcribing and evaluating the information obtained was an extremely time-consuming responsibility. Also, the intelligence information obtained could not be used to prosecute our subjects in a court of law. If we were going to make substantive cases against the Chicago mob, we were going to need information from live witnesses who could testify against these hoodlums as well as the use of court-approved ELSURs. In addition, as cases were developed by the FBI against our subjects, we had to certify to the courts in each and every case that the information developed did not originate from the use of an illegal ELSUR. SA William Roemer was somewhat disappointed over the discontinuance of

ELSURs. He had enjoyed working the intelligence information obtained every day, and he performed his task very well. This development, however, did not dim the enthusiasm of the C-1 agents who were about to make further progress and inroads against the Chicago mob.

TITLE III OF THE OMNIBUS CRIME CONTROL ACT OF 1968

On June 19, 1968, Congress passed Title III of the Omnibus Crime Control and Safe Streets Act of 1968, which set forth rules and procedures allowing federal agencies to obtain court-approved wire tapping and electronic eavesdropping surveillance coverage. This was a huge boost to our criminal intelligence and gambling programs. It gave us the legal authority to further penetrate organized crime on an interstate basis and against its prime source of income, which had been illegal gambling. The C-1 agents embraced this new legislation with contagious enthusiasm and unyielding tenacity. One by one, we obtained court orders against the Chicago mob's interstate gambling network. This was in addition to our numerous local gambling raids based on FBI secured warrants, which were executed by local and state authorities. Over the next several years, we initiated about seventy-five court-approved Title III surveillances, which had a huge disruptive and devastating effect on the mob's ability to operate their gambling network. This caused a substantial loss of revenue to various elements of organized crime in this area and elsewhere. For example, a Title III was utilized on a large sports and horse race gambling operation of Dennis Finn of Aurora, Illinois, with Chicago and Miami connections. The monthly handle was estimated to be $1 million. In 1971, C-1 agents executed ten search warrants at ten wire room locations that resulted in the indictment of thirty subjects. C-1 agent Bobby Gillham did a fine job as the case agent. In addition, C-1 agent James Annes did exceptional work in handling of a complex Title III on Charles Bishop Smith, the largest bookmaker in Lake County, Illinois. Smith was in charge of a large-scale bookmaking operation that included thirty-three subjects that handled an estimated $425,000 in bets per month. Many Title III electronic surveillances followed, and our continuing expanded coverage proved to be a major weapon in the penetration of the mob's activities.

THE ORGANIZED CRIME
CONTROL ACT OF 1970

On October 15, 1970, the Organized Crime Control Act of 1970 became law; and that included as one of its major provisions the Racketeer-Influenced and Corrupt Organizations, more commonly referred to as the RICO statute. This gave the FBI a tremendously effective tool to combat organized crime. This defined a pattern of racketeering activity as two or more violations of state law such as murder, gambling, robbery, extortion, usury, etc., that constituted a violation of the RICO statute. Also included in the act was the Interstate Gambling Business (IGB) statute, which prohibited a gambling organization of five or more people to be in business for more than thirty days or accumulate $2,000 in gross revenue in a single day. We were finally getting the legislative tools we needed to combat the Chicago mob.

As a result of the new IGB legislation, on November 14, 1970, C-1 agents made their first IGB arrests at Morrie's Liquors, 5738 S. Prairie, and at a next-door walk-in bookmaking parlor at 5724 S. Prairie, Chicago, Illinois. Morrie's, a combination tavern and package store, was a front for one of the largest gambling operations in Chicago during the prior twenty years under the control of hoodlum leader Ralph Pierce. Its monthly handle was approximately $100,000. Arrested was Sam Lennett, the owner of Morrie's, and four other subjects. Seized at the time of the raid was an apparent payoff list of thirty police officers, which included three lieutenants, twelve sergeants, and fifteen detectives, that represented various police districts and other police units that allowed this operation to flourish. William Hermann was the case agent and did a remarkable job, assisted by C-1 agents Dennis Shanahan, Herb Briick, and others. All subjects were successfully prosecuted in federal court in Chicago under this new federal law. The liquor license at Morrie's was also revoked.

Vincent "The Saint" Inserro

I was surprised to hear about a Chicago hoodlum whose name was so similar to mine. "The Saint" first came to my attention when C-1 agent Lenard Wolf told me about an arrest he made of a fugitive named Vincent "The Saint" Inserro in 1956, which was prior to the start of the Top Hoodlum Program. His nickname was "The Saint" because he was from St. Louis, Missouri. He had a long history of crime and was known for his violent temper and animal-like behavior. In 1932, he was convicted for armed robbery in Lake County, Illinois, and was sentenced to serve one year to life for that crime. He was received there under the name of Frank Tuffano, and it was some time before his true identity was learned. He had the reputation of never owning anything in his own name, and this was borne out by his auto registration and even his home and phone number, which were in the name of Mario DeStefano, a well-known hoodlum. The crime for which he was convicted in Lake County was a vicious robbery in which he and four other armed men forced their way into the home of a Lake Forest, Illinois, family and robbed the home owner and eight of their guests of money and jewels valued at $150,000. During 1951, Inserro was reportedly involved in the attempted robbery of the Bowman Dairy Company in Chicago during which Rocco Belcastro and Frank Piazza were killed by a Brink's guard. "The Saint" and three other well-known hoodlums were reportedly involved in the crime; however, they escaped. On October 17, 1951, Inserro was arrested for the baseball bat beating of a Northlake, Illinois, civic leader who was attempting to drive organized crime out of that community. Inserro was captured after a wild eighty-mile-an-hour chase, driving a car identical to that observed at the scene of the beating. Although he was tentatively identified, the police were unable to develop enough evidence to warrant prosecution because of lack of witnesses.

On September 22, 1954, Vincent Inserro, while walking down the street with his wife near his residence in North Riverside, Illinois, got into an argument with several construction workers and accused them of whistling at his wife. A worker by the name of Arthur Ebenroth interceded in the argument. Ebenroth told Inserro that the men were only whistling at a new car. Inserro became enraged, pulled out his knife, and stabbed Ebenroth to death and fled. The Chicago Police Department issued a murder warrant for the arrest of Inserro. Because they were unable to locate Inserro, they requested the assistance of the FBI because they believed he had left the state of Illinois to avoid prosecution. An FBI wanted flyer was issued on "The Saint," and a fugitive case was assigned to our prolific fugitive hunter SA Lenard Wolf. It did not take long for SA Wolf to locate and arrest Inserro who was submissive at the time of his arrest. He showed no remorse for the murder and commented to the agents that, "Ebenroth got what he deserved." He was subsequently turned over to the Chicago Police Department.

Inserro was later tried by a Cook County, Illinois, jury on the murder charge and was acquitted after only three hours of deliberation. The local press severely criticized the decision and the manner in which the case was prosecuted. Fear and intimidation were reported to be factors in his acquittal in this case.

Vincent "The Saint" Inserro

Inserro's connection with the Chicago outfit was that of an enforcer and hit man. He was a made member of the Chicago mob and was reported to have been involved in a number of murders in the 1950s. He reportedly worked over the owner of the MGM Lounge in Cicero, Illinois, with a baseball bat and thereby became a partner in that business. The North Riverside Police Department had numerous dealings with Inserro who was well known to them because of his violent temper. They had answered disturbance complaints at his residence, including the reported discharge of firearms. Officers of that department had seen his wife badly bruised after frequent beatings. On one occasion, the police telephoned Inserro at his home to advise him that they had a warrant for his arrest rather than face him in person at his residence and be confronted with his violent temper. On September 29, 1963, a cab driver went to the Inserro residence to collect a cab fare. Inserro smashed the driver across the face with a fireplace poker, kicked him in the groin, and shoved him down a flight of cement stairs. The cab driver filed assault charges against Inserro, and when Inserro appeared in court on that charge, he went berserk. The North Riverside Police had to use drawn guns and handcuffs to restrain him. He was sentenced to ten days in the county jail.

Inserro was also in charge of a group of youthful burglars and robbers who shared their "earnings" with the Chicago hierarchy through Inserro. I heard nothing more about "The Saint" until I met Captain Frank Pape, Robbery Detail of the Chicago Police Department. Upon hearing my name, Pape laughed out loud and told me that he was hoping to catch up with my namesake. Pape had set up a trap at a warehouse where a load of stolen goods was stored. Inserro was expected to claim it, and he was ready for him. I assumed he meant that a gun battle would take place and that the suspected mobster would be on the receiving end. Captain Pape had the reputation of being the toughest cop in Chicago. He had sent nine suspects to the grave and never received an injury. Unfortunately for Captain Pape, as a result of a warrantless raid on a suspect's south side home in 1958, the suspect's family filed a federal civil rights suit against Captain Pape, which was upheld by the US Supreme Court and eventually contributed to his retirement in 1972.

In the mid-1960s, I began to receive telephone calls from some of my neighbors who told me that deputies from the Cook County sheriff's office were in the neighborhood inquiring about me. It was apparent that they had assumed that I was identical with "The Saint" and were attempting to find out about my activities. I had to contact Sheriff Richard Ogilvie and tell him that his officers were investigating the wrong man. I was the good guy. Since my phone number was listed in the phone book, I also began receiving calls at my home from unknown callers asking to speak with "The Saint." My wife was also receiving visitors at our home during the day, asking for "The Saint," only to be told that they had the wrong address. She became greatly concerned so I finally removed my listing from the phone book. Little did they know that they were talking to the FBI.

I opened a criminal intelligence case on the "The Saint" and assigned it to Agent John Dallman. He learned that Inserro was an associate of Cicero boss Joseph Aiuppa. He still had the reputation as a hit man for the Chicago mob and had been responsible for a number of murders. He was scarcely five feet tall and weighed only about 130 pounds, but he had the reputation of being a vicious cold-blooded killer. Agent Dallman determined that Inserro failed to file federal income tax returns for the years 1959 through 1963, while having earned substantial income from vending machines in Cook and Kane counties for that period of time. This information was turned over to the Internal Revenue Service, and Inserro was indicted by a federal grand jury. He entered a plea of guilty on May 31, 1966, in federal court of failure to file tax returns for the five years in question. Federal Judge Hubert Will sentenced Inserro to serve two years in the federal penitentiary and one year on probation following his jail sentence. That put "The Saint" out of circulation for the time being.

Sam "Teets" Battaglia

Joseph "Joe Shine" Amabile

Joseph "Joe Shine" Amabile was a prime lieutenant of hoodlum leader Sam Battaglia. In 1966, investigation by C-1 case agent John Dallman disclosed that Amabile had been convicted in January of 1947 of possessing counterfeit federal sugar rationing stamps and had been sentenced to one year in prison and fined $10,000. It was noted that Amabile paid only $500 of the fine and owed the government $9,500, claiming to have been a pauper and unable to pay the balance. It was obvious that Amabile was living a lifestyle of a very prosperous individual. He had recently sold property in Northlake, Illinois, to Greyhound Van Lines for $250,000 and had invested this money along with Sam Battaglia in a new nightclub known as "Strangers in the Night" in Melrose Park, Illinois. Amabile also purchased a $70,000 home in Addison, Illinois, where he resided. As a result of Amabile's apparent assets, this information was made available to the US attorney's office, and a judgment was pursued by the government against Amabile for payment of the $9,500. On October 24, 1966, US Attorney Edward Hanrahan advised the FBI that his office received a cashier's check for $9,500 in full payment of Amabile's fine. It was learned that Chicago hoodlum attorney Joseph I. Bulger strongly urged Amabile to pay his fine in an effort to get the government off his back.

Efforts by Amabile and Battaglia to obtain a state liquor license for the new nightclub, "Strangers in the Night," had been stalled. The nightclub was scheduled to open on August 3, 1966; however, Amabile had been unable to obtain the approval of a state liquor license from the Illinois Liquor Control Commission (ILCC). Based upon the background information provided by the FBI to Howard Cartwright, chairman of the ILCC, each of Amabile's proposed hoodlum licensee applicants for "Strangers in the Night" had been rejected. The attorney for Amabile sought a rehearing, and the liquor license was again denied. It was reported that Amabile was considering selling the nightclub so that he could recoup his $250,000 investment in this stalled venture. The nightclub was still closed after a four-month period. Robert Wiedrich, crime reporter for the *Chicago Tribune*, wrote an article exposing Joseph Amabile's criminal background and his futile efforts to open his new hoodlum nightclub on behalf of Sam Battaglia. He also highlighted the FBI's role, which resulted in Amabile paying his 1947 debt to the US government. FBI investigation centered around four other clubs under the control of Sam Battaglia in Melrose Park, Illinois; and they were the Charm Club Inc.; Mary Ann's Tavern aka Mary Lou's; Avenue Lounge, formerly the Casa Madrid, a mob gambling joint; and Club Twenty. These four establishments and the still unopened "Strangers in the Night" comprised the nucleus of Sam Battaglia's vice and gambling operations in hoodlum-dominated Melrose Park, Illinois. Additional information was confidentially furnished to the chairman of the ILCC regarding recent violations that occurred at the Charm Club and Mary Ann's Tavern. Both club owners were subsequently given citations and notified to appear at a hearing to show cause why their state liquor license should not be suspended or revoked. In November 1966, Sam Battaglia was seen twice conferring with his liquor licensee John Zito, at Mary Ann's, concerning the prospects of more trouble with his Melrose Park locations, which had long been a haven for the Battaglia group. Melrose Park Mayor Chester Carson was contacted by the FBI and tactfully declined to cooperate in this matter citing fear of retaliation against himself and his family.

During the course of this investigation, it was noted that Sam Battaglia owned a four-hundred acre, $500,000-horse breeding farm in Pingree Grove, Illinois. He had been dumping old rusty cars and trucks and miscellaneous farm equipment on his property without displaying proper state license plates. This information was disseminated to local authorities who apparently were reluctant to act until this situation was exposed by a headline article on November 19, 1966, by *Chicago Tribune* crime reporter Robert Wiedrich, which was supported by photographs. The Battaglia farm was referred to as "a cancer on the landscape." Kane County, Illinois, zoning officials and the Illinois State Police were dispatched and began a crackdown on the use of all vehicles on the farm to ensure that Battaglia cleaned up his farm and complied with the law.

The ILCC held hearings on December 6, 1966, on the Charm Club and Mary Ann's. The Charm Club was granted a continuance until January 3, 1967, to prepare its case. Representing Mary Ann's Tavern was attorney Stuart Spitzer, an associate of hoodlum attorneys Bieber and Brodkin. Spitzer was observed consulting with attorney Mike Brodkin and Anthony Champagne, Sam Giancana's attorney, all during the hearing, indicating the full force of the mob's legal talent being employed to thwart efforts of the ILCC and the FBI. Spitzer moved for a continuance because his chief character witness, attorney Joseph I. Bulger, had been killed in a weekend plane crash, and his second character witness operated the funeral home handling Bulger's wake and funeral. Mary Ann's Tavern hearing was also granted a continuance until January 3, 1967.

It was noted that Joseph Imburgio Bulger's true name was Joseph Imburgio, and he had been a hoodlum attorney for the Chicago mob for the prior three decades. Bulger's double life was exposed by his death on December 2, 1966, when his private twin-engine Aero Commander plane piloted by him crashed in the wooded hills of Tennessee. It was determined at that time that Joseph Bulger had the luxury of two wives, two families, and two homes. His two wives were Mrs. Elsie Bulger in Melrose Park, Illinois, and Mrs. Sallee Bulger in Miami, Florida, whom he visited on practically a weekly basis by plane. Many questions still remain about his bizarre lifestyle and the millions of dollars that he reportedly managed for the Chicago mob. Bulger would have made quite the character witness for Battaglia.

In late December, 1966 the attorneys representing "Strangers in the Night" filed a motion in the Circuit Court of Cook County before a judge more "friendly" to their cause; however, this attempt was thwarted, and a ruling was not expected for thirty days. License revocation hearings before the ILCC were held on January 3, 1967, regarding Mary Ann's Tavern and the Charm Club. Mayor Chester Carson and Chief of Police Anthony Iosco were subpoenaed and testified. Both were pawns of Sam Battaglia. The hearing for Mary Ann's Tavern concluded with testimony tying in licensee John Zito to Battaglia's former notorious gambling casino at the Casa Madrid in Melrose Park for which Zito held a federal wagering stamp. This case had been taken under advisement prior to a final decision. The attorneys representing the Charm Club, operated by Frank Parillo, whose father-in-law, Rocco Salvatore, was the gambling overseer for Battaglia in Melrose Park, attempted to surrender his liquor license at the hearing, which was refused by the ILCC. This would have allowed a new licensee to operate the club, whereas a license revocation would prevent any liquor from being sold at this location for one year from the date of revocation. The attorneys for the Charm Club were surprised by a new ILCC citation charging the Charm Club with having a convicted gambler Rocco Salvatore, as a corporate officer that was additional grounds for revocation. The Charm Club attorneys moved for a continuation and change of venue on grounds that the ILCC was under pressure from the US attorney's office and the FBI to close these locations. They also complained of prejudicial newspaper accounts. This case was also taken under advisement. ILCC sources advise that pressure on Chairman Howard Cartwright continued to be extremely intense from politicians and other contacts of the Chicago crime syndicate in an effort to discourage him from taking positive action against the licensees of these locations, which were lucrative sources of income for the Chicago mob. In the meantime, FBI efforts continued to maintain pressure on Battaglia's nightclub and gambling operations in Melrose Park, Illinois. Devastating gambling raids were conducted during the prior two years culminating in the triple raids of Sam Battaglia's gambling operations on January 14, 1967, in Melrose Park by the Cook County sheriff's police, based on local search warrants obtained by the FBI. In addition, the ILCC subsequently revoked the liquor licenses for Mary Ann's Tavern as well as the Charm Club. It was also determined that the Esquire Club in Melrose Park, another notorious Battaglia vice den, was in violation of the state liquor laws. This information was also furnished to the ILCC, and the license for the Esquire Club was soon to be revoked. Information was received that a local citizen group had been formed in hoodlum-dominated Melrose Park based upon recent damaging publicity concerning that community, resulting from the continuing FBI investigations there; and the group had demanded "good government" in that community. Throughout this entire investigation, Agent Dallman was capably assisted by C-1 agents Peter Kotsos, Edward Bloom, Lenard Wolf, and Harold Johnson.

Following the incarceration of Sam Giancana, Sam "Teets" Battaglia, a powerful Chicago West Side boss, reluctantly accepted the position of acting boss of the Chicago mob. His problems, however, were just beginning and his reign was about to be short-lived. In 1966, C-1 Agent John Dallman commenced a joint FBI and IRS investigation of Sam Battaglia and one of his top lieutenants Joseph Amabile. The investigation centered around a conspiracy to extort money from William G. Riley, president of the Riley Management Corporation, during the construction of the King Arthur Apartments in Lansing, Illinois. They were responsible for conspiring to obstruct shipments of building materials in interstate commerce in violation of the Federal Hobbs Act extortion statute. The case was prosecuted by Dave Schippers, chief of the Strike Force, assisted by Sam Betar and Joseph Lamendella. This case was one of the most significant cases of the year involving crime syndicate chieftain Sam Battaglia and his lieutenant Joseph Amabile. C-1 agents acting as agents of the federal grand jury served a subpoena on Riley and seized fifty-three boxes of business records, which were reviewed and used throughout the grand jury and the trial. The trial commenced April 24, 1967. One week prior to the trial, the Chicago hoodlum hierarchy had obtained a number of copies of the prospective jurors in this case. The purpose apparently was to determine, which juror would be most susceptible to an approach to vote for an acquittal. Chicago hoodlums Phil Alderisio, Ralph Pierce, and Gus Alex were in charge of supervising the background investigation of the jurors. A female juror was allegedly approached and reportedly agreed to vote not guilty; however, this unidentified juror became quite concerned and later decided to vote guilty. Chicago hoodlum leader Gus Alex expressed his deep indignation to Phil Alderisio that the Chicago hoodlums, who had been assigned to tamper with the jury, reportedly bungled the job. It was noted that only one juror's ballot was taken and it was unanimous for guilty as charged. In addition, information was confidentially received that a Chicago police officer named Ronald O'Hara, reportedly on a leave of absence from the Chicago Police Department, had been working on a confidential basis for veteran defense attorney Maurice Walsh on this case. O'Hara was conducting background investigations of witnesses and other confidential work to assist Walsh in defending the subjects. O'Hara had been reported to be closely associated with Chicago North Side gambling boss Leonard Patrick.

On May 9, 1967, the jury returned a verdict and found all subjects, namely Sam Battaglia along with his lieutenant Joseph Amabile and construction manager Dave Evans, guilty as charged on conspiracy to violate the Federal Hobbs Act extortion statute. Federal Judge Julius Hoffman refused a motion of all defendants to be admitted to bond and placed them in custody of the US Marshal until sentencing. On May 29, 1967, Judge Hoffman sentenced Battaglia to fifteen years in prison and fined him $10,000. Joseph Amabile was also given a prison sentence of fifteen years and fined $10,000, and Dave Evans received a ten-year sentence and fined $5,000. The three subjects were also ordered to pay a total of $6,000 in costs for the three-week trial. Judge Hoffman denied a motion for an appeal bond because the three key witnesses in this case, as well as the family of William Riley, had been threatened by the subjects. Judge Hoffman stated, "This is one of the most serious cases in the federal criminal courts. It would be dangerous to the community, based on the evidence, to have any of the defendants admitted to bail. I would be derelict in my responsibility if I admitted them to bail. I find each one of the defendants to be dangerous. I cannot assume the responsibility of letting these defendants go about threatening people with baseball bats." Also as a provision to the sentence, Judge Hoffman stated that all subjects remain confined until the fines and costs were paid. He then ordered each defendant to be taken into the custody by the US Marshal to begin their sentences immediately.

While at the Cook County jail waiting to be transferred to the federal penitentiary in Leavenworth, Kansas, Sam Battaglia was reportedly being given preferential treatment similar to that of Sam Giancana because of his important hoodlum status. Cook County Sheriff Joseph I. Woods was notified and initiated an investigation and corrected the situation. Sheriff Woods advised that the federal tier of the Cook County jail was now crowded with prominent Chicago hoodlums, noting that Marshall Caifano and Rocco Pranno were confined there along with Sam Battaglia and Joseph Amabile. Woods was experiencing some difficulty in keeping these prisoners separated so that members of organized crime could not conspire with each other in jail. As a result, Battaglia was confined in the same general area as Richard Speck, a recently convicted murderer of eight student nurses in Chicago, a situation that was disturbing to Sam Battaglia.

Following the convictions of Battaglia and Amabile, the US attorney's office took immediate steps to ensure that the fines and costs levied by the federal judge were not lost to the government as a result of a possible transfer of assets by the subjects. This included an injunction that specified that Joseph Amabile must pay the $10,000 fine plus the $2,738 in court costs prior to selling his $250,000 investment in the Strangers in the Night. The Chicago news media carried extensive articles on these convictions because of the notoriety and importance of Sam Battaglia as acting boss of the Chicago mob and his lieutenant Joseph Amabile and attributed the successful results to the cooperative efforts of the FBI and IRS. Attorneys for Sam Battaglia, Joseph Amabile, and Dave Evans appealed their convictions to the US Court of Appeals; and their convictions were upheld. They petitioned for a rehearing, which was refused.

It was noted that there were three key witnesses who testified for the government in this case, namely William G. Riley, president of Riley Management Company and victim of the extortion conspiracy; Michael DiVito, a suburban contractor; and Henry LaKey, president of the Carlson Construction Company. LaKey was the principal witness against Sam Battaglia and was present during a conversation at Battaglia's horse breeding farm that tied Battaglia into the shakedown conspiracy. Following the trial, government witnesses William Riley and Michael DiVito were given new identities and were relocated to other parts of the country. Henry LaKey declined to be relocated from the Chicago area and changed his name to Henry Rufo and moved to Lombard, Illinois. On December 15, 1971, the body of Henry Rufo, true name Henry LaKey, was found in the trunk of a stolen car in Freeport, Illinois. He was the victim of a brutal gangland slaying. Rufo's body was viciously beaten and showed signs of knife wounds, cigarette burns, and other forms of torture. A rope was still fastened around his neck, which apparently had been used to suspend his body throughout the torture. There was no known publicity of LaKey's killing in the Chicago news media. The reason for the killing was never established, but it was obvious that it was the work of the Chicago outfit sanctioned by Sam Battaglia. It was known that Henry LaKey had been fronting for Joseph Amabile in the Carlson Construction Company and had been a willing participant as a subcontractor in the shakedown conspiracy of William Riley. Also, LaKey had been paid $20,000 as seed money and had reportedly absconded with a portion of the funds. To withhold funds and to testify against Sam Battaglia, the mob boss, proved to be fatal. It was unfortunate that LaKey did not accept the government's offer to relocate to another part of the country. In the meantime, Sam Battaglia served six years in prison, and because of his bad health caused by cancer, he was released during the summer of 1973. He died eleven days later at the age of sixty-four. Amabile died in 1976 shortly after his release from prison. Battaglia never got to enjoy the prestige and wealth that accompanied his lofty position as acting boss of the Chicago mob. His tenure as mob boss was an unpleasant experience and lasted for only about a year.

Photo of Sam Battaglia

ROCCO PRANNO

Rocco Pranno, a prominent Chicago West Side boss and underling of Sam Battaglia, was in complete control of the western suburbs of Stone Park and Northlake, Illinois. The Pranno investigation was also handled jointly by C-1 agent John Dallman and his IRS counterpart. On March 9, 1968, Rocco Pranno was found guilty of conspiring with Northlake officials Wayne Seidler and Peter Anderson to extort $23,000 from two contractors who were attempting to build industrial plants in Northlake in violation of the Federal Hobbs Act statute. On April 27, 1966, Chief Federal Judge William J. Campbell sentenced Rocco Pranno to serve fifteen years in prison, and he was denied an appeal bond. Seidler and Anderson were sentenced to serve five and three years, respectively.

In 1966 before Rocco Pranno was sentenced to jail, Pranno was an active participant in a closely related shakedown case involving Joseph Amabile and other Northlake officials of William G. Riley, a contractor who was also building the King Arthur apartments in the town of Northlake, Illinois. Joseph Amabile, Henry Neri, former mayor of Northlake, and two other former Northlake aldermen, Joseph Drozd and Leo Shababy, along with hoodlum plumbing contractor Nick Palermo were shaking down Riley by withholding necessary zoning and building permits during the construction of this facility. Although Rocco Pranno was not charged in this case, his name was mentioned prominently throughout the trial. Amabile and his co-conspirators were found guilty of extorting about $250,000 over a three-year period from victim Riley in violation of the Federal Hobbs Act statute. On October 28, 1968, Joseph Amabile and his co-conspirators received lengthy sentences; however, these convictions were subsequently overturned by the US Court of Appeals, and the subjects were reindicted by the federal grand jury. Joseph Amabile was deleted from the second trial because of a ruling of double jeopardy. On March 23, 1971, Federal Judge Frank McGarr sentenced former Mayor Henry Neri and Nick Palermo, a relative of former Chicago crime boss Anthony Accardo, to serve five years each in prison. Also, former Northlake City aldermen, Leo Shababy and Joseph Drozd, received jail sentences of three and seven years, respectively.

STERLING-HARRIS FORD AGENCY SCAM

Leroy Silverstein, alias Leroy Sterling, and George Harris owned the Sterling Harris Ford Agency in Chicago. Harris was a former business partner of Larry Rosenberg, a former secretary-treasurer of Twin Food Products, a hoodlum-dominated company in which Leo Rugendorf was president. Rugendorf was a major jewelry fence and chief underling of hoodlum leader and enforcer Milwaukee Phil Alderisio. During the weekend of March 4-5, 1961, the owners of this agency sold over three hundred cars to Chicago hoodlums and their families and friends at prices far below cost. They received over $225,000 from the sale of these cars. A short time later, they declared bankruptcy, and the creditors could only locate about $5,000 in assets. Also, the records of the agency had conveniently disappeared. Agents of the FBI investigated the matter as a National Bankruptcy Act (NBA) scam committed by the Sterling Harris Agency under the aegis of Leo Rugendorf upon instructions of Milwaukee Phil Alderisio. C-1 agent John Bassett, while investigating another matter, happened to stumble upon the missing records of Sterling Harris, which solidified the case against Silverstein, Harris, Rosenberg, and Rugendorf. In court testimony, locating the missing records without benefit of a search warrant was allowed and referred to as "serendipity." On July 10, 1964, all four subjects were indicted and later found guilty of conspiracy to conceal assets in violation of the NBA. Federal Judge Joseph Perry sentenced each of the four subjects to five years in prison and a fine of $19,000. Subjects appealed the sentences and were granted a new trial. In March of 1968, Leo Rugendorf and Leroy Silverstein entered pleas of guilty and were each sentenced to one year and a day in prison. In September of 1968, George Harris was sentenced to one year in prison, which was later vacated because he had served sixty days in jail and had been making restitution. In October 1968, Larry Rosenberg was found guilty and sentenced to one year in prison and fined $10,000.

JOSEPH Y. STEIN

Joseph Y. Stein was another scam operator associated with Leo Rugendorf and Milwaukee Phil Alderisio. Stein and Larry Rosenberg were charged with violating the mail fraud statute by defrauding their victims under the guise of obtaining mortgage loans for them. On December 11, 1970, Joseph Stein entered a plea of guilty. US District Court Judge Frank McGarr sentenced Stein to four years in prison followed by five years on probation. Charges against Larry Rosenberg were dismissed.

IRWIN "PINKY" DAVIS ET AL.

I rwin "Pinky" Davis along with Alan Rosenberg, Burton Wolcoff, and Harris Jacobs were professional financial swindlers associated with Chicago hoodlum leader and enforcer Milwaukee Phil Alderisio. In 1963, subjects traveled to Bettendorf, Iowa, where they negotiated the formation of a company known as the Harris Discount Center. Over a period of time, they ordered merchandise for the company that exceeded $100,000, which they converted to their own use and allowed the company to go bankrupt without paying its creditors. The merchandise was reportedly shipped to Chicago and disposed of by Alderiso, who profited from the scam. On August 16, 1966, all four subjects were convicted in federal court in Des Moines, Iowa, of mail fraud conspiracy and violating the federal bankruptcy statute; and each was subsequently sentenced to serve five years in prison. Also, Davis and Rosenberg were fined $10,000 each, Wolcoff was fined $5,000, and Harris was fined $1,000. The information leading to the successful prosecution of this case was developed by C-1 agents Peter J. Wacks and Gus Kempff. Alan Rosenberg was murdered in gangland fashion on March 17, 1967, while on bond, appealing his conviction. On May 21, 1968, the US Court of Appeals affirmed the convictions in this case. This case was very significant because it would cause Irwin "Pinky" Davis, while serving his prison sentence, to become a government witness, whose testimony would ultimately result in the conviction of hoodlum leader Milwaukee Phil Alderisio on a similar type of financial scam operation.

Felix "Milwaukee Phil" Alderisio

Milwaukee Phil Alderisio had been one of the most powerful members of organized crime in Chicago and a ruthless mob enforcer. He had been reported to be involved in numerous gangland slayings. He had over thirty-five arrests ranging from assault and battery to murder and had managed to avoid prosecution until just prior to taking control of the Chicago mob in about 1967, following the jailing of acting boss Sam Battaglia. Alderisio's reign as acting boss was suddenly about to unravel. His partner, an enforcer during the late fifties, was Chicago hoodlum Charles Nicoletti. On May 2, 1962, the Chicago police responded to a call about a suspicious looking black car during the early morning hours and found Alderisio and Nicoletti crouched on the floor. They claimed they were just waiting for a friend and had no idea who owned the car. They were taken into custody and released on bond. The police discovered that the car was obviously a "hit car" that was fictitiously registered and had a hidden compartment to hold weapons. Both were charged only with disorderly conduct.

On October 2, 1964, the FBI in Miami filed a complaint against Alderisio, charging him with interstate travel to commit extortion. Alderisio reportedly assaulted a Denver Colorado banker while in Miami and threatened the banker's daughter. Alderisio was subsequently arrested by C-1 agents at his Riverside, Illinois, residence after he refused entry to the agents who had to use force to enter his home. He also threatened the agents who placed him under arrest. Alderisio was transported to Miami to stand trial and was released on a $25,000 bond. On October 29, 1964, Milwaukee Phil Alderisio's charmed life would continue for a while longer, because a federal jury in Miami found Alderisio not guilty of the extortion charges brought by the Denver banker.

Alderisio, while free on bond in the Miami case, could not behave himself. He was indicted again by a federal grand jury in Denver, Colorado, along with Chicago hoodlum enforcer Americo DiPietto and two Las Vegas gamblers Ruby Kolod and Willie "Ice Pick" Alderman. They had threatened to kill and extort money from Robert Sunshine, a disbarred Denver attorney, in violation of the interstate extortion conspiracy statute. Alderisio also threatened to harm Sunshine's wife and family. On February 4, 1964, Alderisio was released on a $100,000 bond in Chicago.

On March 29, 1965, the trial began in Denver, and the jury began hearing testimony. Chicago C-1 agents Ralph Hill, Marshall Rutland, Robert Malone, Gus Kempff, Bill Roemer, and I were called by the defense to testify in this case. Alderiso was represented by prominent attorney Edward Bennett Williams. Attorney Williams attempted to show that this case was based on information obtained illegally from eavesdropping devices, which was not the case. Subjects Kolod and Alderman wanted Alderisio to testify on their behalf to establish their innocence, but Alderisio refused. He wanted no part of being a witness.

On April 7, 1965, the federal jury in Denver returned a verdict of guilty against Alderisio, Kolod, and Alderman on count 1 of the indictment. On May 14, 1965, Federal Judge Arraj sentenced subjects as follows:

- Alderisio: four and one half years in prison and a fine of $7,500. He was permitted to remain free on a $50,000 bond while he appealed his conviction.
- Kolod: four years and a $5,000 fine
- Alderman: three years and a $7,500 fine

Americo DiPietto was acquitted on both counts; however, he was currently serving a twenty-year sentence for conspiring to sell narcotics.

In July 1969, another case was developed by C-1 agents involving Milwaukee Phil Alderisio and his co-conspirators. A fraudulent firm named the Chemical Mortgage Investment Company of Chicago was created by Alderisio's underlings, Irwin "Pinky" Davis, then serving a seven-year sentence for a mail fraud scheme, and the late Alan Rosenberg, a master swindler who was killed in gangland fashion in 1967. Alderisio financed this shell operation with a payment of $5,000. Subjects applied for nineteen home improvement loans, most of which were fictitious or had insufficient collateral. With the aid of Richard Jackowski, a former loan officer of the Parkway Bank in Harwood Heights, Illinois, they defrauded the bank of approximately $89,000. On July 25, 1969, the federal grand jury in Chicago returned a suppressed indictment charging Alderisio with conspiring to defraud a suburban bank in violation of the Federal Reserve Act statute by obtaining $89,000 through the use of fraudulent applications for nonexistent home improvement loans. Also named in the indictment, as co-conspirators were Alan Rosenberg and Richard Jackowski. Irwin Davis was named as an unindicted co-conspirator. Arrest warrants were issued and on Sunday, July 29, 1969, at 10:45 a.m. Alderisio was arrested at his residence 505 Berkeley Road, Riverside, Illinois, by C-1 Agents Dennis Shanahan, John Bassett, Bill Roemer, and I. Agents Gus Kempff, Ray Shryock, John Roberts, and Max Fritschel, the case agent, conducted a search of the residence.

Present at Alderisio's home at the time of his arrest was Joey "The Clown" Lombardo, a hoodlum enforcer and protégé of Alderisio. It was known that

Alderisio held regular Sunday meetings at his home for his hoodlum associates to discuss plans for the upcoming week's activities. Some of the hoodlums, who arrived to attend the meeting, noted the presence of agents and quickly departed from the area without comment. Those identified approaching Alderisio's residence were Joseph Glimco, president of Local 777 of the Taxicab Union; Frankie Schweihs, a notorious mob hit man; and Patrick Ricciardi, a bail bondsman and cousin of Alderisio. Since the arrest was made on a Sunday, Alderisio was taken to police lockup for the night and was subsequently released on a $100,000 surety bond on Monday July 30, 1969. A joint news release was made by US Attorney General John Mitchell and FBI Director J. Edgar Hoover because of the obvious stature of Felix Alderiso as a top leader of organized crime in Chicago. The indictment and arrest of Alderisio culminated a four-year investigation by C-1 agents.

At the time of Alderisio's arrest, an elaborate gun vault was discovered at his home by FBI agents that contained a large collection of thirty-three weapons. This included fourteen handguns and nineteen rifles and/or shotguns. Because Alderisio was a convicted felon, possession of these weapons appeared to be a violation of federal law. With the consent and approval of the then US Attorney Thomas Foran, the matter was referred to the Alcohol, Tobacco, and Firearms Division (ATFD). Based on an FBI affidavit, the ATFD agents seized the thirty-three weapons with FBI agents as observers and rearrested Alderisio the very next day, July 30, 1969, for illegal possession of weapons by a convicted felon. Alderiso was released on a $25,000 surety bond on the firearms violation. It was determined that one of the handguns in his possession had been reported stolen in a burglary of a Chicago resident about six years ago, and a burglary report had been filed by the Chicago Police Department. Alderisio initially claimed that these guns belonged to his son Dominic but later withdrew that claim when he realized it could cause problems for his son. Also part of his gun collection included a match pair of .22 caliber Colt derringers that were last known to be owned by Nick Danolfo of Las Vegas. It would appear that Danolfo was identical with Nick "Peanuts" Danolfo, last known to have been employed at the Desert Inn Casino in Las Vegas and a known associate of Sam Giancana. Not only did this indictment serve as a basis for revoking Alderisio's appeal bond on his extortion conviction in Denver in 1965, but it also led to his immediate imprisonment in September of 1969. Alderisio's problems were far from over. On September 3, 1969, he was arrested by state authorities for failure to comply with the Illinois Gun Registration Act on the basis of an affidavit executed by C-1 agents Gus Kempff and Ray Shryock. Alderisio posted an additional $1,000 bond.

In January 1970, the Alderisio trial on the federal bank violation commenced. The principal witness in this case was Irwin "Pinky" Davis, a convicted underling of Alderisio, who was serving a seven-year prison term for mail fraud. Davis was greatly concerned for his own safety as well as the safety of his family because he greatly feared retaliation by Alderisio. Davis was personally contacted by US

Attorney Thomas Foran at the US Penitentiary in Terre Haute, Indiana, where his cooperation in this matter was secured. Davis made an outstanding witness and testified that he participated with Alan Rosenberg, Milwaukee Phil Alderisio, and Richard Jackowski, the loan officer to defraud the Parkway Bank out of a large sum of money by utilizing fraudulent home improvement loans. On January 23, 1970, at midpoint during the trial, Alderisio withdrew his not guilty plea and entered a plea of nolo contendre. At the same time, he changed his plea of not guilty to guilty for the illegal possession of firearms. He was subsequently found guilty on January 23, 1970, on the federal bank violation. On January 30, 1970, Federal Judge Alexander Napoli sentenced Alderisio to serve the maximum penalty of five years in prison on the bank violation and two years on the federal firearms violation to run concurrently with the four-and-one-half-year sentence previously imposed by the federal court in Denver in 1965. The Alderisio case was personally handled by US Attorney Thomas Foran and his capable assistants Richard Makarski and Jeffery Cole. They did an outstanding job prosecuting this case. It was later declared in open court that reliable information had been received that a $50,000 hit contract had been placed on the life of witness Irwin "Pinky" Davis by the Chicago hoodlum element because of his cooperation. Following the testimony of Davis, Mr. Foran had Davis transferred to another penal institution for his safety and had his family relocated to a secure place to ensure their personal safety.

It was noted that the federal firearms violation against Alderisio was withdrawn by Judge Napoli and prosecution was deferred to the State of Illinois on the charges of violating the State Gun Registration Act. In a local Cook County court, Alderisio was subsequently fined $500 and sentenced to serve one year in jail on the gun charge, to run concurrently with all of the sentences previously imposed. On September 25, 1971, Milwaukee Phil Alderisio died of a heart attack at the federal penitentiary in Marion, Illinois, at the age of fifty-nine. This brought an end to the brutal history of one of the most vicious hoodlums in the Chicago mob.

In September 1971, following the death of Alderisio, information was received that he had a safety deposit box at the Cermak-Oak Park Safety Vault Co. This information was provided to the IRS who obtained a court order and opened the box on October 1971. The total content of the box was estimated to be $58,000, which was seized by the IRS.

Milwaukee Phil Alderisio

JOSEPH DIVARCO AND JOSEPH ARNOLD

Joseph "Caesar" DiVarco and Joseph Arnold were top lieutenants in charge of organized crime affairs on Chicago's near North Side nightclub area for hoodlum leader Ross Prio. During the course of many debriefings of incarcerated hoodlum underling Irwin "Pinky" Davis by C-1 agents, which resulted in the conviction of hoodlum leader Milwaukee Phil Alderisio, additional information was obtained concerning hoodlum activities in the Chicago area. Pinky Davis also advised that in1965, when he and Alan Rosenberg (deceased) operated the Chemical Mortgage Investment Corp. (CMIC), a dummy corporation set up for the purpose of defrauding the Parkway Bank of Harwood Heights, DiVarco and Arnold approached him and told him to furnish them with fraudulent W-2 forms so that they could report income of about $12,000 from commissions and fees from the CMIC to conceal their income from illegal sources. This information was turned over to the US attorney's office and the IRS. This information was confirmed by the IRS, and on March 7, 1972, DiVarco and Arnold were indicted for filing false income tax returns in 1965. Pinky Davis was listed as a co-conspirator and testified during the trial. The jury found DiVarco and Arnold both guilty as charged; and on August 8, 1972, Judge Hubert Will sentenced them each to one year in prison and five years on probation. US Court of Appeals denied subjects' appeal. US Attorney James R. Thompson made a news release and described the outcome as significant convictions against organized crime members. AUSA Michael Siavelis did a fine job in handling the prosecution of this case, which was made possible by information from a C-1 source.

THIS IS YOUR LIFE, SAM GIANCANA

E ach year, SAC Marlin W. Johnson would travel to FBI headquarters for his annual conference with FBI Director J. Edgar Hoover. Johnson wanted to present Hoover with some sort of a memorable photographic display that would be reflective of the work and accomplishments of the Chicago Division. Because Mr. Johnson had the embarrassing distinction of having been convicted for contempt of court in the civil suit brought by Sam Giancana against the FBI in 1963, his fellow agents thought that a book narrating the life and incarceration of Sam Giancana would be appropriate. We prepared a large loose leaf notebook, with the FBI seal on the cover, and included about twenty-five choice photographs of Sam Giancana and his associates along with some caption comments. SAC Johnson thought that this was a good idea and took the notebook with him for his interview with Mr. Hoover in 1966. Apparently, SAC Johnson's interview and the large notebook containing pictures of Giancana went over well with Mr. Hoover. The following is a sampling of some of the pictures that had been included in this book as they were displayed to FBI Director J. Edgar Hoover.

This is your life Sam Giancana - You were born in Chicago, Illinois on June 15, 1908, to immigrant parents Antonio Giancana and Antonia nee DeSimone, natives of Italy, who entered the United States in 1906. Throughout your humble beginnings you resided in a poorer section of Chicago, but with success came affluence. In the 1930's you moved to a more fashionable area of Chicago and resided in a five room flat on Chicago's near west side as pictured above.

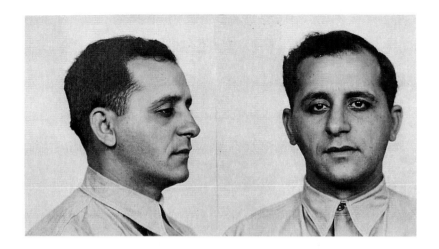

Criminal History - Sam Giancana's life of crime began at an early stage in his career.

1925 – At age 17, Larceny of an auto, sentenced to serve 30 days in the House of Correction

1926 – At age 18, Indicted by Cook County Grand Jury along with 2 co-defendants on a charge of murder committed during a robbery. Following several unsuccessful attempts to bribe the prime witness in this case, the witness was shot gunned to death in his home. The case against Giancana was dismissed.

1926 – Indicted by Cook County Grand Jury with 2 co-defendants on charges of burglary. Giancana implicated by a co-defendant but case dismissed.

1926 – Arrested several times for various minor offenses resulting in subsequent fines.

1926 – 1928 Arrested as a prime suspect in a number of homicides. No convictions

1927 – Auto theft, case dismissed

1929 – Entered guilty plea to a reduced charge of attempted burglary. Sentenced to 1 - 5 years in State penitentiary, Joliet, IL.

1939 – Federal prohibition violation. Sentenced to 4 years, US penitentiary, Leavenworth, KS

1933—At the age of 25 Giancana was beginning to enjoy the finer things in life.

1939 - GIANCANA'S FIRST BOUT WITH THE
GOVERNMENT RESULTED IN FOUR YEARS AT
TERRE HAUTE AND LEAVENWORTH FEDERAL
PRISONS FOR BOOTLEGGING.

1946 – IN KEEPING WITH HIS POSITION AS ONE OF THE NATION'S TOP RACKETEERS, GIANCANA MOVED INTO THIS SPACIOUS, EXPENSIVE BUT UNPRETENTIOUS HOME, COMPLETE WITH A GOLF PUTTING GREEN IN SUBURBAN OAK PARK, ILLINOIS

1959 – GIANCANA MAKES HIS 3RD APPEARANCE BEFORE THE
GRAND JURY IN CHICAGO, WHERE HE CONTINUES TO EVADE ALL
QUESTIONS BY INVOKING THE 5TH AMENDMENT. HIS DEPARTURE
FROM THE COURT HOUSE, WHILE PRETENDING TO BE READING
A CHICAGO NEWSPAPER, DID NOT GO UNNOTICED.

1959 - GIANCANA BEGAN FIRST OF SEVERAL
LEGAL BOUTS WITH GOVERNMENT. ALTHOUGH
NOW THE TOP MAN IN CHICAGO GIANCANA
APPARENTLY DESIRES ANONYMITY.

1962 - FIRST PHOTO OF SAM AND PHYLLIS WAS TAKEN IN A LONDON, ENGLAND, NITE CLUB IN COMPANY OF PHYLLIS' SISTERS. GIANCANA WEARING WEDDING RING.

1963 - AS A PLAINTIFF AGAINST THE
GOVERNMENT, GIANCANA APPEARS TO
ENJOY THE LIMELIGHT. ON HIS LEFT
IS SON-IN-LAW ANTHONY TISCI THEN
THE ADMINISTRATIVE ASSISTANT TO
U. S. CONGRESSMAN ROLAND LIBONATI.
ON RIGHT, GEORGE LEIGHTON, HIS
ATTORNEY, PRESENTLY A COOK COUNTY
CIRCUIT COURT JUDGE.

FRANK SINATRA IS ALSO NUMBERED AMONG
THE CLOSE FRIENDS OF GIANCANA, HAVING
FURNISHED HIS PLANE AND HOME TO GIANCANA
ON NUMEROUS OCCASIONS.

BECAUSE OF YOUR FRIENDSHIP WITH SINATRA,
HE WAS FORCED TO DISPOSE OF HIS NEVADA
CASINO HOLDINGS WHICH INCLUDED THE CAL-
NEVA LODGE AT LAKE TAHOE, NEVADA

THE MC GUIRE SISTERS AS THEY APPEARED AT
CAL-NEVA IN 1963. SHORTLY THEREAFTER, THE
TRIO DISBANDED BECAUSE OF UNFAVORABLE
PUBLICITY RESULTING FROM THE PHYLLIS MC GUIRE –
SAM GIANCANA RELATIONSHIP. THEIR SUBSEQUENT
APPEARANCES AS A TRIO HAVE BEEN FEW AND FAR
BETWEEN.

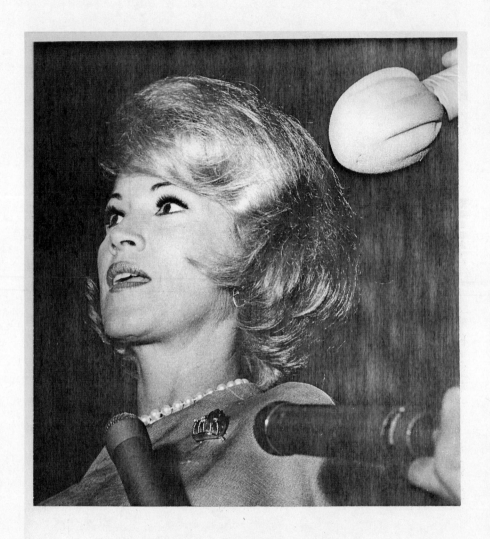

1965 - PHYLLIS MC GUIRE, NATIONALLY
KNOWN ENTERTAINER, WAS THE LATEST IN
A LINE OF GIRL FRIENDS UPON WHOM
GIANCANA LAVISHED GIFTS AND AFFECTION.

1965- COCKY GIANCANA, FLANKED BY
REPORTERS, APPEARS IN FEDERAL BUILDING
FOR APPEARANCE BEFORE FEDERAL GRAND
JURY.

1965 - PHYLLIS RESORTED TO HIGH PRICED
LEGAL REPRESENTATION WHEN HIRING E. BENNETT
WILLIAMS TO HANDLE HER GRAND JURY APPEARANCE.

JUNE 1, 1965 - LAST PHOTO TAKEN OF
GIANCANA PRIOR TO HIS APPEARANCE
BEFORE FEDERAL JUDGE WILLIAM CAMPBELL,
WHO REMANDED HIM TO CUSTODY OF U. S.
MARSHAL WHERE HE REMAINS TO DATE.

Giancana released from jail, as he ponders his options.
May 31, 1966

GIANCANARELEASEDFROM JAIL, FLEES TO MEXICO

Sam Giancana, who was incarcerated in the Cook County jail on June 1, 1965, on contempt of court charges, was released one year later on May 31, 1966, upon the expiration of the term of the federal grand jury. It was the intent and desire of C-1 agents and David Schippers, chief of the Chicago Strike Force, to issue another subpoena for Sam Giancana to appear before a new federal grand jury. However US Attorney General Nicholas Katzenbach would not approve of another grant of immunity to Giancana. US Attorney Edward Hanrahan was willing and prepared to proceed against Giancana; however, he was told not to take any further action against him. Chief Judge William J. Campbell issued a statement to the grand jury at the time of their dismissal claiming that US Attorney Hanrahan in Chicago was under strict orders from the US attorney general not to proceed against Sam Giancana for obstruction of justice or contempt of court, nor consent to any further prosecution. Judge Campbell was critical over the reluctance and the inconsistency of the attorney general's decision not to bring this matter to a logical conclusion. The Chicago news media was also very critical of the attorney general and the US Department of Justice for not allowing Hanrahan to proceed and permit the federal grand jury to indict Giancana.

Sam Giancana was not about to wait around to see whether the FBI was going to serve him again with a grand jury subpoena, and he decided to make himself scarce. He had not been seen at his residence, usual hangouts, and meeting places, or at his headquarters at the Armory Lounge, which had been sold to restaurateur Nick Giannotti. It was now known as Giannotti's Restaurant and Lounge. His close associates Butch Blasi and Chuck English were also conspicuous by their absence. Sources reported that Giancana left Chicago to avoid the possibility of further confinement and to escape the intense scrutiny of FBI. He had previously implied that he may travel to South America. His sudden departure was entirely voluntary and anticipated because his presence in Chicago was a huge burden and an embarrassment to the leaders of organized crime. The mob was extremely unhappy with all of the unprecedented attention focused on the entire structure of organized crime as a result of Giancana's flamboyant style of leadership. Also, the smoldering dissension in the mob may have contributed to his decision to step down. Because of Giancana's incarceration and subsequent absence, there had been no strong leadership of the Chicago criminal group. This had caused disputes and dissatisfaction among various factions of the hoodlum element.

On August 5, 1966, Sam Giancana appeared at the American embassy in Guatemala City, Guatemala, and applied for a US passport valid through August 4, 1969. He stated that he was headed for South America. It was also determined in October 1966 that Samuel Giancana applied for immigrant status in Mexico.

RICHARD CAIN

Richard Cain, true name Scalzitti (Scalzetti), was one of the most devious and corrupt police officers on the Chicago Police Department. Cain was a direct link to organized crime and received his orders through the First Ward Secretary Pat Marcy from Sam Giancana. When Richard B. Ogilvie was elected sheriff of Cook County, Illinois, in the early 1960s, he was in search of a chief investigator for the sheriff's department. He called me and offered me the position, and I declined because I felt it was temporary because of the political nature of the job. Besides, I was completely satisfied with my current position with the FBI. A short time later, Mr. Ogilvie called me again and told me that he was considering Richard Cain for the position of chief investigator. I was shocked to think that a man of Ogilvie's background and experience would consider such a person. I told him very emphatically that Richard Cain was a horrible choice because he was completely untrustworthy and had serious links to organized crime. His reply was that he had never been convicted of anything in the past. I told him that it was just a matter of time. I was aware that Jack Mabley, the well-known Chicago newspaper reporter and columnist, had been friendly with Richard Cain and thought that Cain was a great police officer. Mabley may have influenced Ogilvie to hire Cain. Ogilvie subsequently hired Richard Cain as his chief investigator, and we now had to be circumspect about our relationship with Richard Ogilvie and his sheriff's department because of Richard Cain's position and influence.

Information was received from our confidential source that Richard Cain was in contact with Pat Marcy of the First Ward. Cain advised Marcy that reporter Jack Mabley of the Chicago American was planning to do a newspaper expose on some of the vice clubs in the town of Cicero. Cain had agreed to accompany Mabley to point out the notorious strip clubs in question. Cain suggested to Marcy that Joey Aiuppa, hoodlum boss of the town of Cicero, be alerted as to the time and date of their appearance so that they could tone down their activity to preclude any excessive exposure. Cain joined Mabley and they toured the hoodlum vice joints in Cicero so that Mabley could write his undercover story on the notorious clubs of Cicero.

During October 1963, unknown subjects burglarized the Louis Zahn Drug Company in Melrose Park and stole a quarter of a million dollars worth of drugs. In December 1963, the Chicago FBI received confidential information that Richard

Cain, chief investigator of the Cook County sheriff's office, was attempting to negotiate with the insurance firm and act as a go-between in selling $40,000 worth of the stolen drugs back to the drug company. This information was furnished to the Cook County State's attorney's office, which led to an investigation of Cain's interest in this matter.

On January 1, 1964, Richard Cain led the sheriff's police in a raid on a Rosemont, Illinois, motel named the Caravelle, where he recovered what purported to be $100,000 worth of stolen drugs. The Caravelle was formerly the River Road Motel in which Sam Giancana had a financial interest. No arrests were made, no examination was made for fingerprints in the motel room, and Cain took custody of the registration card for the room where the stolen loot was located. It was obvious that the robbery and the raid was a set up by Cain. Subsequent investigation revealed that Sergeant John Chaconas, an assistant to Cain, was the individual who reportedly registered for the room where the loot was found. Richard Cain, Sergeant Chaconas, and Lieutenant James Donnelly were indicted on charges of conspiracy to commit perjury arising from this matter. Reporter Jack Mabley offered to be a character witness for the subjects but was turned down by the defense attorneys.

On December 15, 1964, Richard Cain was discharged by Sheriff Ogilvie as chief investigator for the sheriff's office. On December 29, 1964, Cain and his codefendants were sentenced to prison terms from one to three years. The sentences were subsequently overturned by the Illinois Supreme Court. This was just the beginning of the problems waiting for Richard Cain, who in 1966 left the Chicago area to be the courier and bodyguard chauffeur for Sam Giancana who was in a self-imposed exile in Mexico.

WILLIAMDADDANOANDHIS
ROBBERY-BURGLARYGANG

W illie "Potatoes" Daddano had been one of the upper echelon leaders of organized crime in Chicago for years and a close associate of Sam Giancana. On September 23, 1963, the Franklin Park Bank in Franklin Park, Illinois, was robbed by four armed men wearing masks, who escaped with about $43,000 plus in cash, following a shoot-out with the local police. The bank robbers were successful in eluding the police in their stolen car. Since the bank was federally insured, it was a violation of the federal bank robbery statute, and Chicago FBI agents responded to the robbery. Frank DeLegge Jr., a well-known robber, had called the Franklin Park Police Department and reported a false bomb threat at a school in the opposite direction of the bank as a diversionary tactic. Frank DeLegge Sr., a former convicted robber, was the driver of the "crash car" that was to ram into any police cars that might be in pursuit of the getaway car.

The robbers were subsequently identified as Joseph D'Argento, a convicted bank robber; Michael LaJoy, a nephew of Willie Daddano; Gerald Tomaszek; and Guy Mendolia Jr., also known as Guy Mendola, a notorious thief. Patrick Schang, a convicted bank robber and hijacker, was identified as the driver of the getaway car. On September 27, 1963, just four days after the robbery, FBI agents arrested Joseph D'Argento and Michael LaJoy for the Franklin Park Bank robbery; and each was released on a $50,000 bond. Other members of the gang were also taken into custody and included Gerald Tomaszek and Patrick Schang. Immediately following the robbery, dissension arose among the subjects over the amount of the loot, which had been left in the possession of DeLegge Sr. and DeLegge Jr., a father-and-son robbery team. They were reluctant to acknowledge the true amount of the loot. Dissension also arose among the subjects concerning one of them being a possible informant that allowed the FBI to identify and apprehend them so quickly after the bank robbery.

These sudden arrests were also disturbing to hoodlum leader Willie Daddano, who had the responsibility for the supervision of major thefts and burglaries. He felt that someone in his criminal organization was an informant for the FBI. He reached out and made contact with Richard Cain, who at the time was the chief investigator of the Cook County sheriff's office. Daddano requested that Cain arrange to have polygraph tests conducted for the members of his robbery gang. Cain then contacted William Witsman, one of his subordinates in the sheriff's office, to conduct the exams. At that time, Cain and Witsman were operating a company known as Accurate Laboratories that performed polygraph tests for the sheriff's office. Cain furnished Witsman with the five questions to be asked, which included "Have you ever given truthful information to a law enforcement officer in the past few weeks?" During the fall of 1963, Witsman took the polygraph machine to the Leyden Hotel in Melrose Park, Illinois, and met Rocco "Schnibble Nose" Montagna, a bail bondsman closely associated with Willie Daddano. The gang was told by Willie Daddano, "I want you guys to take lie tests. There is a stool pigeon in this case." Witsman then gave polygraph tests to LaJoy, Schang, D'Argento, and Tomaszek and gave the results to Rocco Montagna, who in turn gave them directly to Daddano. Apparently, all had passed their polygraph tests.

A short time later, Deputy Witsman was requested to give additional lie tests at the home of Rocco Montagna to DeLegge Sr., DeLegge Jr., and Guy "Lover" Mendolia Jr. It was reported that Mendolia failed the lie test three times. Daddano felt that Mendolia was the informant and obtained approval from Sam Giancana to dispose of Mendolia. On August 31, 1964, at about 1:30 a.m., as Mendolia was entering his garage in his Cadillac in Stone Park, Illinois, he was shot and killed instantly by multiple shotgun blasts. Mendolia was an ex-convict and a member of the notorious Paul Panczko burglary and robbery gang. It was suspected that Chicago mobster and hit man Anthony Spilotro was responsible for the killing of Mendolia. The only problem here for Willie Daddano was that Guy Mendolia Jr. was not an informant for the FBI and had nothing to do with the solution of this case other than being one of the subjects involved in this bank robbery. Subjects Joseph D'Argento, Michael LaJoy, Jerry Tomaszek, and Patrick Schang were subsequently indicted; and in 1965, all were convicted for the Franklin Park Bank robbery, and each was sentenced to serve fifteen years in prison.

In 1968, prosecution of this case continued and was now being handled by US Attorney Thomas A. Foran, who had replaced Edward Hanrahan. Foran was a bright, energetic, and tenacious attorney, who along with his assistants James B. Casey and Michael B. Nash did a remarkable job in the war against organized crime. This was the first time in recent memory that a US attorney personally prosecuted a major organized crime case in US District Court in Chicago.

David Schippers, chief of the Strike Force, who handled the earlier prosecution of the above four bank robbery subjects in 1965, retired from government service in 1967 to pursue the private practice of law in Chicago. After his departure, he defended many former agents from various federal agencies, who were in need of an attorney and did so on a pro-bono basis. We are all grateful for the outstanding services rendered by Mr. Schippers as chief of the Strike Force. Also, in April 1998, Mr. Schippers was named chief investigative counsel for the House Judiciary Committee by then US Representative Henry Hyde, who at that time was assigned to look into the impeachment of President William Jefferson Clinton. This was an awesome responsibility, and Mr. Schippers and his team of investigators did a tremendous job during those highly charged and controversial hearings.

On March 5, 1968, a federal grand jury returned a five-count indictment charging five additional defendants with violations of the bank robbery statute and conspiracy. Included in the indictment were William "Potatoes" Daddano, Richard Cain, Frank DeLegge Sr., Frank DeLegge Jr., and Rocco Montagna. Richard Cain declined the services of an attorney and represented himself at the trial.

Prior to the trial, Richard Cain contacted the FBI and wanted to speak to US Attorney Thomas Foran on a very confidential basis. A meeting was arranged between Mr. Foran and Cain, at which time Cain told Foran that he would not have any objections if the government would bring a deportation suit against him in lieu of having to stand trial in the bank robbery case. Cain felt that he had been framed and that his chances of acquittal were slim. Cain also wanted to include Willie Daddano in any such deportation arrangement. Mr. Foran told Cain that he could not go along with him under his conditions; however, if Cain would implicate some of his associates such as Sam Giancana, the government would have more interest in working something out. Cain's response was "I wasn't a tattletale in school, and I won't be one now." Foran told Cain that he would only contact the judge for leniency with specific facts showing his cooperation and only after his conviction in this case. They departed on amicable terms.

Testifying as government witnesses were Michael LaJoy, Joseph D'Argento, and Patrick Schang, all of whom were willing and active participants in the bank robbery. D'Argento agreed to testify only after the Chicago mob made threats against his life while he was in prison. They had been previously sentenced along with Jerry Tomaszek to serve fifteen years for their role in the Franklin Park Bank robbery. They stood up well under grueling cross-examinations. US Attorney Thomas Foran's performance throughout the trial was brilliant, and his closing arguments and presentation were very effective and contributed to the successful results achieved.

On October 3, 1968, the federal jury found the five additional defendants guilty as charged on the Franklin Park Bank robbery conspiracy. Judge Julius Hoffman sentenced the subjects as follows:

> William Daddano, fifteen years in prison and a total fine of $13,000
>
> Richard Cain, four years in prison and a fine of $15,000
>
> Rocco Montagna, three years in prison and a fine of $13,000
>
> Frank DeLegge Sr., fifteen years in prison and a fine of $5,000
>
> Frank DeLegge Jr., seven years in prison and a fine of $5,000

All subjects were committed immediately to the custody of the US Marshal without bond until all costs of the trial and fines were paid. On October 1, 1970, the US Court of Appeals unanimously affirmed the convictions of all subjects.

On September 9, 1975, William Daddano died of a heart attack while in the US penitentiary at the Marion, Illinois, Memorial Hospital at the age of sixty-three.

John "The Bug" Varelli et al.

Also intricately associated with the above subjects in the Franklin Park Bank robbery case were additional members of the Willie Daddano robbery-burglary-hijacking gang. They were indicted by a federal grand jury in 1967 on one or more of twelve separate major thefts valued at more than $5,000,000, occurring between 1962 and 1967. They included Johnny "The Bug" Varelli, a prominent member of the robbery-burglary gang who helped plan the Franklin Park Bank robbery, but he did not participate in the actual robbery. Varelli along with more than thirty of the most notorious thieves, burglars, and fences associated with organized crime were subsequently convicted in federal court on one or more of these multiple thefts. These included various violations of the anti-racketeering statute, bank burglary, bank robbery, hijackings, interstate transportation of stolen property, thefts of interstate shipments, robberies, armed robberies, and a home invasion. Part of the loot included more than $1,000,000 in silver bullion. A number of these subjects were already serving time on previous convictions. During separate trials from 1968 to 1970, most were found guilty and received prison sentences, some to run concurrent with their previously imposed sentences. John Varelli reportedly attempted to commit suicide while en route from the US penitentiary in Leavenworth, Kansas, to Chicago for a trial set for September 9, 1968.

Varelli, while incarcerated on three separate cases, entered a guilty plea to the hijacking of a Spector Freight Company interstate tractor trailer containing Polaroid film and cameras, valued in excess of $200,000, in August of 1964. The driver of the trailer had been abducted at gunpoint. Varelli received an eleven-year sentence to run concurrently with sentences previously imposed. Some of his confederates involved in this interstate theft were also found guilty and were sentenced as follows: Thomas Bambulas, Roy Nielson, and Emil Crovedi, received fifteen-year sentences; Kenneth Bratko received a ten-year sentence; and Joseph Rossi an eight-year sentence. Other subjects involved with this theft were Guy Mendolia Jr. and Angelo Boscarino, both suspected as informers and both killed in gangland fashion. Boscarino had numerous ice pick holes on his body and apparently was brutally tortured before being shotgunned to death.

In other related interstate theft cases, Frank Cullota, a master burglar, was found guilty on May 27, 1969, and received a ten-year sentence to run concurrent with a five—to fifteen-year sentence imposed in 1968. Also found guilty with Cullota in the theft of a trailer load of eighty-five Zenith TV sets were James Catalano, sentenced to six years; Vincent Moscatello, sentenced to ten years; Michael Swiatek, sentenced to ten years; and Donald Trznadel, sentenced to four years.

Anthony Borsellino, a notorious thief, received a thirteen-year sentence that covered three separate hijackings of silver shipments; and Albert Cardenas and Max Heckmeyer were sentenced each to serve seven years in prison for possession of stolen silver shipments. Cardenas's sentence was to run consecutive to a five-year previously imposed sentence for theft from an interstate shipment. James D'Antonio entered a plea of guilty to possession of stolen property and was sentenced to six months in prison and five years on probation to run concurrent with a previously imposed sentence of five years. Richard Urso entered a plea of guilty to being an accessory to an interstate theft shipment and was sentenced to three years on probation. Morris Saletko, also known as Maishe Baer, a prominent Chicago bookmaker and loan shark, who participated in disposing of the stolen silver bullion and Polaroid camera hijackings, was sentenced to serve eight years, later reduced to five years in prison and fined $5,000. Saletko was killed in gangland fashion on July 13, 1977. Thomas Fornarelli entered guilty pleas to two hijackings and was sentenced to serve one year and a day plus three years on probation. James Cartin entered guilty pleas to two armed robberies of Brink's armored trucks in 1962 and 1965. He was sentenced to serve one year and a day plus three years on probation. Cartin along with Marty Garity, recently deceased, specialized in Brink's truck robberies and reportedly had a tipster at Brink's who furnished them with keys and information. Eugene Cacciatore entered a guilty plea and was sentenced to serve eighteen months in prison plus five years on probation on an interstate hijacking charge. Roy Arthur Nielson entered guilty pleas to armed robbery of the Silver Leaf Savings Bank in 1966 and the bank burglary of the Laramie Federal Savings and Loan Association in 1967 and was sentenced to serve three years in prison to run concurrent with a previous fifteen-year sentence. Joseph Moskovitz and Gerry Cole entered guilty pleas to receiving stolen furs and apparel. Moskovitz was sentenced to three years on probation, and Cole received three months in prison and five years on probation. Americo DiPietto entered a plea of guilty to charges of interstate theft in 1963 and was sentenced to seven years in prison to run concurrently with the twenty-year sentence he was currently serving for a narcotics conviction.

Frank DeLegge Sr., Frank DeLegge Jr., John Caldarazzo, Philip Barone, and Robert Brown were found guilty by a federal jury in Chicago in July of 1969 of violating the Federal Hobbs Act statute. The case involved an armed robbery of jewelry salesman Ralph Wegner in 1964 while he was traveling to Wisconsin and the armed robbery and home invasion of Ralph Wegner's residence in Crystal Lake, Illinois, in 1965. Also entering guilty pleas in both of the armed robberies of Wegner were Steve Tomares and Paul "Peanuts" Panczko, both major thieves and burglars. Panczko also entered guilty pleas to the two armed robberies of the armored Brink's trucks as well as a number of the Chicago interstate shipment thefts. DeLegge Sr. and DeLegge Jr. were sentenced to fifteen years and ten years in prison, respectively;

Caldarazzo was sentenced to eight years; Barone was sentenced to four years; Robert Brown was sentenced to seven years; Tomares was sentenced to serve six months in prison and three years on probation. Panczko was sentenced to serve twelve years in prison to run concurrently with previous twelve-year and fifteen-year sentences.

Prior to the trial of home invasion victim Wegner, he advised C-1 agents of several vicious phone threats that had been received by him and his family if he and his son were to testify in this case. These threats did not deter Wegner and his son from courageously testifying at the trial and indentifying the armed robbers involved in the home invasion. Federal Judge Alexander Napoli was made aware of the threats prior to the sentencing of subjects and took it into consideration during the sentencing.

On October 27, 1969, Frank DeLegge Sr. entered a plea of guilty in connection with the robbery of the Citizen's National Bank of Chicago in 1963 and was sentenced to serve eight years in prison to run concurrently with two fifteen-year and one eight-year sentence previously imposed for theft of a tractor and trailer in interstate commerce. Frank DeLegge Jr. also entered a guilty plea and was sentenced to eight years on the same theft case as his father to run concurrent with a ten-year and a seven-year prison term previously received. On January 20, 1976, Frank DeLegge Jr.'s frozen body was found slain in gangland fashion, with his throat slashed, in Elmhurst, Illinois.

Maurice Friedman was a close associate and a former partner in several Chicago liquor stores with William Daddano. Friedman was arrested by FBI agents and charged with possession of more than a $1,000,000 worth of stolen drugs and miscellaneous appliances from interstate commerce. During the trial, Friedman was described as "the biggest fence-handling stolen merchandise from William Daddano." Friedman was found guilty in federal court; and on July 30, 1968, Judge Hubert Will sentenced Friedman to serve ten years in prison. He was denied an appeal bond and immediately was taken into custody by the US Marshal's office.

The above convictions received favorable and continuing news media coverage throughout the trials because of the notoriety of the individuals involved. The C-1 agents who resourcefully contributed to the incredible outcome to all of the above organized crime cases with their vital sources of information and astute investigation, which led to the solution of these cases and the prosecution of numerous organized crime subjects, were Merle Hamre, Frank Ford, Thomas J. Green, John Oitzinger, Lenard Wolf, Harold Johnson, Max Fritschel, William Roemer, Robert Malone, John Roberts, Thomas Parrish, John Dallman, and other C-1 agents. These convictions virtually decimated the Willie "Potatoes" Daddano robbery-burglary-hijacking gang; and as a bonus, it included the conviction and incarceration of Richard (Scalzetti) Cain, former chief investigator of the Cook County sheriff's office, one of the most blatantly corrupt police officers in the Chicago area.

Michael LaJoy, Joseph D'Argento, and Patrick Schang were government witnesses throughout the above trials and were active and willing participants during a number of these crimes. They were completely debriefed on a continuing basis by FBI agents. Without their cooperation, the remarkable accomplishments achieved could not have been possible. They had been sentenced to fifteen years in prison for their role in the Franklin Park Bank robbery. The Chicago hoodlum element had made a concerted effort to learn the whereabouts of their families apparently to take action against them. These witnesses and their families had to be relocated to different areas of the country by the US attorney's office to ensure their personal safety.

JOSEPH PAUL GLIMCO

In 1958, Joseph Paul Glimco, also known as Joey Glimco, was elected president of Local 777 of the Taxicab Driver's Union, International Brotherhood of Teamsters in Chicago, and was a close associate of former Teamster President James R. Hoffa. Glimco was also closely associated with Paul "The Waiter" Ricca, Milwaukee Phil Alderisio, and other well-known Chicago hoodlums during the period of mob dominance of Chicago unions. Glimco had about thirty-eight arrests over the years but had never been convicted of a felony. On December 16, 1964, a federal grand jury in Chicago, under the direction of David P. Schippers, chief of the Strike Force, returned a seventeen-count suppressed indictment charging Joey Glimco with violating the Taft Hartley Labor Law and conspiracy. Glimco was subsequently arrested by C-1 agents the following day. This indictment culminated a lengthy and intensive investigation by C-1 agent Joseph Servel and others. Glimco was indicted for accepting a Jaguar sports car, tailor-made suits, TV sets, paid trips to New York and Florida from employers, free service and repairs to his personal car, illegal payoffs, and other gifts to members of his family in violation of the Taft Hartley labor law, a bill designed to mitigate the influence of labor unions. Glimco had received and accepted money and other things of value from employers with the intent to influence him in his decisions and duties as an official of a labor union organization. Also named in the indictment were Frank Pesce, an officer and owner of Best Sanitation and Supply Company in which Glimco was also said to have a sizable interest, and Don Ross, also known as Donald Rosenberg, past owner of Midwest Jaguar Company. On February 4, 1969, Glimco finally changed his plea to guilty and was fined $40,000, the maximum penalty allowed under the Taft Hartley Act. Also convicted and fined were Frank Pesce and Don Ross. The case was cleverly developed by C-1 agent Joseph Servel, whose son subsequently followed in his dad's footsteps as an FBI agent.

BENJAMIN R. STEIN, "KING OF THE JANITORS"

Benjamin R. Stein, the "King of the Janitors," was head of the National Maintenance Company, a janitorial service firm that had contracts for the maintenance of McCormick Place, Chicago's largest exhibition hall. Stein was a close associate of hoodlum leader Gus Alex and Joseph Glimco, president of Local 777 of the Taxicab Union. In May 1966, Stein was found guilty of six counts of violating the Federal Taft Hartley labor law by providing illegally expensive gifts to Joseph Glimco and Edward Donovan of Local 755 of the Teamsters Union for allowing Stein to use nonunion labor at McCormick Place. Stein was paying janitors only $1.00 per hour, although contracts called for $2.75 per hour. Federal Judge Richard Austin sentenced Benjamin Stein to serve eighteen months in prison. Stein's conviction was upheld by the US Court of Appeals. C-1 agent Joseph Servel contributed materially to the successful outcome of this case.

PAUL "THE WAITER" RICCA

Paul "The Waiter" Ricca, the elder statesman of the Chicago crime syndicate, took over as boss of the Chicago mob following the suicide death of Frank Nitti in the mid-1940s. He and Anthony Accardo had been sharing the duties as boss during the prolonged absence of Sam Giancana. Ricca had been involved in endless deportation hearings since 1957. Ricca was born in Naples, Italy, under name of Felice DeLucia and had been involved in two murders. He served two and one-half years on the first murder and was convicted in absentia and sentenced to eighteen years on the second murder. He fled from Italy to the United States using the alias of Paul Maglio. In 1957, his US citizenship was revoked, and after many hearings, he was finally ordered deported in 1962. He was told to find a country that would accept him, or show cause, why he had not done so. Ricca had sent letters to forty-seven countries and enclosed newspaper clippings of his notorious hoodlum background and activities, and all forty-seven countries refused to accept him. Italy did agree to accept Ricca; however, Ricca's attorney claimed that this would amount to "persecution," and this began a series of new hearings. In 1965, the US Supreme Court upheld the deportation order of Paul Ricca. In the meantime, the Italian government had revoked his murder conviction and refused to accept him. The US government had no other alternative but to allow Ricca to remain in this country, unless and until they could find a country that would accept him. They were at an impasse.

In November 1968, Paul Ricca's sister Amelia DeLucia arrived in Chicago from Italy on the same Alitalia Airlines flight with Anthony Accardo for a visit with her brother. She was summoned to appear before an immigration (INS) hearing officer on December 5, 1968, to show cause why her visitor's visa should not be revoked. She falsely stated on her visa application that she had never been convicted of a felony, when in fact she had been convicted of murder in Italy several years ago. Rather than appear before the INS as summoned, Amelia DeLucia returned to Italy via Alitalia Airlines on December 4, 1968. Her visit with her brother Paul was cut short. In the meantime, Paul Ricca was somewhat preoccupied with his many scheduled appearances before the federal grand jury in Chicago in December 1968 in connection with the Jack Cerone interstate gambling case investigation.

During his deportation hearings in 1965, Ricca testified under oath that he reported "miscellaneous income" of $80,159 on his 1963 tax return. He claimed that this income was derived totally from gambling during his almost daily visits to Chicago race tracks where he wagered exclusively on horses at the $10 pari-mutuel window. This was the same scheme used by Anthony Accardo in the mid-1950s when he was told by the IRS to be more specific about reporting miscellaneous gambling income. Ricca was well prepared and obviously well coached by tax attorney Eugene Bernstein, who also represented Accardo about miscellaneous gambling income. Ricca displayed charts and records that showed that he placed eighty-six wagers on thirty-seven races and won the $80,159. All of the winning bets were on horses that came in first, which was unbelievable. C-1 agents conducted an exhaustive investigation at the race tracks in question assisted by the race track police. It was determined that Ricca obviously committed perjury inasmuch as there was not enough money wagered at the $10 pari-mutuel windows, which would support the winnings claimed by Ricca. There were also twenty-three discrepancies noted on his "worksheet" on wagers allegedly made at Chicago tracks in 1964. Also, race track police and off-duty police officers at the track who were familiar with Ricca all claimed they had never seen Ricca at any of the tracks.

On April 28, 1966, the federal grand jury in Chicago returned an indictment charging Paul Ricca with perjury, and a warrant was issued for his arrest. Paul Ricca was arrested by C-1 agents on the same day while riding as a passenger in a limousine chauffeured by Jack Cerone and in the company of Anthony Accardo. When arrested, Ricca was very calm and cordial. He said, "I have the greatest respect and admiration for Mr. Hoover who comes along only once a lifetime." He concluded by stating, "The good old days ended when the FBI stepped in." That was one of the finest endorsements ever received by the FBI from a Chicago hoodlum leader.

The perjury trial against Paul Ricca began in November 1967. The race track police testified that they had never seen Ricca at any of the race tracks in question. Also, it was established by the government that there were not enough bets recorded by the race tracks on first-place winners in 1963 at the $10 pari-mutuel windows. Therefore, the winnings claimed by Ricca were a pretext, contrived, and fraudulent to conceal the actual source of his illegally obtained income. The government also produced representatives from three Chicago area tracks who produced records to show that it was mathematically impossible for Ricca to have won as much as he claimed at these tracks. The defense attorney called as witnesses pari-mutuel clerks Charles Ferger, James Picardi Sr., Joseph Krampat, and Marion Pacelli from Washington and Arlington Park race tracks, who claimed that Paul Ricca was a frequent visitor to the race tracks and was a good customer of theirs. With the hoodlum influence in the gambling industry, it was not very difficult for the defense to find witnesses who would testify on behalf of Ricca. Another witness for Paul Ricca was Eugene Albano, owner of Albano's Bake Shop in Elmwood Park, Illinois. Albano testified under oath that it was his almost daily procedure to drive Ricca and Chicago hoodlum Guido DeChiaro to the Chicago area race tracks in 1963 and placed most of the bets for Ricca. Albano was reported to be a cousin of hoodlum

Joseph Amabile, who was convicted of a Federal Hobbs Act violation in 1967. Also, Guido DeChiaro testified that he had accompanied Ricca at the race tracks when he made his incredible string of first place winners. It was noted that Guido DeChiaro operated a jukebox and pinball machine business in Franklin Park, Illinois, and was a close associate of Paul Ricca and Anthony Accardo. He had been subpoenaed in the Sam Giancana federal grand jury investigation in 1965 and invoked the Fifth Amendment. On November 18, 1967, the jury found Paul Ricca not guilty of perjury.

On November 22, 1967, Paul Ricca and Guido DeChiaro were subpoenaed by C-1 agents to appear before the federal grand jury on December 5, 1967, to answer additional questions regarding their reported wagering activities at the Chicago area race tracks. Both Ricca and DeChiaro expressed concern and bewilderment over receiving the subpoenas. Ricca's only comment was "Not again." They appeared as scheduled, and both invoked their Fifth Amendment privilege. Even though Paul Ricca had been successful in avoiding deportation from the United States over the years and had avoided federal prosecution in this perjury case, he was to be used as an unwittingly key witness in the conviction and incarceration of hoodlum leader Jack Cerone in a federal interstate gambling conspiracy case.

It was the intention of US Attorney Edward Hanrahan to seek perjury indictments against all individuals who testified for Paul Ricca in the recent perjury trial of Ricca, including Eugene Albano, and the four pari-mutuel ticket clerks, because all had made contradictory statements on the witness stand believed to be sufficient to constitute perjury. On December 12, 1967, Mr. Hanrahan made available a hand-printed anonymous letter addressed to him that stated in part, "Sir, here is the real truth on Paul Ricca. I am a mutuel clerk. I was approached by John Accardo (Anthony Accardo's brother). I refused, so now I'm on their s— list with the union. The four that testified for Ricca was paid $2,500 apiece. John Accardo was the payoff man. Too bad they don't bring them before the federal grand jury. I know two of them will talk. This is a true story so take it from here. A disgusted mutuel clerk." It was also determined that *Chicago Tribune* crime reporter Robert Wiedrich received an almost identical letter postmarked December 13, 1967, which prompted the *Tribune* to run a front-page item on Sunday December 17, 1967, requesting that the anonymous letter writer contact Bob Wiedrich or the *Tribune* with additional facts regarding the payoff. No follow-up action was taken in this regard because Mr. Hanrahan was soon replaced by Thomas A. Foran as US attorney.

IGNATIUS SPACHESE A.K.A. NED CHARLES BAKES

Ignatius Spachese, also known as Ned Charles Bakes, a Capone-era hoodlum, was a confidence man and a close associate of Paul Ricca and other members of organized crime in Chicago. During the mid-1940s, Spachese was a Cook County deputy sheriff. At that time, Spachese came to the attention of the FBI during the premature paroles of Paul "The Waiter" Ricca, Louis "Little New York" Campagna, and other top organized crime leaders convicted and sentenced in the multimillion-dollar Browne-Bioff movie extortion case in Chicago. Spachese was alleged to have been involved in bribing officials to influence the early release of the Capone mobsters.

On February 4, 1969, Spachese was arrested by Chicago agents in possession of approximately $14,000,000 worth of stolen Westinghouse Electric stock certificates. On November 18, 1969, he was convicted in federal court on charges of interstate theft and sentenced to six years in prison. He was released on a $10,000 surety bond while appealing his conviction. On December 22, 1969, Spachese was again arrested by Chicago agents for unlawfully possessing a quantity of Gulf & Western stock certificates, which had been stolen from the US mail in June of 1968, at Kennedy Airport in NYC. In a bench trial held in Chicago on July 1, 1970, Spachese was found guilty by US District Court Judge Hubert Will, who sentenced Spachese to four years in prison to run concurrently with his previous six-year sentence. Spachese was immediately taken into the custody by the US Marshal to begin his sentence. The case agent was Robert L. Baker, who did an outstanding job in coordinating all of the monitored telephone calls and surveillances in this case, which led to the two convictions of Spachese. He was capably assisted by C-1 agents Merle Hamre and Robert Malone. On December 3, 1975, Spachese was found shot to death in the trunk of his car near his Addison, Illinois, residence. He had been paroled from federal prison in June of 1973.

FRANK TORNABENE ET AL., INTERSTATE PROSTITUTION RING

F rank Tornabene and his associates had long been connected with gambling and vice activities on Chicago's near North Side for the Ross Prio hoodlum group. Eileen "Bunny" Curry, a well-known Chicago madam, operated a house of prostitution for Frank Tornabene assisted by Sam Elia, Thomas Rizzo, and Robert Smith. In 1964, this ring sent approximately six thousand "credit cards" or letters of solicitation through the mail to prospective businessmen throughout the country. They advertised their services and invited them to call Shirley at a specific phone number, which led to their house of prostitution at 1847 N. Cleveland Avenue or at 521 Dickens Avenue in Chicago. The list of the names of businessmen had been obtained from various conventions held at hotels throughout the city of Chicago and included many wealthy persons, doctors, lawyers, and other prominent individuals. The case was developed by C-1 agent Gus Kempff who was assisted by James Dewhirst, John Osborne, and Robert Malone. US Attorney Thomas Foran handled the prosecution of this case, assisted by AUSAs John J. McDonnell and Richard Jalovec. Eileen Curry had a long record of arrests and was designated to be the principal witness for the government. When interviewed she had agreed to testify against the subjects. Tornabene was the ringleader. Elia and Campione were officers of a Chicago near north social club that had been raided in the past for gambling activities. On December 2, 1965, the federal grand jury returned an indictment charging Tornabene, Elia, Campione, and Smith, with operating a $600,000 a year interstate prostitution ring in violation of the federal interstate racketeering laws and conspiracy. Subjects were subsequently arrested by the FBI and released on bond. Eileen Curry was an unindicted co-conspirator because she agreed to testify.

After a series of delays, the trial in this case began on May 9, 1968. Eileen Curry now refused to testify at the trial of the four subjects and invoked the Fifth Amendment. AUSA John J. McDonnell immediately presented the facts to the grand jury regarding Eileen Curry's involvement in the case; and on May 16,

1968, she was treated as a defendant and was indicted on five counts of interstate racketeering and conspiracy. Eileen Curry was arrested by FBI agents and released on bond. The trial resumed, and the first government witness was a young blonde prostitute who made an excellent witness and described the overall operation of the house of prostitution and implicated all of the subjects. She held up well under cross-examination. A number of clients who had been solicited by this ring testified along with an FBI agent, concerning admissions made to him by subject Elia. Federal Judge J. Sam Perry was told that subject Eileen Curry, who was to be the principal witness for the government in this case, had refused to testify because she had been threatened on two occasions by persons she declined to identify, claiming that she was in fear of her life. On May 27, 1968, the jury found all subjects guilty as charged in the indictments. Prior to sentencing, Judge Perry took note of the fact that Eileen Curry had been threatened in this case as well as the past convictions of Tornabene, Campione, and Elia, and their connection with organized crime. Judge Perry sentenced subjects to five years on each of the six counts to run concurrently with their sentences plus costs. Judge Perry directed Tornabene, Campione, and Elia to begin their sentences immediately. Judge Perry allowed Smith to be released on bond, pending a presentence investigation. On June 25, 1969, Judge Perry reduced the previous sentence of Robert Smith to one year in prison, suspended under certain conditions. On September 27, 1968, Eileen Curry appeared before Federal Judge Alexander Napoli and entered a plea of guilty and was placed on probation for three years.

JohnPhilipCeroneA.k.a. Jack Cerone et al.

Jack Cerone, who was referred to as Jackie "The Lackey" because of his subservient role of catering to former bosses Anthony Accardo and Paul Ricca, had been groomed to become the boss of the Chicago mob. According to our confidential source, he had been known to be involved in a number of brutal murders for the mob and had personally boasted about his accomplishments. With former bosses Sam Giancana, Sam Battaglia, and Milwaukee Phil Alderisio out of the picture, Jack Cerone was about take over the Chicago mob with the counsel of former bosses Accardo and Ricca. Unfortunately for Cerone, he was about to encounter some strong head winds as acting boss, which would eventually be his undoing.

LOUIS BOMBACINO

In 1967, the Chicago office of the FBI received a phone call from Louis Bombacino who was previously unknown to us. The call was taken by C-1 agent Paul Frankfurt, an experienced and capable agent. Bombacino was a bookmaker for the mob who was currently in jail on a robbery charge and was seeking help from the FBI. Agent Frankfurt assisted Bombacino who was eventually released on probation. He agreed to help the FBI regarding his mob gambling associates. Bombacino was a bookmaker for a large-scale bookmaking operation under the control of Jack Cerone and hoodlum leader Fiore Buccieri. As time went on, Bombacino was furnishing excellent intelligence information on his hoodlum associates. Unfortunately, Bombacino began to pocket some of the mob's gambling proceeds for his own use and was in serious trouble with the mob. They threatened him to come up with the money or else he would be history. With his life in danger, he went into hiding. His use to the FBI as an informant had run its course, and Bombacino looked to the FBI for help.

This was before the Federal Witness Protection Program was established by the US Department of Justice and administered by the US Marshal's office. We felt that the only course for Bombacino was to cooperate as a witness and testify against his hoodlum associates. We contacted US Attorney Thomas Foran and told him that we had a potential witness who feared for his life and might be willing to testify against Jack Cerone and other members of his hoodlum organization. Mr. Foran recommended that we use his horse farm west of Elgin to house, protect, and debrief Lou Bombacino. This was a great idea; however, it required an around the clock commitment of manpower by C-1 agents John Roberts, Bill Roemer, John Bassett, Dennis Shanahan, Robert Malone, Harold Johnson, John Dallman, myself, and others with Agent Paul Frankfurt taking the lead. The details about the mob's large-scale gambling operation as provided by Bombacino were excellent and established an interstate conspiracy to violate the federal gambling laws. The big problem now was getting Lou Bombacino to agree to testify in open court about his hoodlum partners and their gambling activities. To cooperate with the FBI would mean that the mob would seek to retaliate against him and possibly his family. This was a huge decision for him. He finally decided to cooperate because his life was in danger so why not take the initiative and strike first.

The present plan of US Attorney Thomas Foran and Strike Force Chief Lawrence Morrissey was to offer a grant of immunity to Paul "The Waiter" Ricca, former boss of the Chicago mob, and to serve grand jury subpoenas to fifteen additional hoodlums on this case. Mr. Foran made a special trip to Washington and persuaded a reluctant attorney general to approve a grant of immunity to Paul Ricca. When Ricca was served on December 10, 1968, with a federal grand jury subpoena, he was leaving his residence and had entered a vehicle being driven by Jack Cerone. Other prominent hoodlums subsequently served with subpoenas were Gus Alex, Ralph Pierce, Les Kruse, Fiore Buccieri, Joseph Gagliano, Attorney George Bieber, Dominic Cortina, Don Angelini, and Alfred Meo, owner of the restaurant where the gambling conspiracy took place. Also, Anthony Gruttadauro, nephew of Gary, Indiana, boss Anthony Pinelli; Louis Pranno, relative of hoodlum Rocco Pranno; Eugene Albano, an associate of Ricca, who had testified on behalf of Ricca at his perjury trial; John DiDomenico, an employee of Don Angelini; Charles English, a lieutenant of Sam Giancana; Chris Cardi, loan shark collector; and Nicholas Kokenas, a Cicero nightclub owner were served with subpoenas. All were served by C-1 agents, and subjects were scheduled to appear before the grand jury during December 1968. Paul Ricca was first to appear on December 11, 1968, and initially refused to testify and resorted to invoking the Fifth Amendment. However, when he did so, the Giancana immunity strategy was used, and US Attorney Foran took Ricca before Chief Judge William Campbell and granted him immunity. Ricca was faced with two choices. He could either refuse again to testify and face the certainty of being held in contempt of court and sent to prison immediately as Giancana did. However, he chose the second alternative, and after seven appearances before the grand jury, he talked evasively so as not to implicate himself or others in a federal violation. Hundreds of questions were directed to him. Unwittingly, he gave some answers that corroborated the testimony of Lou Bombacino about a meeting with Jack Cerone at Meo's Norwood House, Harwood Heights, Illinois, in the presence of Paul Ricca, where the gambling conspiracy was discussed and instructions were given to Louis Bombacino by Cerone. The key to indicting Jack Cerone was accomplished by the skillful interrogation of Paul Ricca. His testimony sealed the fate of Jack Cerone in this case. All of the other hoodlums subpoenaed appeared as scheduled and invoked the Fifth Amendment, with the exception of Joseph Gagliano who gave some evasive nonspecific answers and unwittingly made several damaging admissions. Hoodlum attorney George Bieber was most concerned about his situation because he was asked a question about a $5,000 payoff, which reportedly passed from him to a specific Chicago Police Department lieutenant to fix a local case. The attorneys for the hoodlums were somewhat puzzled as to the focus of the federal grand jury. The top leaders were concerned that the government might attempt to show some sort of a continuing conspiratorial pattern of activity and had issued instructions to their hierarchy to discontinue meeting at the customary meeting places for the present time.

Based on the testimony furnished by Louis Bombacino, Paul Ricca, and others before the grand jury on February 6, 1969, an indictment was returned charging the following subjects with violating the interstate gambling conspiracy statute: Jack Cerone, acting boss of the Chicago mob; Donald Angelini, a gambling boss for Fiore Buccieri; and Frank Aurelli, a prominent bookmaker and sponsor of Louis Bombacino. Bench warrants were issued on the same date, and subjects Jack Cerone and Don Angelini were arrested by C-1 agents the following day, with the exception of Frank Aurelli who surrendered through his attorney. Jack Cerone was arrested at the residence of Paul Ricca as Cerone arrived to pick up Ricca in River Forest, Illinois. Ricca expressed great relief to the FBI that he was not being arrested and said, "God, I'm glad it's not me that you want. After seven times before your grand jury, I don't know what to expect anymore." Because of the involvement and importance of Jack Cerone, as heir apparent of the Chicago mob and his prominent hoodlum associates, a joint press release was made by the US Attorney General John N. Mitchell and Director J. Edgar Hoover, which received considerable coverage in the Chicago news media.

In June 1969, US Attorney Thomas Foran and AUSAs James Casey and Michael Nash advised that they would seek a superseding indictment in this case to include three additional subjects, namely Joseph Ferriola, a top lieutenant and enforcer for hoodlum leader Fiore Buccieri; James "Tar Baby" Cerone, a cousin of Jack Cerone; and Dominic Cortina, a gambling partner of Don Angelini. AUSA Casey empanelled a federal grand jury in August 1969, at which time three Cleveland bookmakers, Morton Kaufman, William Weiss, and Herbert Polk, were called to testify because they formerly bet with Frank Aurelli and Lou Bombacino. They were to be immunized if they declined to cooperate. Also, approximately fifteen additional witnesses were to be called to testify before the grand jury. Subpoenas were issued for the following: John DiDomenico, an Angelini employee; Angelo Kokas, former bookmaker; Joseph Gagliano, a Cerone henchman; Fiore Buccieri, prominent hoodlum leader; James "Turk" Torello, a Bucceri enforcer; Salvatore Molose, an Angelini bookmaker; Joseph Giancana, brother of Sam Giancana; John and Louis Manzella, Angelini bookmakers; John Sprovieri, an Angelini lieutenant; Henry Erfurth and Louis Pranno, both Angelini bettors; Jack Garber, former owner of Garfield Printing Shop; and others. All persons in the Chicago area originally scheduled for subpoenas had been served except Joseph Gagliano who was apparently attempting to avoid service. He had departed Chicago aboard his brother-in-law's thirty-six-foot Chris Craft yacht headed for Lake Huron. Through the continuing cooperation of the US Coast Guard Search and Rescue Branch, they were able to locate the yacht on Lakes Michigan and Huron, where they had been for almost two weeks. Gagliano was most surprised at being served aboard his yacht by FBI agents at the Ludington Yacht Club, Ludington, Michigan, at 8:00 p.m. on July 31, 1969. Apparently not known to Gagliano since his departure from Chicago, he had lost his longtime docking slip at Burnham Harbor in Chicago. The Cleveland bookmakers testified completely after a grant of immunity; and John DiDomenico, the Angelini employee who persisted in refusing to testify after a grant of immunity, was held in contempt of court and committed to the custody of the US Marshal. Henry Erfurth and Louis Pranno testified about their betting activities with the group, and all other witnesses took the Fifth Amendment. Testimony before the grand jury was completed; and suppressed superseding indictments were returned on August 19, 1969, charging Jack Cerone, Donald Angelini, Frank Aurelli, Dominic Cortina, James Cerone, and Joseph Ferriola with violating the interstate gambling statutes and conspiracy. Dominic Cortina and Joseph Ferriola were arrested by C-1 agents. Jack Cerone, Donald Angelini, Frank Aurelli, and James Cerone were allowed to surrender through their attorneys.

Also intricately connected with this case was the Angel Kaplan Sports News Service, 236 N. Clark Street in Chicago, which was owned and operated by Don Angelini. Angel Kaplan, a handicapper of sporting events in the Chicago area and one of the largest in the country, furnished a service that was indispensable to bookmaking and the handicapping of sporting events. No bookmaker was able to accept sports bets without the knowledge of the "line" or the "spread" or the "odds" on any particular sporting event. For years, this service had been furnished by Angel Kaplan not only to the Chicago area but also to bookmakers all over the country and in Canada and Mexico. Don Angelini operated under the direction of hoodlum leader Fiore Buccieri, was the expert on handicapping sporting events, and had earned the nickname of "The Wizard of Odds." He was a genius and was a huge money maker for the Chicago mob. Angelini was previously arrested by the IRS on August 25, 1963, based on FBI information for on-track bookmaking. He was convicted on February 17, 1964, and sentenced to sixty days in jail, three years on probation, and fined $2,500.

In March and April of 1968, FBI agents conducted raids at Angel Kaplan on charges of interstate gambling, which all but ended their operation. These raids created chaos among bookmakers and had a disruptive effect on the Chicago mob's sports bookmaking operation in Chicago and throughout the country. The Chicago news media devoted considerable attention to the raids and to the consequences.

The Jack Cerone trial began in April of 1970 before Federal Judge Abraham Lincoln Marovitz. The case was prosecuted by US Attorney Thomas Foran and his assistants James B. Casey and Michael B. Nash. The government did a masterful job in linking all the subjects, including Louis Bombacino, to Jack Cerone. Of course, the key witness was Lou Bombacino, who was cross-examined vigorously for several days by the six defense attorneys. Bombacino held up reasonably well, even though he was visibly shaken and at times was coughing up blood. Paul Ricca testified under a grant of immunity and appeared in court in his pajamas and bathrobe in a wheelchair because he was recovering from a fractured pelvis. C-1 agents had to afford Bombacino protection twenty-four hours a day prior to and throughout the trial. On May 9, 1970, the federal jury returned a verdict of guilty against all six subjects on charges of conspiring to violate the interstate gambling statute. It was a tremendous victory for the government and the FBI to have successfully prosecuted Jack Cerone, the heir apparent of the Chicago mob, and a number of significant members of the hoodlum group. Judge Marovitz, who was known to be somewhat charitable at times when issuing sentences, gave each of the subjects the maximum penalty allowed by law of five years in prison plus a $10,000 fine. Subject Frank Aurelli had to be severed from the trial for medical attention; however, he was later tried, convicted, and sent to prison for eighteen months. It was interesting to note that subject Don Angelini listed Agent Bill Roemer as a character witness in a presentencing report for the Judge, but fortunately, it had no effect on his sentencing. Apparently, Bill Roemer had established a friendly rapport with Angelini during the two FBI raids at Angelini's office at Angel Kaplan, and Angelini tried to capitalize on it. Judge Marovitz denied bond pending appeal and took into consideration the reputation of Cerone as a hit man for the mob and a threat to the life of Louis Bombacino. Attorneys for the subjects filed their appeal for reversal, but all convictions were affirmed by the appellate court. The incarceration of Jack Cerone was another major setback for the Chicago hoodlum group and deprived the mob of its acting leader.

Also, John DiDomenico, an employee of Don Angelini, who refused to testify before the grand jury on August 14, 1969, after a grant of immunity, was committed to prison for civil contempt of court charge. This charge was confirmed by the US Circuit Court of Appeals, and DiDomenico remained in the custody at the Cook County jail until the termination of the July 1969 federal grand jury, almost a year later. In addition, Angelo Kokas, a defense witness for the Angelini group, was indicted by the grand jury for committing perjury in this case. He was arrested by C-1 agents on May 17, 1970, and released on bond. Kokas was a gambler, bookmaker, and a close associate of hoodlums and was employed as a labor union representative. Kokas was convicted in a bench trial, and his conviction was upheld by the US Appellate Court.

The task of what to do with Lou Bombacino now posed a greater challenge. There was no such thing as the Federal Witness Protection Program in existence at that time. FBI headquarters had no solution for cooperative witnesses who felt threatened other than refer the matter to the local police for protection. We called upon FBI agent Walt Peters, who had been on the C-1 squad in Chicago and was now residing in Phoenix, Arizona. Walt Peters agreed to help. We obtained a new identity and social security number for Lou Bombacino, who would now be known as "Joe Nardi." We told Lou, very emphatically, to keep his nose clean and not to become involved in any activity that would focus attention on him because the Chicago mob would be looking for him. He assured us that he would. We helped Lou, his wife, and teenage son with their travel to Phoenix; and we were able to scrape up a few dollars to keep them going until Lou got a job. Walt Peters was able to get Lou Bombacino a warehouse job with the Arizona Public Service in Phoenix.

We maintained contact with Lou over the next few years and even helped Lou to return to Chicago for several visits with his mother. We then heard from Walt Peters that Lou was in trouble with his employer. Lou apparently was accused of being involved with gambling, prostitutes, and thefts, which resulted in Lou being arrested and fingerprinted. This exposed Joe Nardi's true identity as Lou Bombacino. Lou was now vulnerable, and we had him moved to a new residence in Tempe, Arizona. It did not take long for the Chicago mob to find Lou Bombacino. One morning, on October 6, 1975, while backing out of his driveway in Tempe, his leased 1976 Mark IV Lincoln Continental vehicle was blown up, killing Lou Bombacino. Even though the explosion was significant, it was reported that Lou actually died of a heart attack caused by the blast. We had done all we could do to protect Lou. Unfortunately, Lou was his own worst enemy by involving himself once again in criminal activities, which led to his undoing. Shortly after the killing of Bombacino, I received a call from his wife. She was fearful and distraught, and I expressed my sincere sympathy over the loss of her husband. She wanted to know if there was a life insurance policy on her husband so that she could plan accordingly. She was told that we had no insurance policy on Lou and that there was very little we could do at this time.

It was certainly a vivid reminder to others who would dare testify against the mob, especially the acting mob boss Jack Cerone, a ruthless enforcer. It had to be Cerone who sanctioned the killing of Lou Bombacino, who was a courageous but unfortunate casualty in our war against organized crime. The FBI, however, was not finished with Jack Cerone and would see to it that Cerone would spend the major portion of his golden years in prison. In 1986, Jack Cerone and other major hoodlums were found guilty of skimming two million dollars from a Las Vegas casino. Cerone was sentenced to serve twenty years in a federal prison. On November 20, 1996, Jack Cerone died of natural causes just six days after his release from prison.

Fiore Buccieri and Joseph Aiuppa Hoodlum Operations

Notorious Cicero Hoodlum Establishments

Cicero, Illinois, had the reputation of having been under the control of the Chicago hoodlum element dating back to the days of the Al Capone era. Hoodlum leader Joey "Doves" Aiuppa had been regarded as the boss of the town of Cicero. Many other hoodlum figures, such as Fiore Buccieri, were also known to operate in Cicero. One of the most notorious and profitable Cicero "B Girl" strip joints was the Stoplight Lounge, 4759 W. Roosevelt Road, Cicero, Illinois, a hangout for thieves and fences. The lounge had an adjoining snack shop that was a prime meeting place for Fiore Buccieri and his hoodlum group. The lounge was operated by Albert Milstein, a fence and loan shark collector for Buccieri, who was also listed as the president and liquor licensee of the lounge. A background investigation of Albert Milstein and other lounge owners was initiated by C-1 agent John Dallman and assisted by agents Lenard Wolf, Harold Johnson, Peter Kotsos, and Edward Bloom. It was determined that Milstein had falsified his state liquor license application regarding his residency and concealed his previous felony conviction, which disqualified him from having a liquor license. Also, Milstein had been charged in 1966 with refilling liquor bottles by the federal authorities who were not aware of Milstein's background. All of this information was furnished to AUSA Michael Nash, who made it available to the presiding Judge Hubert Will, who in June of 1967 sentenced Milstein to six months in prison plus a $1,000 fine. This sentence was one of the most severe sentences of its kind because this type of liquor violation was usually resolved with a fine. Milstein was released on an appeal bond. This information was also provided to the chairman of the Illinois Liquor Control Commission (ILCC) on June 13, 1967; and Albert Milstein's liquor license at the Stoplight Lounge was revoked. The effect of this revocation was that Milstein could never again be a liquor licensee in Illinois, and no liquor could be sold from the address of the Stoplight Lounge for one year from date of revocation. The Stoplight Lounge was forced to close down; however, the Millstein group attorneys filed an appeal, which was subsequently denied.

Milstein's problems were just beginning. After the closure of the Stoplight Lounge in Cicero, Albert Milstein moved his loan-sharking and fencing operation to the Madison Cafeteria, 5034 West Madison Street, Chicago. Information was received from a reliable Chicago source to the effect that a quantity of battery chargers had been stolen on August 6, 1968, from an interstate shipment and was in possession of Milstein at the Madison Café. FBI agents obtained a search warrant on August 22, 1968, and recovered thirty-eight battery chargers identified from the theft. Also seized was a quantity of gambling and loan-sharking records. Milstein was arrested and charged with interstate theft. His appeal bond on his federal liquor violation was revoked, and Milstein began serving his six-month sentence. Milstein was subsequently convicted on the interstate theft charges; and on October 17, 1968, Federal Judge Hubert Will sentenced Milstein to three years in prison. Bond was denied, and he was immediately incarcerated. We were not quite finished with Albert Milstein because he would be convicted again in 1970 on a loan-sharking violation at the Family Amusement Center in Cicero and would be sentenced to an additional eight years in prison.

The other notorious hoodlum locations in Cicero were the Turf Lounge in the Towne Hotel, which had been the Cicero headquarters of Al Capone and was the headquarters of Joey Aiuppa; the Shoo Shoo a Go Go, a reported Buccieri and James Torello enterprise; and the Towne Revue, reportedly owned by Aiuppa and William Daddano. False residency statements were also found on the state liquor license applications of Richard O'Donnell for Aiuppa's Turf Lounge and Anthony Blazevich for Buccieri's Shoo Shoo a Go Go. Details of false statements and the fact that B girls and prostitution were openly being solicited at the clubs were provided to the ILCC. In order to circumvent license revocation at the Turf Lounge, Aiuppa's hoodlum group formed a corporation known as the Turf Lounge Inc. Richard O'Donnell, the original licensee, was now listed as the incorporator, which bypassed residency requirements. They obtained a local Cicero liquor license and then applied for a state liquor license. The chairman of the ILCC described the action of the Cicero town president in granting the local license to Turf Lounge Inc., when the lounge was already under citation by state officials, as a "brazen attempt to circumvent due process of law." On August 23, 1967, Robert Wiedrich of the *Chicago Tribune* exposed this maneuver in an article and highlighted the Turf Lounge as mob headquarters of the Cicero vice operation since the days of Al Capone. C-1 agents Dallman and Wolf testified at the ILCC revocation hearings on September 12, 1967; and the ILCC made a unanimous decision to revoke the liquor license for the Shoo Shoo Lounge in that Blazevich falsified three consecutive liquor license applications. Also, the Turf Lounge revocation hearing was continued. In the meantime, the Cook County sheriff's police and the Illinois State Police continued to make their open checks of Cicero taverns and nightclubs, all of which had virtually shut down all syndicate-controlled vice locations in hoodlum-dominated Cicero. On September 20, 1967, Aiuppa's nephew Simone Fulco at the Turf Lounge advised C-1 Agent John Dallman, "The show is over. You win," and said that he had fired all the B girls and strippers at the Turf Lounge and that his business was finished.

Regarding the Towne Hotel in Cicero, which was the headquarters of Joey Aiuppa and the daily meeting place for numerous West Side hoodlums, investigation disclosed that the Chicago, Burlington and Quincy Railroad (Burlington Road) had an agreement with the Towne Hotel since 1965, wherein the hotel made available on a permanent basis hotel rooms for the Burlington brakemen laying over between trains. This amounted to over $35,000 a year in income for Aiuppa; in addition, the Eagle Cab Company in Cicero, an alleged Aiuppa enterprise, handled the transportation between rail yards. In March of 1968, Harvey Johnson, former FBI agent and operating director for the Chicago Crime Commission (CCC), was made aware of this arrangement and personally contacted the president of the Burlington Road, a financial contributor to the CCC, and notified him of the situation. The president of the Burlington Road indicated that as soon as other hotel arrangements could be made for his employees, he would cancel the agreement with the Towne Hotel and no longer utilize the Eagle Cab Company. A confidential source advised that without the income from the Burlington, the Towne Hotel would have to operate at a loss or possibly close. The hotel was owned and operated by Rosmar Realty in which Aiuppa was reported to be president.

The Towne Revue, another key Cicero vice den under the control of Aiuppa that employed up to thirty-five people, Agent Dallman also furnished sufficient information to the ILCC for state license revocation in September 1967; and the ILCC issued a citation against this location. Other Cicero vice dens that were closed because of liquor license revocations based on FBI information and/or FBI testimony were Harry's Lounge, a gambling and vice location; the 2900 Club, a fencing and juice operation; and Julius's Lounge, another Aiuppa vice den. The closing of the notorious hoodlum gambling and vice clubs deprived the Chicago mob of one of their highly lucrative sources of income. On the evening of September 20, 1967, thirty-six Cicero civic groups and representatives of major industries in Cicero held a meeting regarding recent disclosures on corruption there, based specifically on FBI vice and gambling investigations, and excluded Cicero City officials. This group planned to convene in 1969 to recommend good government candidates for public office. This change in civic attitude and action in Cicero would hopefully result in the historical ending of the dominating influence of the Chicago mob in that area.

Intensified investigation of Aiuppa's Cicero vice dens continued. On February 9, 1968, the Cook County State's attorney's office raided "Show of Shows" in Cicero, a key vice operation in the building owned by Tarquin "Queenie" Simonelli, brother-in-law of Anthony Accardo, based on FBI information relating to violations of the state anti-B girl solicitation statute. This information was provided to the ILCC; and on April 16, 1966, the ILCC revoked their state liquor license. Additional state violations were detected at Al's Place operated by Alphonso Carlisi, brother of Buffalo, New York, top hoodlum Roy Carlisi. On December 13, 1968, the ILCC revoked the state liquor license of Al's Place. Carlisi was also arrested for a bookmaking operation based on FBI information, and he was found to be in the process of constructing a hidden gambling casino in the back room of his establishment. The Red Velvet Lounge in Cicero, operated by one of Aiuppa's top aides, was one of the last of Aiuppa's B girl strip joints and house of prostitution. On August 22, 1968, ILCC agents and the Cook County sheriff's office raided the Red Velvet Lounge, also based on FBI information. On October 8, 1968, the state liquor license of the Red Velvet Lounge was also revoked.

Violations of state fire prevention laws at the notorious Towne Hotel in Cicero had been referred to the state fire marshal's office by the Chicago Division since late 1967. In 1969, additional specific information on these violations were again furnished to the state fire marshal's office as well as to Bernard Carey, former FBI agent and newly appointed deputy director of Public Safety. Aiuppa, and his aide Anthony "Bucky" Ortenzi reportedly used their influence during the last eighteen months to delay state action; however, they were now given a thirty-day limit for the Towne Hotel to correct these violations. Aiuppa reportedly spent almost $10,000 during the previous thirty days attempting to bring the hotel up to the minimum standards. Ortenzi told Bernard Carey that additional work required by the state would force the hotel out of business because of cost. Carey advised Cook County State's Attorney Edward Hanrahan of the delaying tactics by Aiuppa and requested Hanrahan's office to consider obtaining a court order to close the Towne Hotel. Chicago sources close to the Aiuppa group advised in recent months that Aiuppa's vice and gambling operations in Cicero had become unprofitable because of continuing FBI pressure in the form of gambling raids, liquor license revocations, vice raids on B girl strip joints, and fire law violations. Also, information was received that Aiuppa reportedly was planning to sell the Towne Hotel to a new owner, Dominic Santarelli, effective February 16, 1970. During the early morning hours of February 17, 1970, a Chicago source who resided near the Towne Hotel advised that an explosion occurred at the hotel snack shop that started an extensive fire, which destroyed the historically infamous Towne Hotel in Cicero, Illinois.

ARMORY LOUNGE, AN AIUPPA ENTERPRISE

The Armory Lounge, 7427 W. Roosevelt Road, Forest Park, Illinois, was the longtime headquarters of Sam Giancana, boss of the Chicago mob, and his underlings. Upon his release from the Cook County jail on contempt of court charges on June 1, 1966, Giancana had been in self-imposed exile in Mexico and had not returned to the Chicago area. In Giancana's absence, the Armory Lounge continued to be a regular meeting place for Chicago West Side hoodlums, including Cicero boss Joseph Aiuppa. In April of 1966, Mary Giannotti, wife of Nicholas Giannotti, a hoodlum associate, became the state liquor licensee of the former Armory Lounge and was doing business as Giannotti's Restaurant and Cocktail Lounge. Investigation disclosed that Joey Aiuppa had a financial interest in the building that housed Giannotti's. Subsequent review of the state liquor license application of Mary Giannotti not only listed Aiuppa as the owner of the premises, but that Mary Giannotti was also in violation of the residency requirements of the Illinois State Liquor Control Act. The above data were furnished by Agent John Dallman to Peter Kotsos, former FBI agent and director of the newly formed Enforcement Division of the ILCC. He immediately instituted plans for the license revocation of Giannotti's as well as a hearing to determine the true ownership of the lounge under the beneficial interest provisions of the state act. Subpoenas were issued for Joseph Aiuppa, Aiuppa's brothers Sam and James, Charles English, possibly Sam Giancana if he could be located, and other hoodlums believed to be connected with the Armory Lounge. Mary Giannotti was interviewed by C-1 agents and revealed that she had no lease or any other interest in the premises. She purchased the restaurant business from Doris Fanelli in 1966. Joey Aiuppa would not give her a lease, and after several months in business, Aiuppa raised her rent from $250 to $450 per month. The rent checks were then mailed to Rosmar Realty, an Aiuppa enterprise, and then to hoodlum attorney Eugene Bernstein. She also mailed checks to Joseph Aiuppa at his residence, 4 Yorkshire Drive, Oakbrook, Illinois. It was noted that failure to have a lease for the premises was also a violation of the Illinois Liquor Control Act, and these data were furnished to the chairman of the ILCC. Tax attorney Eugene Berstein was also subpoenaed and ordered to bring books and records that he maintained for Aiuppa on Giannotti's at a hearing that was held on May 15, 1968. Joseph Aiuppa invoked the Fifth Amendment on advice of counsel when questioned about the ownership of the restaurant building and to the receipt of the rent payments. The property was managed by Country Investment Corp. in which Aiuppa's brothers were officers of that company until its dissolution in February 1967. The building was then reportedly sold to one Geneva Cox, not further identified. The existence of a lease became an issue; and Aiuppa, who had been receiving the rent checks, was ordered to produce a copy of the document that he could not provide. On May 27, 1968, Howard Cartwright, chairman of the ILCC, revoked the state liquor license for Giannotti's Restaurant based on the evidence of violating the residency provisions of the State Liquor Control Act and by not having a lease for the premises as well as failure to register with the county clerk under the assumed name statute. This license revocation was responsible for the closing down of a historical meeting place of the top leaders of organized crime. The Chicago news media highlighted the hoodlum history of the Armory Lounge and credited the cooperative efforts of the ILCC and the FBI for its closure. It was the first instance where conclusive evidence had disclosed a direct "behind-the-scene" crime syndicate interest in a large well-known Chicago area restaurant. It was at the Armory Lounge where entertainer Frank Sinatra held his command performance in 1959 for Sam Giancana and his hoodlum associates. It was also the location where Anthony Accardo held his meeting in 1956 to "negotiate" his $65,000 a year salary contract as a beer salesman with the officials of the Fox Head Brewing Company. Last but not least, it deprived Sam Giancana, who had fled to Mexico in 1966, of his prime headquarters and hoodlum meeting location and message center.

LUXOR BATHS, CHICAGO, ILLINOIS

In 1972, when Cicero boss Joseph Aiuppa began his rise to power, he began using Luxor Baths, 2039 W. North Avenue, Chicago, Illinois, as his prime meeting place with his subordinates. Photographic surveillances confirmed that it was becoming a prime meeting place for the Chicago mob. This bathhouse had a storied past dating back to the 1920s and was also known as the Luxor Russian Bathhouse and the Luxor Turkish Bathhouse. It had been built originally as a public bathhouse for immigrants. It later became a commercial bathhouse used by politicians and hoodlums because it was difficult to wiretap inside of steam baths and the pool area. Prostitutes were reportedly available upon request. Plans were formulated to infiltrate this location by using a first office agent, whose background coincided with the ethnic background of the neighborhood of Luxor Baths. The C-1 agent selected was Fernando Mata, who was of Cuban descent and was not known to the Chicago hoodlum element. SA Mata was able to slowly assimilate with the clientele and penetrate this location for a three-month period. On scores of occasions, Mata observed Aiuppa and his associates during their meetings and occasionally was close enough to overhear their conversations. The hoodlums also used a public phone at this location, which enabled the FBI to determine the identity of the recipient of these calls. As a result of SA Mata's continuing observations, along with our photographic surveillances, the Chicago office was able to develop critical intelligence information on the identity and activities of all of the members of the Aiuppa hoodlum group.

Eugene "Gino" Izzi et al.

In 1966, the Chicago Division developed information that Eugene Izzi, a reputed mob enforcer; John Fezekas, a Chicago gambler; and other Chicago individuals were traveling daily from Cicero, Illinois, to establish and operate several large-scale gambling casinos in the Hammond and East Chicago, Indiana, areas under the control of hoodlum leader Fiore Buccieri. Chicago agents, led by C-1 agent Dennis Shanahan, successfully penetrated these gambling operations in May of 1966. On June 2, 1966, three gambling locations were raided by FBI agents from the Chicago and Indianapolis divisions assisted by local authorities. More than 150 patrons were involved at the three locations, and many other patrons fled into the streets. Fourteen persons were arrested. The Forsythe Club was the main location and was a twenty-four-hour-a-day operation with an estimated annual take of six million. Considerable gambling equipment and cash were seized. Eugene "Gino" Izzi, John Fezekas, and three casino dealers were indicted by a federal grand jury for violating the federal interstate gambling statute. On January 11, 1967, Fezekas and three subjects entered guilty pleas, and Eugene Izzi was found guilty following a bench trial. Izzi was sentenced to three years in prison, and the other four defendants received probationary sentences and fines.

SALVATORE DEROSE ET AL.

Salvatore DeRose was a gambling collector, enforcer, and a cartage thief for the Fiore hoodlum group. On November 13, 1967, DeRose and two of his burglary confederates, Anthony DePaolo, a convicted bank robber, and Anthony Mazzone, were arrested by FBI agents in possession of a stolen interstate shipment of Dutch Masters cigars valued at $500,000. The thieves kidnapped and blindfolded the driver of the tractor and made off with the trailer load, consisting of 484 cartons of cigars, just hours before they were arrested at the Turf Farm, US Highway 6 in Tinley Park, Illinois, by FBI agents. The kidnapped driver was located and released, and the entire shipment was recovered. Subjects were charged with violating the interstate theft statute. DeRose and Mazzone were released on bond, and DePaolo was placed in federal custody for being a parole violator. Further investigation disclosed the involvement of an additional subject named Carmen Trotta, who was arrested and also charged in the theft. On June 27, 1968, subjects Salvatore DeRose and Anthony DePaolo entered guilty pleas and were sentenced by Federal Judge Abraham Marovitz to seven years in prison. Subjects Anthony Mazzone and Carmen Trotta were found guilty in a jury trial and on February 17, 1969, were sentenced to seven years and three years in prison, respectively. The case agent Dean J. Mieseler did an outstanding job in the quick resolution of this major theft and kidnapping case and was capably assisted by C-1 agents Merle Hamre and Frank Ford.

MICHAEL BIANCOFIORE

In May of 1968, Congress passed the Truth in Lending Bill. This included the Extortionate Credit Transactions statute (ECT) that gave the FBI a weapon against the mob's lucrative loan-sharking operation also known as shylocking, "juice" loans, usury, or the loaning of money at exorbitant interest rates, which was one of the prime sources of income for organized crime. Whenever gambling occurs, there will always be available a hoodlum money lender who would be happy to advance funds to gamble or to repay gambling debts. Normally, these loans are made at outrageous interest rates, usually around 20 percent per week. If payments are missed, then there are dire consequences resulting in threats or actual violence. Any "juice" operation of any magnitude was controlled by organized crime.

Michael Biancofiore was a lieutenant of the Fiore Buccieri hoodlum group, who operated a segment of Buccieri's "juice" loan operation. In June 1968, one of Biancofiore's juice victims was being threatened for being in arrears on his loan payments. The original loan was for $200, and he had been making weekly payments for the past two years. Victim had need for an additional $200, and his weekly juice payments were about $100 per week. The victim advised Biancofiore that he could no longer make any more payments because he had to care for his family. Numerous threats were made against the victim and his family. The victim was in fear of his life and decided to cooperate with the FBI. In October of 1968, FBI agents hid themselves in the victim's home, at which time Biancofiore arrived and made further threats, which were overheard by the agents. Subject was placed under arrest and was found to have a loaded gun in his possession. In 1969, Biancofiore was indicted by a federal grand jury for violating the ECT statute by threatening a juice loan victim with physical injury for being in arrears with his payments. He was subsequently convicted and was sentenced to serve seven years in prison. However, while on bond, Biancofiore had threatened to kill his paramour of ten years and continued to threaten the juice victim. As a result of these threats, Biancofiore was again arrested and his bond revoked and was immediately incarcerated to serve his sentence. The US Court of Appeals upheld this conviction. This case was developed by C-1 agent Richard Cavanagh and was the first conviction recorded of its kind in the Chicago Division since the enactment of the new ECT statute.

FAMILYAMUSEMENTCENTER

M ichael Biancofiore was a member of the Family Amusement Center (FAC) operation, located at 5913 West Roosevelt Road, Cicero, Illinois. In May of 1968, it was determined that the FAC was the prime headquarters for the loan-sharking activities of the entire Fiore Buccieri hoodlum organization. It formerly operated at the Social Athletic Club, 4755 West Roosevelt Road in Cicero, Illinois. The following hoodlums were identified as frequenting this location: James Torello, Angelo LaPietra, James LaPietra, Steve Annoreno, Vito Spillone, Louis DeRiggi, and George Vertucci. Observations and photographic surveillance by C-1 agents, led by SAs Lenard Wolf and Harold Johnson, on a nightly basis from a fixed plant over a prolonged four-month period of time, established the presence of numerous collectors and victims of the Buccieri loan shark operation. Many of Buccieri's lieutenants were observed directing and controlling this operation, which was believed to be the largest of its kind in the Chicago area. During this time, a steady stream of juice loan victims, collectors, and hoodlums paraded in and out of this location with several victims known to have been assaulted on the premises. Some 250 juice lenders, collectors, and juice victims were observed doing business at this central location. Photos of all persons coming and going at this location were taken. The tedious task began of identifying subjects and victims for the purpose of developing a violation of the federal ECT statute. Steve Annoreno was a rising star in the organization and reported directly to Angelo LaPietra, a lieutenant of Fiore Buccieri. Annoreno's principal collector was hoodlum enforcer Frank Calabrese. Others were George Vertucci, Martin Bucaro, and Lawrence Moretti; and the proceeds would be turned over to Annoreno at his residence every Friday afternoon. Annoreno, at this time, had approximately one million dollars out in juice principal and was collecting from $40,000 to $50,000 every Friday to be turned over to the Buccieri organization. Annoreno appeared to be in charge of this operation. Fiore Buccieri did not make an appearance at the FAC; however, he was known to be in almost daily contact with his lieutenant and bodyguard James Torello and Angelo LaPietra. During September 1968, the lease expired on the FAC, and the group moved out of the building and decentralized their juice loan operation. Over the next several months, C-1 agents began to interview hundreds of juice victims who had been photographed while visiting the FAC. Many were cooperative and furnished details about their juice loans. Those who were uncooperative, out of fear of reprisal by the mob, were handed federal grand jury subpoenas. Ten of the victims took the Fifth Amendment and were granted immunity from prosecution and were forced to testify. Five witnesses, who lied before the grand jury, were arrested for perjury. Two were convicted and received jail sentences for perjury. Four of these witnesses then cooperated with the government.

On September 9, 1969, suppressed indictments were returned, and arrest warrants were issued against ten of Buccieri's top lieutenants and collectors on charges of violating the federal ECT statute. On September 10, 1969, at 7:00 a.m., forty C-1 agents participated in the arrest of the subjects throughout the Chicago and suburban areas on these charges and were arraigned before Federal Judge Edwin Robson. On November 3, 1969, a superseding indictment was returned, naming Martin Bucaro as an additional subject. The trial began on October 5, 1970, and was prosecuted by Special Department of Justice attorney Alan Edelstein who was skillfully assisted by AUSA Anton Valukas, a bright and capable attorney who eventually became US attorney for the northern district of Illinois. This case presented unique and complex obstacles. It was the first of its kind because of the magnitude of the loan-sharking operation. All of the juice victims were initially reluctant to testify in open court for fear of physical reprisal by the Buccieri group, who were noted for their terror tactics. During the trial, twenty-five juice victims testified, and an additional fourteen were not used. Three other corroborative witnesses testified, as did one expert witness and seven C-1 agents. There were over nine hundred exhibits introduced by the government, including over seven hundred photographs taken of victims and subjects at the FAC. On October 19, 1970, the jury found the eleven subjects guilty on all counts of violating the federal ECT statute. One of the juice collectors, who had pocketed some of the collections, was so severely beaten by the mob that he committed suicide a short time later.

On January 7, 1971, in a surprise move, and prior to the sentencing of subjects, defense attorney Louis Carbonaro had obtained subpoenas for the following Chicago C-1 agents to appear on January 11, 1971, as defense witnesses: Vincent L. Inserra, Lenard Wolf, John Dallman, Richard Cavanagh, and Harold Johnson. It was the contention of the defense attorneys that the "government illegally and unlawfully" used electronic eavesdropping devices to convict the subjects. It was noted that Steve Annoreno, Louis DeRiggi, and Albert Milstein were in fact monitored by electronic surveillance (ELSURs) by the FBI in 1963 and 1964 at two previous loan-sharking headquarters locations; however, no such ELSUR coverage was ever maintained at the FAC. Investigation at the FAC by Chicago agents began in May of 1968, well after the discontinuance of the ELSUR program. From January 11 through 19, 1971, the above C-1 agents as well as agents Richard Gliebe and George Perkins all testified in depth about the role they played at the ELSUR hearings before Judge Edwin Robson, who took the matter under advisement. On January 21, 1971, Judge Robson ruled in favor of the government, stating that defendants had not shown any evidence in this case that came from tainted information obtained from ELSURs conducted in 1963 and 1964. Also, the defendants had not shown that the FBI focused on the defendants because of the previous ELSURs. We were confident that this important case was not initiated based on information obtained from illegal ELSURs.

On February 2, 1971, Judge Robson sentenced the eleven defendants as follows:

Steve Annoreno: fifteen years and $10,000 fine

Vito Spillone: twelve years and $10,000 fine

Martin Bucaro: twelve years and $10,000 fine

Louis DeRiggi: eight years

Albert Milstein: eight years to run consecutively with the five years presently serving

George Vertucci: five years

Anthony Delgallo: five years

John Kobylarz: five years

Anthony Spillone: five years

Sam Pullia: three years

Anthony Reno: three years (brother of Steve Annoreno)

All subjects were immediately incarcerated without benefit of an appeal bond because Judge Robson felt they were a danger to the community. The successful outcome of this major case had been given continuous and preferential investigative attention. It required the use of all of the C-1 agents over a prolonged period of time, especially agents Lenard Wolf, Harold Johnson, Eugene Sather, John Dallman, and Richard Cavanagh, all of whom did an exceptionally fine job. AUSAs Edelstein and Valukas did an outstanding job in handling all of the legal challenges faced in prosecuting this highly complex matter. The case received widespread new media attention throughout the entire trial. The US Department of Justice hailed these convictions as one of the most significant cases of its kind in the country in combating the evils of the loan-sharking operation of organized crime in Chicago. All defendants appealed their convictions. On May 26, 1972, the US Court of Appeals concluded that the evidence presented was sufficient to sustain all convictions except for Tony Reno, whose conviction was reversed. The remaining ten defendants appealed their convictions to the US Supreme Court, and they were denied.

Since the successful prosecution of this case, the entire structure of loan shark activity in the Chicago area changed. The Chicago outfit immediately decentralized their juice loan operations and became more selective in loaning to victims, which curtailed a significant amount of juice loan activity. At one time, the juice loan operation in Chicago was one of the major sources of hoodlum income, and after these convictions, their source of income from loan-sharking greatly diminished.

LAS VEGAS JUNKET OF JOSEPH FERRIOLA AND FRANK BUCCIERI

Joseph Ferriola had been a leading lieutenant and enforcer for hoodlum leader Fiore Buccieri and was considered to be his logical successor in the Chicago mob hierarchy. On August 2, 1968, information was received by the Chicago FBI that Frank Buccieri, brother of Fiore Buccieri and also a possible successor to his brother's throne, was departing Chicago via United Airlines for Las Vegas. The Las Vegas FBI office was alerted to the travel and arrival of Frank Buccieri to their territory for their information. Frank Buccieri was greeted upon his arrival in Las Vegas by Chicago hoodlum leader Joseph Ferriola and an unknown female. A bellman in a Caesar's Palace uniform was waiting for the group and drove all three to the Caesar's Palace, where they were assigned two connecting rooms. Frank Buccieri was registered as Frank Bruno of Peoria, Illinois; and Joseph Ferriola and his blonde female companion were registered as Mr. and Mrs. Jay Long, also from Peoria, Illinois. The registration cards bore the notation that the room, food, and beverages were to be complimentary on the authority of Paul Ross, the assistant hotel manager at Caesar's Palace. The Clark County sheriff's office was alerted to the presence of Frank Buccieri and Joseph Ferriola, and they placed subjects under surveillance while at Caesar's Palace. On Saturday August 3, 1968, at 10:45 p.m., Frank Buccieri and Joseph Ferriola were arrested by Clark County detectives at Caesar's Palace. Buccieri claimed his name was Frank White from San Francisco and refused to divulge any other information and had absolutely no other identification on his person. Buccieri asked what the charges were for his arrest; and he was told, "Vagrancy: No Identification Papers," at which time he admitted that his name was Frank Buccieri and that he was from Chicago. He tried to bargain with the arresting officers to keep out of jail, but to no avail. Joseph Ferriola identified himself as Mr. Long from Chicago and declined to furnish any other information. Both were arrested and charged with "Vagrancy: No Identification." Neither subject could understand how they could be arrested for vagrancy, when each had more than

$2,000 in cash in their possession. Subjects were taken out of Caesar's Palace in handcuffs and transported to the Clark County sheriff's office.

Although Frank Buccieri did not like being arrested and having to be photographed and fingerprinted, he was cooperating and taking his predicament rather philosophically. On the other hand, Ferriola was being obstinate and refused to have his photo taken, or to be fingerprinted, and was placed in a jail cell. He finally agreed to be fingerprinted but was completely unwilling to be photographed. When efforts were made to take a photo of Ferriola in a seated position, Ferriola lashed out and hit an officer in the eye with his fist and was then charged with assault and battery of a police officer. It took about five police officers to subdue Ferriola, and he was placed in a padded cell without his clothes for his own protection. In the meantime, Buccieri was able to arrange to have one of his contacts from Caesar's Palace post bail of $25 for his own release from jail. The following morning, on August 4, 1968, Buccieri was able to secure the release of Joseph Ferriola by posting a $50 bond on the charge of vagrancy and a $500 bond on the charge of assault and battery of a police officer. Ferriola was to appear on August 5, 1968, on these charges. Ferriola refused to sign for his property, and when he was told that he would not be released, he reluctantly signed and was released. Both were directed to leave Las Vegas immediately and were designated as "undesirables." A representative from Caesar's Palace assured the Clark County police that Buccieri and Ferriola would be escorted to the Las Vegas airport as soon as possible so that they could return to Chicago. The C-1 agents who received the intelligence information in this matter were Harold Johnson and Lenard Wolf. The above situation had to be extremely embarrassing and frustrating for Fiore Buccieri's top lieutenants, Frank Buccieri and Joseph Ferriola, because they had become accustomed to VIP treatment in Las Vegas as well as in Chicago. Ferriola, who had been known for his muscle tactics in Chicago and was one of the mob's chief enforcers in the past, should have taken a more calm and diplomatic approach with the Las Vegas police officers, especially because he had a serious heart condition. Joseph Ferriola's problems, however, were just beginning because he would be indicted and convicted with Jack Cerone and others in an interstate gambling violation in 1970, for which he would serve three years of a five-year sentence in prison. Joseph Ferriola died at the age of sixty-one.

Photo of Joseph Ferriola reacting violently to being processed by the Clark County sheriff's detectives in Las Vegas, Nevada, on August 3, 1968

FRANK TEUTONICO ET AL.

Frank "The Calico Kid" Teutonico was a prominent loan shark collector for the Fiore Buccieri hoodlum group. Teutonico and his two confederates, Anthony Schullo and John Zizzo, were conducting their loan-sharking operation out of the Coolidge Hotel in Chicago, where Teutonico and Schullo both lived. Approximately thirty-five victims of this operation were identified by C-1 agents Lenard Wolf, Harold Johnson, James Bonner, and Phil Heil; and all the victims were subpoenaed to testify before the federal grand jury. A majority of the loan shark victims were Chicago cab drivers. On June 28, 1971, the three subjects entered guilty pleas to the federal ECT statute; and on August 6, 1971, each of the subjects received a five-year suspended sentence and five years on probation and was ordered to serve six months in prison.

HARRY ALEMAN

Harry Aleman was one of the most feared and cold-blooded hit man for the Chicago mob. He was the nephew of outfit leader Joseph Ferriola; a key lieutenant of Fiore Buccieri. In 1971, based upon a joint investigation into the income of Harry Aleman by the IRS and the Chicago FBI, it was determined that Harry Aleman had made false statements to the Lincoln Federal Savings and Loan in order to obtain a mortgage loan for a house he wanted to purchase. Aleman also made false statements on a loan application with the Silver Leaf Savings and Loan. Handwriting samples were obtained before the federal grand jury, confirming Aleman's signature; and Harry Aleman was convicted in US District Court on August11, 1971, for violating the Federal Reserve Act statute. On September 13, 1971, Harry Aleman was sentenced to three years on probation and fined $450.

Being on federal probation did not deter Harry Aleman from living up to his reputation as a ruthless hit man. In 1973, William Logan, a Teamster Union Shop Stewart, was killed by two shotgun blasts at close range in Chicago. In 1977, Harry Aleman went on trial for the killing of Logan and was acquitted during a bench trial because of an alleged $10,000 bribe to Cook County, Illinois, Judge Frank J. Wilson. During February of 1990, Judge Wilson committed suicide with a self-inflicted gunshot wound to the head after the bribe scheme was made public. In 1997, Harry Aleman was retried on the murder charge of William Logan after a higher court ruled that there was no double jeopardy involved in a fixed murder case acquittal, a landmark decision. Harry Aleman was subsequently convicted in local court of first-degree murder and sentenced to one hundred to three hundred years in prison. On May 20, 2010, Harry Aleman died in a prison hospital at the age of seventy-one.

ARREST OF FIORE BUCCIERI

Fiore "Fifi" Buccieri, a prominent hoodlum leader and at that time perhaps the most powerful hoodlum in the Chicago mob, was indicted on November 25, 1970, by the Dupage County, Illinois, grand jury for theft, soliciting others to commit theft, and possession of stolen property, which included various heavy construction equipment valued at about $200,000, all based on FBI information. The stolen equipment was recovered on the grounds of the Santa Fe Saddle and Gun Club, a west suburban hangout for Buccieri and his mob. It was noted that in 1967, Billy Falbo Jr., a Chicago entertainer, was the secretary of the Santa Fe Saddle and Gun Club who hosted a testimonial dinner for Fiore Buccieri at the Edgewater Beach Hotel's grand ballroom in Chicago. Popular singer Vic Damone entertained the crowd of about one thousand people and called for a round of applause for his good friends Fiore and his brother Frank Buccieri. Also in 1964, Vic Damone unwittingly allowed himself to be appointed president of the Vic Damone Pizza Co., which was later determined to be a front for a loan-sharking operation of Frank Buccieri and his collectors Donald and Joseph Grieco.

The information that led to Buccieri's indictment was provided by a confidential source of the C-1 squad who had been turned over to former C-1 agent Richard Gliebe, then head of the organized crime unit of the Illinois Bureau of Investigation (IBI). Also charged in the indictment were subjects Frank Nitti and Jan Sacks, who were arrested by agents of the IBI. Buccieri surrendered to local authorities on November 30, 1970, and was released on a $5,000 bond. In March of 1971, information was received that Fiore Buccieri was recently operated on for lung cancer at the Cedars of Lebanon Hospital, Beverly Hills, California. Buccieri's left lung was removed, and his right lung was badly infected. He was reportedly recuperating from surgery in Palm Springs, California, at a home rented by his brother Frank. The illness of Buccieri, which was believed to be terminal, could precipitate another power struggle in the Chicago mob. James "Turk" Torello, Buccieri's most trusted lieutenant, had been the operating director of Buccieri's interests during his illness. On August 4, 1971, Buccieri's attorney Louis Carbonaro provided the judge with a letter from the doctor that stated that Buccieri's physical condition made it uncertain whether he would be physically able to stand trial. On March 20, 1972, the trial of Fiore Buccieri was postponed indefinitely because of his physical condition. Following the death of Fiore Buccieri on August 17, 1973, James "Turk" Torello took over the leadership of the Buccieri hoodlum group. In April of 1979, Torello died of cancer at the age of forty-nine.

JAMES FALCO ET AL.

James "The Hawk" Falco, an old-time Chicago West Side mobster and convicted armed robber and cartage thief, and his enforcer associate Samuel Annerino Jr., who was on appeal after having received a two-year sentence for a similar offense, were convicted on November 11, 1974, in federal court of violating the federal ECT statute for using terror tactics, while collecting a $5,000 loan from an Oak Park, Illinois, businessman. The victim testified that he had been beaten severely, mainly by Annerino, a former light heavyweight boxer who participated in the 1964 Olympics. Also, both men threatened to break his bones with a baseball bat and kill him with a shotgun. On November 24, Judge William Lynch sentenced Annerino to five years in prison to run consecutively with the two-year sentence he was presently serving. Falco received a three-year sentence. Three of the victim's company trucks were badly vandalized following the sentencing of subjects, and the judge adamantly refused to reinstate subjects appeal bonds and remanded them to the custody of the US Marshal to begin their prison sentences immediately. All aspects of this sensitive case were handled in a very proficient manner by C-1 agent Richard Cavanagh, who was capably assisted by SAs James Annes and Dane Hill.

CARMEN PETER BASTONE ET AL.

Carmen Peter Bastone was a longtime protégé of Sam Giancana and was closely associated with hoodlum leaders in Chicago. In 1965, Bastone represented Sam Giancana and gambling boss Les Kruse in an attempt to set up a gambling operation in the Dominican Republic. A rebellion in that country caused him to be evacuated before accomplishing his mission. On December 9, 1971, Carmen Bastone was indicted by the federal grand jury on two counts of filing false applications for federal home improvement loans. Bastone entered a plea of guilty to the federal charges before Judge Abraham Marovitz; and on March 17, 1972, he was sentenced to three years on probation and ordered to make restitution to the Bank of Lincolnwood, Illinois. Bastone, while on probation, continued to involve himself in criminal activities. In 1972, Carmen Bastone and other well-known Chicago cartage thieves were indicted in a multimillion-dollar interstate semi-trailer theft ring, which had been operating during a four-year period. On January 29, 1975, Carmen Bastone and six other cartage thieves, including a Melrose Park, Illinois, police officer, were found guilty of interstate theft conspiracy charges. On May 6, 1975, Judge Thomas McMillan sentenced Carmen Bastone to five years in prison and took into consideration that this violation occurred during the time Bastone was on federal probation. Other sentences ranged from two years in prison to probation. The C-1 agents who materially contributed to this case were James Bonner and Philip Heil. They were assisted by other agents of the Chicago Division because of the overall complexity of this case.

ERNEST SANSONE ET AL.

Ernest Sansone, a prominent Chicago hoodlum and former convicted bootlegger, was a close associate of Charles Nicoletti, a Chicago mob enforcer. In 1943, Sansone and Nicoletti served time on federal narcotics charges. In 1966, Sansone operated a nationwide horse race results dissemination service that utilized numerous employees and serviced a large number of customers across the country. As a counterpart to sports betting, the Sansone operation provided fast race results, which was essential to horse betting by Chicago area bookmakers and elsewhere. A four-year investigation aided by several court approved Title III electronic surveillances, resulted in the return of two federal grand jury indictments, charging Ernest Sansone and seven Chicago gamblers with violation of the interstate gambling statute, which involved the dissemination of fast race results to bookmakers in the Midwest. As a result, Chicago area bookmakers no longer had rapid race results, which greatly hampered the volume of their bookmaking business and severely diminished their income. All subjects were arrested by C-1 agents. In 1968, subjects Milton Ruthstein and Joseph Vazzano were convicted and sentenced to three years in prison. In 1969, Ernest Sansone and five other subjects entered pleas of guilty to similar interstate gambling charges and received sentences ranging from six to eighteen months in prison and placed on probation for a period of five years each. C-1 agent Herb Briick, as the case agent, did an outstanding job in coordinating all of the aspects of this highly complex case and was assisted by SA Paul "Pete" Neumann and many other C-1 agents.

This investigation was far from over. Information had been obtained from the Sansone Title III electronic surveillance that disclosed a substantial link to a large-scale Detroit gambling operation handled by gambler Thomas Emon. The Detroit office requested assistance from Chicago in executing numerous arrest and search warrants in connection with their Emon investigation. The Chicago office dispatched forty-five C-1 agents and twenty-two bureau cars to assist the Detroit office. On May 11, 1970, Chicago and Detroit agents conducted numerous gambling raids and arrests throughout the Detroit area on the Thomas Emon operation, which successfully disrupted a major organized crime gambling network.

MICHAEL POSNER ET AL.

Information was also received that Michael Posner, a south side Chicago bookmaker and wire room operator for gambling boss Ralph Pierce, had taken over the race results service when Ernest Sansone was sentenced to prison. C-1 agent Herb Briick was assigned to the Posner case in view of his familiarity with the Sansone case. SA Briick immediately submitted an affidavit to support a court-authorized Title III surveillance. This coverage documented a huge network of the Chicago mob's gambling network and led to additional court-authorized Title III surveillances. Based on the evidence developed, Strike Force Attorney Alan Edelstein authorized the arrest of five principal subjects and the execution of sixteen federal search warrants in connection with the Michael Posner interstate gambling operation. On June 19, 1970, approximately one hundred agents conducted twenty-one gambling raids in a massive crackdown on the mob's gambling network and arrested Michael Posner, Ernest Sansone, who had just been released from jail, Lionel Issacs, Pasquale Amore, and Benay Franklin. Huge amounts of records, gambling paraphernalia, and cash were seized. These raids involved the greatest number of FBI agents ever to take part in a single operation against a multimillion-dollar horse betting racket. From a review of the material seized, twelve additional subjects were added to this investigation. On March 23, 1971, the case was presented to the federal grand jury by Chief Strike Force Attorney Sheldon Davidson, and fifteen subjects were indicted and arrested in the Posner gambling operation. All of the subjects eventually entered guilty pleas and received various jail and probationary sentences. SA Herb Briick's performance in this matter was again remarkable; and he was assisted by C-1 agents Dennis Shanahan, William Hermann, Paul "Pete" Neumann, James Annes, and the entire C-1 organized crime squad and others.

FRANK "SKIPPY" CERONE ET AL.

Frank "Skippy" Cerone was a prominent Chicago hoodlum and a cousin of former acting boss Jack Cerone. Frank and Jack Cerone and others were reportedly involved in the attempted murder of Chicago labor union leader Frank Esposito in Hollywood, Florida, in 1962. In July of 1971, information was developed by C-1 agent James York that Frank Cerone was in control of a large-scale bookmaking operation. Several complicated, court-authorized Title III surveillances were instituted; and numerous physical surveillances were required to identify the entire network of Cerone's bookmakers. SA York capably assisted by agent Joseph Doyle and other C-1 agents spent long and arduous hours working late into the night and on weekends in order to obtain maximum results. On August 10, 1971, fifteen simultaneous gambling raids were successfully conducted, and extensive gambling paraphernalia and evidence were seized. At one location, bookmaker George Columbus destroyed gambling records, which resulted in his arrest and subsequent conviction for obstructing justice. The federal grand jury in Chicago returned indictments against five subjects, who were later convicted for violating the federal gambling statute. Based on information provided by SAs York and Doyle, the grand jury was in the process of indicting Cerone; however, he died of natural causes in 1973, which concluded the FBI investigation into this matter.

HENRY "RED" KUSHNIR

Following the demise of Chicago North Side boss Ross Prio in December of 1972, Henry "Red" Kushnir had been for decades one of Prio's top bookmakers and loan shark operators. Kushnir decided to retire from the rackets because of poor health. Kushnir was called before the federal grand jury and invoked the Fifth Amendment to all questions asked. He was granted immunity and decided to furnish false testimony. C-1 agents James Dewhirst and Lee Farmer, based upon a prior in depth investigation of Kushnir, were able to contradict Kushnir's testimony. Kushnir was subsequently indicted and arrested for perjury. On June 18, 1973, Kushnir changed his plea to guilty and was sentenced by US Judge James Parsons to serve two years in prison.

FBI CONVICTIONS OF
ORGANIZEDCRIMEFIGURES

Fiscal Year	Convictions
1966-1967	38
1967-1968	41
1968-1969	44
1969-1970	59
1970-1971	60
1971-1972	72
1972-1973	117
1973-1974	137
1974-1975	153

Chicago successfully recorded over seven hundred convictions of organized crime figures since the passage of the organized crime statutes. Since the main contributors to the coffers of organized crime had been income from gambling and loan-sharking operations, particular emphasis had been placed on these illegal activities. The successes achieved by the C-1 agents of the Chicago Division in the areas of illegal activity have been vividly illustrated by the unprecedented disruption caused by our relentless investigations, which resulted in significant prosecutions and subsequent incarceration of numerous organized crime figures on every level of authority.

Gambling Raids Based on FBI-Secured Warrants and Information

The Chicago Division made a significant contribution to the Criminal Intelligence Program through the initiation and utilization of the local gambling raid technique. Since gambling was the main lifeblood of the Chicago underworld, C-1 agents since 1963 have continued to exert intensive pressure on all forms of gambling, which according to sources, had dwindled the proceeds of organized crime to a new low.

This unique and aggressive action had been accomplished through gambling raids conducted by local, county, state, and federal law enforcement officers based on FBI affidavits, which served as the basis for execution of search and/or arrest warrants by the authorities. As a result of this technique, through dissemination of this information to reliable law enforcement agencies, it enabled local and federal authorities to establish prosecution of gamblers who had carefully avoided violations of FBI jurisdiction. From 1963 through 1975, there had been 562 local raids conducted by various law enforcement agencies based on FBI warrants and/or FBI information. These raids resulted in the arrest of 3,767 gamblers and the confiscation of huge quantities of cash, countless gambling records, and numerous dice tables, roulette wheels, and other miscellaneous gambling equipment destroyed or confiscated. Sources reported that the loss of revenue suffered by the organized criminal element in the Chicago area had been significant as a result of this action. In all instances, the local authorities made news media comments, giving credit to the FBI for making these raids possible.

One of the most damaging blows to organized crime occurred on August 24, 1963, when a raid was conducted by the IRS on fifteen illegal on-track bookmakers at Sportsman's Park. This raid was made possible by C-1 agents, who initiated the investigation and developed all the information concerning this operation for the IRS. The various bookmakers were pointed out, and their respective locations within the clubhouse and grandstand were noted. Fifteen well-known bookmakers belonging to the Chuck English and Fiore Bucceri hoodlum groups were arrested and $23,000 was confiscated. All fifteen subjects were successfully prosecuted in US District Court in Chicago, which included such prominent gamblers as Don Angelini, Joseph Accardi, William Russo, Joseph Altieri, William Greco, Joseph Amore, Michael Falco, and others. Prosecution resulted in $11,000 in fines, twenty-two and one-half months in jail, and 165 months on probation. It was reported that each bookmaker and his runner were paying $240 per week to police and track officials to permit them to operate their business openly at the race track. This raid caused the formation of the Illinois Bureau of Race Track Police headed by Francis Crosby, former FBI agent, as executive director. The C-1 agents that made this raid possible were William Meincke, Joseph Shea, Eugene Sather, Gerhard Maisel, and Harold Johnson. As an indication of the huge loss of revenue to organized crime resulting from this raid, the Illinois State racing authorities publically announced that the increase in pari-mutuel take at the Illinois tracks for the first six months of 1964 showed an increase of over $30,000,000, and an increase in taxes to the state of Illinois of $1,700,000, while the increase in attendance was only 3.3 percent.

As a further indication of the effectiveness of these gambling raids, on March 22, 1964, the Illinois State Police, led by Director John Newbold, a former FBI agent, raided the mob's big floating gambling casino in Highwood, Illinois, based on an FBI warrant. The local police were notified while the raid was taking place. The raid was timed with the arrival of a railroad train at 10:00 p.m. so that the sound of the arrival of the raiding party would be muffled by the noise of the train. Arrested were scores of gamblers and customers, including the gambling keeper of the operation, "Slicker Sam" Rosa, a close associate and golfing partner of Sam Giancana. All of the gambling equipment was either confiscated or destroyed, and a large quantity of cash was seized. Sam Rosa had recently accompanied Sam Giancana on a trip to Hawaii in January 1964, where Rosa and Giancana played in a golfing foursome with baseball legend Joe DiMaggio, at the Waialae Country Club in Honolulu, Hawaii.

In April 1964, our confidential source advised that Sam Rosa was in contact with Sam Giancana and was looking for financial assistance, apparently to resume their gambling operation and/or a job position in his organization. Giancana turned down "Slicker Sam" on both requests, to the bitter disappointment of Rosa. This raid virtually put an end to the mob's large floating gambling casino in the Chicago suburban area, which operated with great impunity and police protection over the years.

On August 2, 1963, Chicago FBI agents executed a federal search warrant at Albert Cohn's Alco Steel Service Company warehouse in Joliet, Illinois, and seized approximately fifty slot machines, mostly one-arm bandits and numerous parts. These machines, valued at about $50,000, were seized under the provisions of the Gambling Devices Act of 1962, which required dealers in gambling devices to register with the attorney general as required by federal law. Albert Cohn was not a registered dealer and was storing these machines for organized crime, because of local and federal pressures against the mob in northern Indiana and southern

Cook County areas. A portion of these machines were reportedly transported from the Hammond, Indiana, area. Cohn was also reported to be an associate of Francis Curry, a Joliet area hoodlum who had the reputation as being the "slot machine king" of the Joliet area. These machines were being stored until arrangements could be made by the south side hoodlum group to place them on location again.

On September 16, 1964, Chicago C-1 agents William Hermann and Logan Pickerl culminated a two-and-a-half-year investigation, by obtaining twenty-one local warrants based on FBI affidavits regarding one of the largest Chicago South Side policy operations run by Cubie Coleman, known as Room Board and Inn. The annual take on this policy wheel was estimated to be approximately $3,000,000. The raids were conducted by Lieutenant John Corless and officers of the gambling unit of the Chicago Police Department. These warrants contained all phases of Coleman's operation, including all route men, headquarters personnel, tons of their entire policy paper supply, the policy cash bank, the pulling station, and Cubie Coleman himself. All of the warrants were successfully executed, and the Coleman policy wheel was completely destroyed for the time being. More importantly, a police payoff list was discovered among the records seized and disclosed the names of three hundred police officers who were on the payroll from two police districts, along with the amounts of their payoffs to allow this policy wheel to operate. According to our informant, the largest single payoff to one individual was to a highly placed police official who received $300 per month. This was handled personally by Coleman for protection as well as payments to the Cook County State's attorney's office. The Chicago news media highlighted the raid and alluded to the corruption that permitted this policy wheel to exist. Similar local gambling raids were subsequently conducted on other major policy wheels, controlled by organized crime in Chicago, with positive results.

The significant results achieved, through the utilization of this technique, were vividly illustrated during September 1964 from a highly confidential source in New York. This source reported that Thomas Eboli, a prominent New York organized crime member, had been in contact with Sam Giancana and inquired of Giancana as to how things were going. According to the New York source, Giancana told Eboli, "The boys are finding it rough making a living. The G is knocking everything over in Chicago."

In addition, on May 5, 1966, Attorney General Nicholas Katzenbach and FBI Director J. Edgar Hoover held a news conference with President Lyndon B. Johnson in the cabinet room and spotlighted Chicago as an example of cooperation between federal and local authorities in the war against organized crime. Katzenbach cited the below gambling summary, which at that time was from 1963 to April 1966, to illustrate that seventy-nine gambling raids were made by local authorities based on FBI secured warrants against the Chicago mob. When asked if there were other examples comparable with Chicago, the attorney general said, "If there were some more dramatic, we would have used that."

Local Gambling Raids Summary (February 1963 to December 1975)

Number of Raids Conducted	562 (232 based on FBI secured warrants)
Number of Individuals Arrested	3,767
Convictions	1,348
Value of Gambling Paraphernalia	
Confiscated and/or Destroyed	$984,714
US Currency Confiscated	$437,623
Estimated Monthly "Handle" of Gambling Places Raided	
Bookmaking:	$23,149,347
Casino Gambling:	$14,768,000
Policy and Numbers:	$13,683,000

In addition to the positive results set forth above, it should be noted that in many instances when local gambling raids were conducted at taverns and other places of business, it resulted in the revocation of their licenses by local authorities.

In 1972, SAC Roy K. Moore decided to reduce the number of agents on the C-1 squad. It was getting to be an administrative hardship for me to continue supervising such a large squad of agents as well as handling our heavy case load of work. He created a separate gambling squad and called it Criminal Squad #10 (C-10) and assigned about twenty-five of my agents to the C-10 squad. The supervisor appointed to the C-10 squad was my gambling coordinator Dennis Shanahan, later replaced by Supervisor Robert Dolan; and our squads worked very well together. I was designated as the coordinating supervisor of the Organized Crime and Gambling Programs and retained about thirty-five C-1 agents to handle the hoodlum, loan-sharking, interstate racketeering, police corruption, and RICO cases as part of the overall Criminal Intelligence Program.

HOODLUM COMMENTS

The following quotations of upper echelon leaders of organized crime in Chicago offer expert commentary on the effectiveness of the investigations of the C-1 squad agents of the Chicago Division of the FBI over the years:

Sam Giancana

During an interview with FBI agents at O'Hare Airport in 1961: "You #!*$%!#&, obscene FBI, obscene, obscene."

In 1965, Giancana had a conversation with Thomas Eboli, a New York City hoodlum leader who inquired how things were going in Chicago. Giancana replied, "Terrible! The boys can't make a living. The FBI's got everything closed down."

Ross Prio

During a conversation with his lieutenant Dominic DiBella in 1964, Prio complained, "I can count the men working for me on one hand."

215

Jack Cerone

To some subordinates in 1966, he said, "Keep your hands in your pockets (no violence). The rackets are all washed up." To a close friend in 1966, he said, "The government is out to break up the outfit and doing a pretty good job of it."

Fiore Buccieri

During conversation with bureau agents in 1965, Buccieri said, "You guys have ruined everything. You have torn down what it took us many years to build."

Rocco Potenzo

North suburban gambling boss in May 1967 said, "The FBI has knocked me out of my gambling operation. I've got fifty men out of work. Nothing left but my liquor store, and now the FBI got my liquor license revoked." In 1964, following a local gambling raid of a wire room in Rosemont, Illinois, based on an FBI warrant, Mayor Donald Stephens contacted Charles Giancana and told him to notify his brother Sam Giancana to have Potenzo's gambling locations removed from Rosemont because it was harming his two-million-dollar real-estate investment.

Richard Cain

Just prior to his arrest by the FBI in 1967, he said, "The FBI has destroyed me, Giancana, and the outfit. You have just about wiped out gambling and vice, and there is nothing left to support the effort."

Marshall Caifano

On arrest by FBI agents in October 1966, he described the syndicate as a "group of gamblers, each having his own territory." He said, "There was no longer any decent gambling in Chicago because of FBI pressure."

Willie Daddano

Following his court appearance in connection with his June 1966 arrest said, "I swear I wish my kids would go blind, rather than have them suffer the grief that I have gone through over this thing."

Ralph Pierce

Chicago South Side gambling boss bitterly complained to agents on numerous occasions over FBI intervention in local gambling matters based on FBI secured warrants. "What business has the FBI to intervene with gambling in Chicago? It's got so bad now that wherever you go you bust us up."

Leslie Kruse

Lake County, Illinois, gambling boss in January 1969 said, "I've been through a lot of crises over this thing through the years, but no time has it been as bad as this." In 1964, Kruse complained about FBI actions in Lake County, Illinois, "The overhead of buildings formerly used for gambling purposes are now standing idle are now costing a small fortune with gambling employees out of work."

John D'Arco

Former First Ward Alderman in 1964 said, "I'm hurting financially. There ain't nothing going anymore, Nothing. There ain't no more money coming in. There just ain't no more rackets." D'Arco lamented and said, "We got to start something legitimate," to which his administrative assistant Pat Marcy replied, "We've never been in anything legitimate before."

Pat Marcy

In August 1964, following the gambling raid based on an FBI-secured warrant in Chinatown, "I don't know if we can go again, if the (obscene) 'G' is going to come in and pinch us again. See what the 'G' does. They know right where they are going and they are right on you and they go out and get the (obscene) coppers and the coppers don't even know where they are going. You know that everything is down on us. And we are supposed to be the power. They just don't give an (obscene) I'm not afraid of cops, but I'm afraid of the G."

Paul Ricca

Upon his arrest for perjury on April 28, 1966 said, "I have the greatest respect and admiration for Mr. Hoover, who comes along once a lifetime. The good old days ended when the FBI stepped in."

During the February 7, 1969 arrest of Jack Cerone, Paul Ricca said, "God, I'm glad it's not me you want. After seven times before your grand jury, I don't know what to expect anymore."

POLICE CORRUPTION

Shakedown of Homosexuals (Homex)

The code name of this multi—million-dollar international sex extortion ring investigation was HOMEX. It was initiated upon information furnished by a Chicago informant in 1965. John J. Pyne, a Chicago police officer who was on sick leave for a period of years, was the mastermind and ringleader of this gang that consisted of a team of about twenty subjects operating in the Chicago area and in various jurisdictions throughout the United States. Pyne claimed that he was too sick to work but found time to travel across state lines to become involved in this scheme. The ring specialized in the shakedown of homosexuals by subjects, who posed as legitimate police officers in this scheme. They would show false Chicago Police ID and tell the victims they had arrest warrants filed against them in Chicago when they were on a business trip. It was suggested that the matter could be quietly taken care of for a price ranging from $5,000 to $10,000. Pyne furnished the extortionists with badges, arrest warrants, and extradition papers as well as names of potential victims, police protection, bond money, travel expenses, attorneys, and in general acted as the overseer of this massive extortion ring. Some the victims of this extortion ring included military officers, college professors, Hollywood celebrities, politicians, government employees, judges, prominent businessmen, and many others. They preyed upon these high profile victims at nightclubs, national conventions, conferences held at various hotels throughout the country, and lured them into compromising situations while posing as legitimate police officers, pretending to be making arrests. The victims, to avoid being arrested and to avoid any unfavorable or embarrassing publicity, would pay off subjects in cash or post a sizeable cash bond, supposedly to be returned later, less than a 10 percent bonding fee. These amounts were never returned. This scheme was in operation for years and was a highly lucrative plan that reaped in millions of dollars until several of the victims were encouraged to cooperate and testify. The case was developed by C-1 agent Richard Cavanagh, who was assisted by SAs Peter Kotsos, Harold Johnson, Richard Gliebe, and Lenard Wolf. They did an incredible job in identifying these high-profile victims and solicited their cooperation in this very sensitive case. All members of this nationwide ring were identified, convicted, and sent to prison. John J. Pyne, the ringleader, was convicted on multiple counts of interstate extortion; and on January 30, 1968, he was sentenced to serve five years in prison and a $10,000 fine to run consecutively with a previous conviction of five years and a $5,000 fine. Pyne was a Chicago police confidence unit instructor who gave lectures on sex crimes and confidence games. He forgot to mention that there were serious consequences for committing these crimes, which violated the federal interstate extortion statute.

POLICE SHAKEDOWN
OF TAVERN OWNERS

15th Austin Police District

In early 1970, articles were written by two veteran crime reporters, Robert Wiedrich of the *Chicago Tribune* and Art Petacque of the *Chicago Sun Times*, regarding alleged police corruption in the 15th Austin Police District of the Chicago Police Department. Bob Wiedrich and Art Petacque were two of the finest watchdog crime reporters in Chicago, who were not only personal friends of mine but closely associated with the FBI. They had written about the demotion of Commander Mark Thanasouras of the Austin District and about complaints of shakedowns by the police of tavern owners who were being forced to pay a standard fee of $100 per month for protection. Thanasouras had a meteoric rise in rank in the Chicago Police Department, having gone from patrolman to commander in just twenty months, and news of his demotion was noteworthy. Allegations of shakedowns by the Chicago Police were not uncommon at the time and were primarily the investigative responsibility of the Chicago Police Department. The FBI had received intelligence information several years prior about the so-called $100 a month shakedown club at the Austin Police District. The superintendent of the Chicago Police Department at the time was James B. Conlisk Jr., who had replaced Orlando W. Wilson in 1967. Things had not changed much under new leadership. Apparently, these articles did not go unnoticed and caught the eye of Attorney James Featherstone, then chief of the Chicago Strike Force. It was Featherstone's theory that if these shakedown allegations could be documented, it could possibly be a violation of the extortion provision of the Federal Hobbs Act statute, which applied to businesses involved in interstate commerce. Since tavern owners and liquor stores received their products through interstate commerce, that factor could supply the necessary requirement to give the federal government jurisdiction in this matter. It had never been done before and appeared to be an overreach on the surface. Hobbs Act violations were normally handled by Criminal Squad #4, which was supervised by Leo Pedrotty. Featherstone called a conference to discuss the matter with me, and Supervisor Pedrotty. Pedrotty was not overly enthused about the possibility of committing considerable manpower to an uncertain and potentially drawn out investigation. Even though the Hobbs Act violation was not my primary responsibility, I finally agreed to accept the investigation because I felt that organized crime and police corruption go hand and hand and depend on each other to exist. It was further decided that the C-1 squad would accept the Austin District case but would assign sufficient manpower on a preliminary basis to determine whether further investigation would be warranted.

The Austin District case was assigned to C-1 agent John Dallman, one of the most dedicated and capable agents on the squad. He was assisted by agents Harold Johnson, William Thurman Jr., and Dane Hill. Other C-1 agents would be assigned as required. The complexity of this investigation was enormous and involved identifying the unknown victims as well as the unknown police subjects involved in the shakedowns. Naturally, we received limited and reluctant cooperation from the Chicago Police Department. They had been asked for photos of police officers from several districts as well those from the Austin District during the past five years to prevent them from knowing our specific interest in the Austin District. There was a considerable delay before we received the photos. More than five hundred past and presently assigned officers from the Austin District were potential subjects. This also involved over four hundred taverns, liquor stores, and restaurants with liquor licenses, because all were potential victims. It was an enormous task. The greatest single problem was fear and a great reluctance on the part of the tavern owner victims to cooperate when interviewed. The thought of having to testify in court when called upon to do so was unimaginable for the tavern owners. All expressed great fear of reprisal, not only for themselves but also for their families. They felt that the corrupt police officers assigned to the Austin District were worse than criminals and could destroy them financially, if not kill them outright to forestall the investigation. Our first sampling of interviews with tavern owners was not too productive. It was obvious that the tavern owners were not being very cooperative.

In the meantime, in early 1970, Attorney James Featherstone was recalled to Washington and would not have the opportunity to see whether his Hobbs Act theory would eventually materialize. The Austin District investigation was placed on hold for the time being. Featherstone was replaced as chief of the Chicago Strike Force by a veteran US Department of Justice attorney by the name of Sheldon Davidson, a bright and capable attorney. Mr. Davidson would be assisted by a new Strike Force attorney named Herbert Beigel. The following year, Attorney Herbert Beigel, Agent John Dallman, and I conferred at length about the best plan of action for the Austin District investigation. Without the unwavering support and tenacity of Strike Force attorneys Davidson and Beigel, the Austin District investigation could not have survived. It was decided that a federal grand jury was the best way to proceed, especially with the limited information developed to date. The Strike Force intended to use limited grants of immunity in the grand jury to several key vice squad officers of the Austin District. Also, police officers or public employees who were subpoenaed to testify, who invoked the Fifth Amendment could be subject to suspension or dismissal from the police force. We were beginning to make progress into this massive police shakedown scheme.

All officers, totaling about thirty, who served under Mark Thanasouras in the Austin Police District were subpoenaed to appear before the federal grand jury, including Thanasouras and two others, who had been convicted in local court for shakedowns and were no longer on the force. Crime reporters Bob Wiedrich and Art Petacque continued, unabated with their articles, highlighting the federal probe into the shakedown scheme of the Austin Police District, much to the dismay of Superintendent Conlisk. The publicity from the news coverage was incredible and resulted in the identification of additional witnesses as well as other pertinent information. The first officer to be called before the grand jury was Mark Thanasouras. After stating his name, he read from a piece of paper and invoked the Fifth Amendment privilege. Since Thanasouras had been demoted, he subsequently resigned from the police department in early 1971. Thanasouras was represented by Attorney James Demopolous who also represented all of the other police officers, an obvious conflict of interest. Fourteen of the police officers that followed invoked the Fifth Amendment. In March of 1972, the federal grand jury returned nine indictments charging eight police officers with extortion and perjury, including two lieutenants, one sergeant, five patrolmen, and one former police officer. The Chicago Police Department was in the process of suspending or discharging officers who took the Fifth Amendment before the federal grand jury.

Individual trials of the indicted police officers began. Strike Force Attorney Beigel handled the first trial against Walter Moore, who had resigned from the police department. Beigel, assisted by C-1 Agent Dallman, did a fine job with what was considered to be a relatively weak case. The jury, however, returned a verdict of guilty of attempted extortion. Moore was sentenced to two years in prison. This case set the tone for the other trials that were to follow. AUSA Allan Lapidus handled the second trial. Sergeant George Demet, who had been suspended from the force, was found guilty of extortion and sentenced to one year in prison. AUSA Dan Webb and Herbert Beigel handled the trial of Lieutenant Frank Gill, and Sergeant James Fahey retired. A limited grant of immunity to a police officer as well as several key witnesses who furnished critical information led to the conviction on all counts of the indictment against Lieutenant Gill and Sergeant Fahey who received prison sentences of four and three years, respectively. U S Attorney James R. Thompson, who later became governor of the state of Illinois, and the Chicago Strike Force attorneys were very pleased with the progress made so far in the Austin District Police investigation.

3rd Grand Crossing Police District

In an unrelated case in April of 1972, information had been received by C-1 agents William Hermann and Sherman Noble that the proprietors of the Bryn Mawr Bowling Lanes, 2015 East Seventy-First Street, Chicago, Illinois, had been making monthly payoffs to police officers of the 3rd Grand Crossing Police District for at least the past four years. These payments were usually made on the fifteenth of each month in cash to the same unknown police officer. Strike Force attorney Herbert Beigel authorized the arrest of the police officer when he attempted to collect his monthly shakedown payoff, which would be a violation of the Federal Hobbs Act statute. Owners of Bryn Mawr were interviewed and were cooperative. They confirmed the shakedown payments and agreed to pass marked money on the next payoff to the unknown officer. On April 14, 1972, Supervising Sergeant Robert Crowley, Chicago Police Department, was arrested by C-1 agents Hermann and Noble as he immediately departed the bowling lanes after receiving the marked money from the victim. The marked money was found in his possession as he was about to enter a police car that had two police officers as occupants. Sergeant Crowley was turned over to the custody of the US Marshal's office and was released on a $2,000 bond. Chicago news media devoted considerable coverage to the above incident, in the wake of the recent indictments of police officers on similar charges arising out of Police Shakedown of Tavern Owners in the Austin District. On April 28, 1972, Sergeant Robert Crowley was indicted by the federal grand jury for violating the Federal Hobbs Act statute. During the trial, Sergeant Crowley testified that the payoffs were "sort of a secondary employment" to provide police protection to the bowling lanes when he was off duty. He could not explain what services he had provided at any time at the bowling lanes. The federal jury had difficulty arriving at a decision but eventually returned a verdict of guilty. On March 27, 1973, Judge Frank McGarr sentenced Sergeant Crowley to two years in prison. The president of Bryn Mawr Lanes expressed his thanks and appreciation to the FBI for putting an end to police shakedowns at his place of business.

18th East Chicago Police District

In the early 1970s, information had also trickled into the FBI and from the *Chicago Tribune* newspaper accounts of Robert Wiedrich, which indicated that a similar type of shakedown activity was reportedly taking place in the 18th East Chicago Avenue Police District, which encompassed the popular Rush Street area of nightclubs and taverns. Sheldon Davidson and Herbert Beigel contacted me once again and made a request for additional agents to expand our investigation to include the 18th Police District. Because there was a strong link between organized crime and the vice detectives in the Rush Street area, which was under the control of Chicago North Side boss Ross Prio, and with the successes achieved to date, I was willing to go along with their request knowing that it would take considerably more manpower to accomplish this task. C-1 agent James Annes, a former California police officer, who was one of my very bright and aggressive young agents, was assigned exclusively to this case to be assisted by SAs Dane Hill and Herbert Briick. At least four other agents would assist as needed. The same problems were encountered with the Rush Street tavern owners who were in fear of economic and/or physical reprisal. Finally, several Rush Street tavern owners decided to cooperate and wanted assurances that they would not be prosecuted and were promised immunity. Slowly but surely, we were obtaining the names of a few of the vice officers involved in these shakedowns. Apparently, there were two shakedown clubs in existence, one for the vice officers and one for the uniformed police. By mid-1972, we had developed sufficient information to warrant a new federal grand jury investigation. Twenty officers, including Captain Walter Maurovich of the 18th Police District, were subpoenaed to testify. Captain Maurovich and his vice coordinator, William Simpson, resigned from the police force just prior to their scheduled appearance before the grand jury. Apparently, Maurovich, who was eligible to retire, wanted to protect his pension. Some of the tavern owners agreed to testify. All of the officers subpoenaed either invoked the Fifth Amendment or denied any involvement in any wrongdoing. An indictment was subsequently returned against three of the principal vice squad officers, namely Edward Rifkin, Sal Mascolino, and John Cello. We had only scratched the surface, and the Strike Force was again considering the judicious use of limited immunity against several key vice officers. Also subpoenaed was the former commander of the 18th District, Clarence Braasch, who was now the chief of Traffic and the fourth highest-ranking officer in the Chicago Police Department. Braasch testified that he knew nothing about any payoffs while he was Commander at the 18th District.

Strike Force attorneys Davidson and Beigel decided to grant limited immunity to officers Mascolino and Cello. If they refused to testify, they could be held in contempt of court for the duration of the grand jury, which would expire in about eighteen months. If they lied under oath, they could be subjected to perjury. Cello and Mascolino both refused to testify; and Chief Judge Edwin Robson ordered them both to be taken into custody, where they remained in jail until they were ready to testify.

In an effort to facilitate the investigation of the Austin District case Davidson and Beigel granted immunity to David Holder, former Austin vice coordinator, who had been convicted in local court for tavern shakedowns, and George Demet, who was recently convicted of extortion in federal court. Both Holder and Demet appeared before the federal grand jury and failed to implicate any other police officers. Also, Cello and Mascolino were still languishing in jail after several months for refusing to testify. There was no indication at this time that they were going to cooperate with this investigation, even though they faced an additional sixteen months in jail. For the time being, we seemed to be at a standstill; however, C-1 agents John Dallman and Jim Annes continued to push ahead by identifying additional tavern owners in the 15th and 18th police districts who were being victimized in those districts. Strike Force Attorneys Davidson and Beigel were not discouraged and continued to select targets for possible grants of immunity. They also planned to immunize Eddie Rifkin, a principal bagman of the 18th District Vice Club. Rifkin also refused to testify after a grant of immunity and joined his fellow officers Cello and Mascolino in jail.

A short time later, the strategy and patience of Davidson and Beigel finally began to pay off. They were now being assisted by AUSA Dan Webb, who was a brilliant protégé of US Attorney Jim Thompson. They received word that Cello and Mascolino, after spending three months in jail, wanted out and wanted to talk. They were ready to tell the Strike Force attorneys all about their involvement in detail about the corruption in the 18th Police District. Eddie Rifkin also wanted out of jail and wanted to cooperate. Their cooperation made it much easier for FBI agents Annes and Hill to identify and gain the cooperation of the tavern owners, who had been paying off the vice club officers hundreds of thousands of dollars over the years. With a breakthrough in the investigation of the 18th Police District, Herbert Beigel suddenly resigned from the Strike Force to enter the private practice of law. That came as a complete surprise because the 18th District investigation was just starting to gain traction. Dan Webb, however, would be a very worthy replacement and would assist Sheldon Davidson in bringing this investigation and the prosecution of the police subjects to a successful conclusion. Davidson and Webb also immunized Lieutenant Robert Fischer, who was a key witness and had been a vice coordinator for former commander Clarence Braasch at the 18th Police District. He was also willing to testify along with Cello, Mascolino, and Rifkin. Another important witness was vice officer Charles DuShane, who had been told by his superiors to notify a specific crime syndicate gambling boss before making any arrests of bookmakers in that district. Not only were the police shaking down tavern owners, but they were also allowing syndicate bookmakers to operate with impunity by paying for protection.

On December 29, 1972, two indictments were returned against thirty police officers that included twenty-three officers of the vice squad club and seven officers, who managed the uniformed club, on charges of extortion and perjury. Also included were Captain Clarence Braasch and two of his lieutenants. As a result of the indictments, two additional police officers who had been indicted, namely Lieutenant James Murphy and Vice Officer Lowell Napier, volunteered to testify. The publicity emanating from these indictments was enormous and continued for several days calling for the resignation of Police Superintendent Conlisk. No action was taken by Mayor Daley's office because this was primarily an indictment and was only the first step toward prosecution. They were going to wait and see what happened in this case. The government still had the huge task of bringing this highly complex matter to trial under the untested extortion provision of the Federal

Hobbs Act statute involving tavern owners. The persistence and determination of the Strike Force attorneys Sheldon Davidson and Herbert Beigel, along with AUSA Dan Webb in concert with the FBI, were finally making progress in breaking the code of silence within the Chicago Police Department.

On August 15, 1973, the long awaited police corruption trial involving the 18th Police District began before US District Court Judge William J. Bauer. There were seven veteran and highly experienced defense attorneys representing the twenty-three police officers. The government attorneys would have their hands full. Dan Webb was assisted by AUSAs Farrell Griffin and James Holderman, who would later become a federal judge. Attorney David Schippers was representing six of the defendants. Schippers had been chief of the Chicago Strike Force during the mid-1960s and played a key role in the incarceration of Sam Giancana until he resigned in 1967. Clarence Braasch was represented by George Cotsirilos, a highly skilled defense attorney. Fifty-three tavern owners were listed in the indictment and testified about the harassment by the vice squad, which led to the payoffs for protection. The number of tavern owners and police subjects would have been greater had it not been for the expiration of the statute of limitations, which prevented additional officers, including two former commanders, from being included in this indictment. The tavern owners were followed by the seven police officers who were cooperating in this case. They testified in great detail about how the vice squad club was organized and operated. Lieutenant Fischer went into detail about the "big club," which included payments from ten Rush Street nightclubs that made large monthly payments of $3,600 for Commander Clarence Braasch from the mob's bookmaking operation in the 18th District. This monthly amount went as high as $6,810 at one time and was provided by mob gambler Bill Gold, a master political fixer and bag man for hoodlum boss Ross Prio. Gold was later replaced by North Side hoodlum gambler Mike Glitta. The Fischer testimony linked Commander Braasch to the payoffs. Braasch took the stand in his own defense. Dan Webb did a masterful job in skillfully rebutting his testimony, especially when he got Braasch to admit that the 18th District, during the last three and one half years of his command, never made one arrest in the fifty-three taverns belonging to the $100-a-month vice club listed in the indictment. That said it all. Webb's closing arguments were also brilliant. No one could have done it better. The trial lasted about seven weeks and concluded on October 3, 1973. It did not take the jury long to reach a verdict. Nineteen subjects, including former Commander Clarence Braasch, were found guilty as charged; and four police officers were acquitted because of weak circumstantial evidence. The Chicago news media had followed the trial closely, and the guilty verdicts against nineteen police officers received unprecedented coverage in the Chicago news media. Clarence Braasch would receive a seven-year jail sentence, and the other defendants received varying amounts of jail sentences. All of the convictions were affirmed by the US Court of Appeals in October of 1974.

A short time after the convictions were announced, James B. Conlisk Jr., who had been superintendent of the Chicago Police Department since 1967, resigned from the force. Speculation was rampant as who would be Conlisk's replacement. The *Chicago Today* newspaper, a *Chicago Tribune* publication dated Friday October12, 1973, ran a front page banner headline titled "FBI Agent in Race for Conlisk's Post," with a subtitle of "Inserra Headed Police Corruption Probe." The article was written by Jack Mabley, a veteran journalist. Other newspaper accounts followed, speculating that I was in the running for the superintendent's post. The articles came as a complete surprise to me. I had not been contacted by anyone prior to the newspaper articles, nor had I contacted anyone in that regard. The SAC of the Chicago office, at the time was Richard Held, who summoned me into his office and asked me about the articles. I told him that I had no idea as to the source of the articles; perhaps it was a slow news day, and the articles were pure speculation with absolutely no basis in fact. Even though I was eligible to retire from the FBI, applying for the position of superintendent of the Chicago Police Department, a politically volatile appointment, was the last thing on my mind. As a result of the newspaper articles, I received several phone calls from friendly members of the Intelligence Unit of the Chicago Police Department, urging me to apply for the position of superintendent. They were desperately looking for police reform. I was flattered by their confidence in me; however, I had absolutely no intention of applying or being considered for the job. On February 11, 1974, Mayor Richard J. Daley appointed James M. Rochford as superintendent of the Chicago Police Department. I was acquainted with Mr. Rochford, and he had an excellent reputation for honesty and integrity. Trying to change the culture of corruption, which had permeated the Chicago Police Department, was an insurmountable task. It had been about ten years since I provided a police corruption report to former Superintendent Orlando W. Wilson at the request of the then Attorney General Bobby Kennedy, listing twenty-nine police officers reportedly on the payroll of the Chicago mob, including some high-ranking police officers. Mayor Daley at that time publicly scoffed at the report and called the information rumor and gossip. Things had not changed. As that colorful character of Chicago's political history, Mathias "Paddy" Bauler once said, "Chicago ain't ready for reform."

Shortly after the news publicity had subsided about the convictions of Clarence Braasch and the vice squad officers of the 18th Police District, information was received that the seven remaining subjects, who belonged to the police uniformed shake down club, all entered guilty pleas to the charges as set forth in the second indictment. AUSA Dan Webb officially withdrew from any further police corruption follow-up after his strenuous involvement in the recently concluded police corruption investigation in the 18th Police District. Strike Force Chief Sheldon Davidson also indicated that he would be resigning from his position soon to enter the private practice of law. With Dan Webb, Herbert Beigel, and Sheldon Davidson no longer in the police corruption probe, Agent John Dallman and I felt somewhat let down because we only had scratched the surface in the corruption investigation in the Austin District. That was the district where it all began almost four years ago at the request of the Strike Force.

Agent John Dallman was not to be denied. He insisted that we continue and bring the Austin matter to a logical conclusion. We discussed the best way to proceed with the investigation, keeping in mind that something had to be done soon to preclude the five-year statute of limitations from running out. We had already successfully prosecuted a handful of police officers from the Austin District in separate trials. We decided to follow the strategy used in the 18th Police District case, in which key targets were selected for limited immunity before a federal grand jury. Dallman went to AUSA Michael Mullen, a capable young prosecutor for assistance. Mullen was briefed about the Austin District case but was not too impressed with our chances for success. Only after Dallman used his persistent persuasive powers did Mullen finally acquiesce. They reviewed possible key targets remaining in the Commander Mark Thanasouras case. The two logical targets were Thanasouras's vice coordinator, Frank Bychowski, who had taken the Fifth Amendment in December 1971. He had retired and was now the chief of Police in the small town of Bayfield, Wisconsin. The other target was Charles Ekenborg, a former member of the Austin vice squad under Thanasouras and a close friend of Bychowski. Dallman contacted Bychowski and Ekenborg, both of whom agreed to be interviewed in the Chicago office of AUSA Mullen. They insisted on having their attorney James Demopolous present at the time. They appeared as scheduled in the office of AUSA Mullen. Demopolous did all the talking, and nothing was accomplished at this meeting. Demopolous was the original attorney in 1970 representing about thirty police officers, including Commander Mark Thanasouras from the Austin District. This was an obvious conflict of interest, but it did not bother Demopolous who was totally uncooperative. Bychowski and Ekenborg were not interviewed because of Demopolous but were told that they would have to return at a later date to appear before the grand jury. It was decided by Mullen and Dallman to grant limited immunity to Bychowski. Approval was granted by the US Department of Justice, and Bychowski appeared as scheduled in the presence of a different attorney. Demopolous was unavailable, which was very fortunate for us. When Bychowski was granted immunity, he agreed to cooperate only in the event that his good friend Charles Ekenborg would also be given immunity from prosecution. Mullen and Dallman struck pay dirt. Bychowski was the key bagman for Thansouras and Ekenborg was his assistant. They also had two shake down clubs in existence in the Austin District, one for the tavern owners called "The Friendship Club," a monthly $100 club, and one from the Chicago mob to allow gambling to flourish in the district. The monthly proceeds from the mobs gambling club amounted to about $2,000 a month that went to Thanasouras and Bychoski. Bychowski also identified the tavern owners in question, which made Dallman's task much easier during his follow up interviews to solicit their cooperation. Mullen and Dallman were shocked to discover that Attorney James

Demopolous reportedly was the bagman for Thanasouras at the Café Chablis, whose owner was having difficulty obtaining a liquor license. Only after the owner paid Thanasouras through Demopolous a total of $3,000 was he issued a liquor license. Demopolous was subpoenaed before the grand jury and denied any involvement in the payoff.

Based upon the information furnished by Bychowski and Ekenborg and the tavern owners, on August 23, 1973, three indictments were returned by the grand jury. The first indictment charged Thanasouras and Demopolous with extortion in the Café Chablis case, and Demopolous was also charged with perjury. The second indictment charged Thanasouras and thirteen vice officers for extorting about $300,000 from twenty-eight tavern owners, and the third indictment charged Thanasouras and three of his vice officers with extorting $300 a month for four years from the Blue Dahlia nightclub. Thanasouras surprised everyone by entering a guilty plea in February 1974 to all of the charges. He seemed to lack the will power to contest the charges. He was sentenced to serve forty-two months in prison and was fined $20,000. Attorney James Demopolous, who had been a contentious defense attorney throughout the entire Austin proceedings, was tried separately and was found guilty of extortion in the Café Chablis case as well as perjury. He was sentenced to serve eighteen months in prison. This appeared to finalize the Austin Police District tavern shakedown case. Of the twenty-two police officers indicted in this case, twelve entered pleas of guilty, seven were found guilty, and three were acquitted for a total of nineteen convictions including Attorney Demopolous. This case attracted considerable publicity but not as much as the Clarence Braasch case, probably because most of the officers in the Austin case entered guilty pleas. It was however a most important case because it was the first case ever to utilize the Federal Hobbs Act statute against police officers for shaking down tavern owners in Chicago. The performance and tenacity of John Dallman and the many other C-1 agents that assisted him in this case was incredible in every respect.

This was not the end, however. Thanasouras through his attorney wanted to make a deal for a reduction in sentence. Thanasouras wanted to cooperate further and give evidence against the four watch commanders at the Austin District as well as other information on police corruption in other districts. We decided to listen to what he had to say. Thanasouras claimed that he provided his four watch commanders with a portion of his monthly payoffs from the Austin District collection. These officers were not involved in any direct shake down; however, they were aware of the club and had received money from Thanasouras. He was granted immunity and testified before the federal grand jury against his former commanders, all of whom were longtime members of the force. On October 16, 1974, the three police captains and a retired police captain were indicted by the grand jury, namely commanders John Foley, Mathew McInerney, John O'Shea, and Edward Russell who retired in 1973. I had prepared a communication to notify FBI headquarters of the indictment and personally notified SAC Richard

Held of the four indictments because of the anticipated news media coverage. Mr. Held's response was somewhat unexpected. After invoking the name of our Lord, he said, "What are you trying to do, ruin our relationship with the Chicago Police Department?" I told him very calmly that if he had any objections about prosecuting corrupt police officers, he might want to discuss the matter with the US attorney's office. He made no further comment. The Chicago media gave extensive coverage to the recent indictments of the four watch commanders. Mark Thanasouras's sentence was reduced to eighteen months when he agreed to testify against his previous watch commanders, all of whom were eventually acquitted. On July 22, 1977, Thanasouras was shotgunned to death in Chicago shortly after his release from prison. His murder remains unsolved.

14th Shakespeare Police District

Mark Thanasouras also claimed that when he was demoted in 1970, he became a watch commander in the 14th Shakespeare Police District and immediately began receiving monthly payments that represented his captain's share. The Chicago gamblers in the district were making monthly payments for protection. They were Andy "the Greek" Louchious and Lottie Zagorski, both under the control of Chicago hoodlum William "Smokes" Aloisio. Zagorski and Louchious were two of the biggest gambling operators on Chicago's northwest side. These payments were made from1960 through May of 1974. The gambling operation of Zagorski was raided several times by the Intelligence Unit of the Chicago Police Department based on FBI-secured warrants obtained by C-1 agents Logan Pickerl and William Hermann. This contributed to the gradual curtailment of Zagorski's gambling operation in the Shakespeare District.

Agent John Dallman and AUSA Michael Mullen decided to explore the allegations of police protection payoffs from the mob. They continued to use the federal grand jury to their advantage. Grants of immunity were given to bookmakers Andy Louchious and Lottie Zagorski, both of whom died of natural causes after their grand jury testimony. A retired Chicago Police Sergeant Fred Forsberg, who was identified as the payoff man for Louchious to the watch commanders in the 14th district, also testified after a grant of immunity. He began collecting money from Louchious and distributing the payoffs to the commanders of the Shakespeare District on a monthly basis. He gave each watch commander $150 a month and continued paying watch commander Thomas Flavin until May of 1974. Commander Thomas P. Flavin of the Shakespeare District was indicted by a federal grand jury on February 11, 1976, for conspiring to obstruct the federal Interstate Gambling Business (IGB) statute for reportedly taking payoffs from bookmakers and failing to pay taxes on these amounts. Captain Flavin had received from $150 to $300 a month from about 1969 to 1974. US Attorney Samuel Skinner said this indictment was the first time a federal charge of obstructing justice under the IGB statute had ever been used against a police official in the northern district of Illinois.

The persistent efforts of C-1 agent John Dallman and the skillful handling of the legal aspects of the federal grand jury by AUSA Michael Mullen were primarily responsible for the successful results achieved.

19th Town Hall Police District

Our investigation into the shakedown of tavern owners by the "vice club" in the 19th Town Hall Police District continued. This case was developed by C-1 agent John Osborne, who was assisted by agent Robert Long and other C-1 agents. They did an exceptionally fine job in canvassing numerous tavern owners who had been making payoffs to the vice squad for the past eight years. In July of 1974, Captain Jerome Callahan, former watch commander at the Town Hall Police District, was convicted of violating the Federal Hobbs Act statute by extorting more than fifty cases of whiskey over a period of six years from Southport Crown Liquors in Chicago. He was sentenced to ninety days in prison. AUSA Charles Kokoras was in charge of the prosecution and would later become chief judge of the US District Court in Chicago. The strategy in this case was to impanel a federal grand jury and offer limited immunity to Joseph Thomas, a former vice officer in the Town Hall District who had agreed to testify. Also testifying were seventeen tavern owners who had been making extortion payments of $50 to $200 a month to the vice squad for a period of eight years. The total amount paid to the vice officers during this period was estimated to be $160,000. On November 14, 1974, the federal grand jury returned a one-count indictment charging five present and three former Chicago police officers with violating the Federal Hobbs Act. Indicted were former Town Hall police officers William Abraham, Robert Herman, David McGee, Richard Weingart, and Gene Benjamin. The three others indicted, who were no longer police officers, were Ronald Henkin, Donald Herman, and Francis Mulligan. Before the trial began, officer Gene Benjamin, who was the organizer of the vice club at the Town Hall police district eight years ago, entered a plea of guilty. Also found guilty in the federal trial were William Abraham, Ronald Henkin, and Francis Mulligan. Judge Frank McGarr sentenced each defendant to terms ranging from one year to eighteen months in prison. Acquitted at this time were David McNee and Donald Herman. Also, the jury failed to reach a verdict on Richard Weingart and Robert Herman. There appeared to be some confusion in this trial because there were two separate shake down conspiracies in the Town Hall police district and the government only charged the defendants with a one-count Hobbs Act conspiracy. Chicago news media continued to devote considerable attention to the large number of policemen involved in the extortion of taverns and nightclubs since the FBI investigation began in 1970.

Shakedown by Area 1 Police Detectives

In September 1973, a former confidential source of C-1 agent Richard Cavanagh related a series of events depicting an effort by three detectives assigned to the Area 1 robbery/burglary detail of the Chicago Police Department to utilize source in a shakedown of a Chicago jeweler of questionable reputation by planting stolen property in the store of the jeweler. The source was in extreme fear for his personal safety. Agent Cavanagh very adroitly persuaded the source to cooperate and wear a microphone to monitor his evidentiary conversations with the subjects. The US attorney general's office was reluctant to authorize in this matter; however, through the tactful efforts of AUSAs Charles Kocoras and Gary Starkman, approval to proceed was obtained. There was great reluctance on the part of the source and the jeweler victim, both of questionable character, to cooperate because of fear of public exposure and police reprisals. Also, there were unusual difficulties inherent in such an investigation with the surveillance coverage of the sensitive police shakedown payoff. SA Cavanagh, assisted by SA Joseph Doyle and other C-1 agents, covered this extremely delicate situation without jeopardy to the source or victim. Source's fears were heightened when he was subsequently searched by the police officers but escaped harm by claiming the tape on his body was for his bad back. The police officers demanded a payment of $350 from the jeweler to overlook his arrest for the stolen property planted in his possession. Agents were able to identify the detectives as Michael McCarthy, Ronald Uginchus, and Harold Durkee Jr. On January 11, 1974, the federal grand jury returned a two-count Hobbs Act indictment charging the three police officers with extortion. A lengthy jury trial followed, and the source and victim were subjected to brutal cross-examinations by three experienced defense attorneys. The three defendants testified in their own defense and were unsuccessful in trying to explain away the government case. On September 23, 1974, the jury found the three defendants guilty as charged; and officers McCarthy, Uginchus, and Durkee received sentences ranging from nine months to two years in prison. This was the first known case in Chicago of the use of the Federal Hobbs Act extortion statute against corrupt police officers in other than a tavern shakedown situation. SA Cavanagh was primarily responsible for handling this highly sensitive case, which led to a successful conclusion. Agent Doyle participated throughout the entire investigation in a very professional manner. The performance of AUSAs Kocoras and Starkman as trial attorneys in this matter was outstanding.

As a result of the emphasis and importance placed on police and political corruption, and its alliance with organized crime, the C-1 squad continued to intensify and expand its investigative efforts in this most vital area. In April 1975, information was received from a former Chicago police officer that he and other members of the 4th Police District vice unit shook down nearly every tavern in that district. Investigation by C-1 agent Joseph Doyle and other C-1 agents had confirmed these payoffs and were in the process of presenting this matter to a federal grand jury with the assistance of AUSA John Gleason. It was also disclosed that these shakedown cases were prevalent in the area and had spread into the 3rd, 5th, and 6th Chicago police districts.

GIANCANA'SSELF-IMPOSED EXILE IN MEXICO FOR EIGHT YEARS

Giancana, following his release from the Cook County Jail on May 31, 1966, where he spent one year on a contempt of court violation, did not waste too much time in Chicago to find out whether he was going to be recalled to the federal grand jury a second time. Giancana had previously arranged to have Pat Marcy, administrative aid to the Regular Democratic Organization of the First Ward, notify Richard Cain that Giancana wanted to meet with Cain upon his release from jail. Within hours following his release, Giancana met with Cain and his longtime bodyguard chauffeur, Dominic "Butch" Blasi, who drove them to St. Louis, where Blasi chartered a plane and flew them to El Paso, Texas. Phyllis McGuire, who was Giancana's girlfriend at the time, met Giancana, Cain, and Blasi in El Paso and spent the night there. The next day, proper credentials were prepared for Giancana in his true name; and Giancana and Cain crossed the border into Juarez, Mexico, and subsequently traveled to Mexico City, Cuernavaca, and other cities in South and Central America, where Giancana intended to live a life away from the intensive scrutiny of the FBI. It was apparent that Sam Giancana was resigned to abdicate his top leadership position from organized crime in Chicago and to live in self-imposed exile in Mexico. Richard Cain was now acting as Giancana's courier and bodyguard chauffeur.

On August 5, 1966, Giancana applied for a US passport in Guatemala City, Guatemala. He later applied for immigration status in Guatemala but was denied residency because of his criminal record. On September 10, 1966, Giancana, accompanied by Richard Cain, arrived in Panama City, Panama; and they departed together on September 13, 1966, for Guatemala. They then traveled to Merida, Yucatan, Mexico, and on to Mexico City. Cain, who had previous experience in Mexico and spoke Spanish, introduced Giancana to a prominent attorney in Mexico City by the name of Jorge Castillo Zepeda, who had close ties to many of the leaders of the government of Mexico. Giancana and Castillo were to become close personal friends through whom Giancana would be purchasing real estate in Mexico.

On December 19, 1966, Phyllis McGuire, Giancana's longtime affectionate lover, traveled from NYC to Mexico under the name of Jean McGuire to visit Giancana, whom she had been longing to see during his prolonged absence. She was greeted at the airport in Mexico City by Richard Cain. Giancana was at the airport; however, he did not approach McGuire or made any contact with her. Cain and Phyllis McGuire took an airport taxi to the elegant Maria Isabel Hotel in Mexico City. Along the way, Cain and Ms. McGuire appeared to be necking in the taxi cab. Giancana followed in a white Oldsmobile convertible, bearing Illinois license PG 5000 registered to Harriette Blake, wife of Richard Cain. Giancana joined them at the hotel. Giancana apparently was cautious and acted as an observer, checking to see if Phyllis McGuire had been followed from the airport. Phyllis McGuire checked out of the hotel the following day. Cain's role as bodyguard chauffeur for Giancana would be short-lived because he would soon be indicted and convicted on bank robbery conspiracy charges, along with Willie Daddano and others in Chicago as reported in the Franklin Park Bank robbery case. On April 30, 1967, the Mexican Government issued an exclusion order against Richard Cain, denying him entry into Mexico under any circumstances. Phyllis McGuire departed Mexico to perform with her sisters at the Sheraton Hotel, San Juan, Puerto Rico, in January, 1967. Giancana did not accompany her on this trip. Upon the conclusion of her performance, Ms. McGuire left San Juan and returned to her apartment in NYC on January 19, 1967, in the company of her new and current romantic interest, Mike Davis, a wealthy mogul from Denver, Colorado, who was married to Helen Bonfils, a wealthy widow of the founder of the *Denver Post* newspaper. Apparently, Mike Davis, who was president of Tiger Oil in Denver, had been the constant companion and paramour of Phyllis McGuire during the absence of Giancana. Davis had been occasionally mistaken for Sam Giancana because there was a slight resemblance to him. Davis reportedly purchased a lavish home in Las Vegas as a hideaway for himself and Phyllis McGuire whom he planned to marry in the near future. It appeared at this time that Sam Giancana was not only a man without a country but also a man without a girlfriend.

From the summer of 1966 through the end of 1967, Giancana and Cain traveled to practically every part of the world. This included Central America, South America, the Caribbean, and Europe. During this period, Cain made most of the arrangements for Giancana to travel, and it was reported that Cain brought about one to two million dollars in cash to Giancana from Sam Battaglia, who succeeded Giancana as the leader of organized crime in Chicago. Dominic Blasi and Rose Flood, an aunt of Giancana, were also used to deliver large amounts of money to Giancana from the Chicago area. Giancana had not returned to the Chicago area since his release from the Cook County jail on May 31, 1966.

Shortly after Sam Giancana arrived in Mexico in the summer of 1966, he purchased a luxurious home in Cuernavaca through his attorney Jorge Castillo. This home was located in an isolated area surrounded by a high wall in the subdivision of Rancho Tetela and was staffed with many servants. The address was Calle de Nubes #2 Rancho Tetela, Cuernavaca, Mexico. Giancana paid about $125,000 for the property and gave the owner a down payment of $5,000 in cash, which he took from his money belt. Giancana wanted to pay the $120,000 balance in cash, but the owner refused. They had to transport the huge cash balance in $100 bills to a bank in order to obtain drafts drawn on a New York bank. Sam began residing there under an alias, and his mail was received at the post office under the name of Richard Scalzetti (Cain). At the home in Cuernavaca, Giancana maintained a permanent staff of at least two gardeners, a cook, and a maid on a full-time basis. When guests were living in the home, he would hire additional part time help to assist with the chores. The property records show that the house was owned by "Las Nubes S.A.," a company dealing in real estate; and the administrator of the company and the property was Jorge Castillo, the attorney representing Giancana. Such companies were common in Mexico to allow Americans to buy property without any restrictions. Giancana spent part of his time at this residence and at the adjoining golf course. Cuernavaca is located about fifty-five miles south of Mexico City and had been referred to as the Beverly Hills of Mexico.

Photo of Giancana's Residence at Nubes #2, Rancho Tetela, Cuernavaca, Mexico

Chicago sources reported that Giancana continued to reside in Mexico and did not intend to return to the United States except perhaps to attend special occasions, such as the impending wedding of his youngest daughter, Francine. Giancana's absence from the Chicago area continued to disrupt the orderly and aggressive leadership of the Chicago hoodlum group. Francine Giancana, the youngest daughter of Sam Giancana, was scheduled to be married at Saint Bernadine Catholic Church in Oak Park, Illinois. The wedding was to be a highly elaborate affair, attended by hundreds of guests with a lavish reception thereafter. Because her father was unable to attend, she decided to be married with as little publicity as possible, with only a handful of immediate family members in attendance. Francine was married on August 16, 1967, to Jerome DePalma. It was noted that shortly after the death of Giancana's wife Angeline, in 1954, he donated $13,000 for a communion rail and $500 for several stained-glass windows to Saint Bernadine's in memory of his wife.

The Mexican Immigration authorities had not as yet become aware that Sam Giancana was currently residing in their country. He was on their "stop list" at various points of entry into Mexico, and his entry was to be denied as an undesirable person. It is not known how Sam Giancana and Richard Cain were able to enter and leave Mexico at will, because both were not welcome in Mexico according to Mexican authorities. Should the Mexican authorities become aware of Giancana's presence in Mexico, it could lead to his immediate expulsion. During January 1968, the Mexican Immigration Service became aware that Giancana was residing in Cuernavaca, Mexico; however, no follow-up action was taken at that time. Giancana's attorney, Jorge Castillo, had petitioned the Mexican Government to review their decision not to grant Giancana immigration status in Mexico, claiming Giancana was not part of the underworld and had not returned to Mexico for several years. It was obvious that Castillo was not being truthful with Mexican authorities, and his intercession on behalf of Giancana may have temporarily prevented the authorities from taking action. Giancana appeared to be living on borrowed time in Mexico.

In 1969, Sam Giancana, in addition to his Cuernavaca estate, also leased and resided in a lavish penthouse apartment in Mexico City. The address was Amsterdam #82, Penthouse #1, Mexico City, Mexico; and the name he used was Sam DePalma, which was similar to the name of his newly acquired son-in-law, Jerome DePalma. Apparently, Giancana spent more time at his penthouse suite than he did at his home in Cuernavaca. Giancana leased this penthouse suite for about two years through his attorney Jorge Castillo. During August of 1969, Giancana was visited briefly over a weekend by his two daughters and their husbands in Mexico City. They were Bonnie and Anthony Tisci and Francine and Jerry DePalma. He was also visited by Richard Flood, a relative from Chicago, whose name Giancana had frequently used in the past. Giancana also made reservations at the Acapulco Towers, an exclusive resort facility in Acapulco, Mexico, for the Christmas holidays in 1969.

In May 1967, Giancana visited Nice, Cote D'Azur, France, and Majorca, on the Island of Palma, off the coast of Spain. In December 1968, he also had visited the Acapulco Towers and met with Sidney Korshak, a powerful hoodlum attorney, with offices in Chicago and Los Angeles. Korshak was reported to be an investor in Acapulco Towers. The manager of Acapulco Towers was Moe Morton, who also had a financial interest in the resort. Morton was a close associate of Sam Giancana and had invited Sam for cruises and deep sea fishing aboard his yacht. Giancana was known to always pick up the tab at group gatherings and paid all of his bills in cash. During the Christmas holidays in 1969, Giancana was visited by his daughter Bonnie and her husband Anthony Tisci in Mexico City. There was no indication that Sam Giancana ever entertained his eldest daughter Antoinette "Toni" Giancana, also known as "the Mafia Princess," while in Mexico. Apparently, Toni fell out of favor with her father when she divorced her husband Carmen Manno. Giancana was opposed to divorce among Italians. Ms. Giancana later married Robert J. McDonnell, a Chicago hoodlum attorney.

Phyllis McGuire, who resided in a lavish home in Las Vegas, reportedly provided by her paramour Mike Davis, was visited by Sam Giancana in Las Vegas on two occasions during the summer of 1969 at her specific request. Apparently, she and Mike Davis had received an extortion letter with a demand for money, and because they were concerned about their safety, she sought the assistance of Sam Giancana. She was able to contact Giancana by phone in Mexico City.

The Mexico City daily newspaper dated December 10, 1969, contained an article that read in part that "Salvatore (Momo) Giancana often connected with the Cosa Nostra, had lived for some time in Cuernavaca and was known as DePalma." Since that article appeared in Mexico City, Giancana had been very cautious about his activities and associates. He had made several trips to the United States and had visited New York City, Miami, Los Angeles, and Jamaica but had not returned to the Chicago area as far as it could be confirmed. Apparently, Giancana had no problem with the Mexican authorities while departing from and returning to Mexico.

Giancana reportedly purchased another very expensive new home in an exclusive area of Quinta San Cristobal, Colonia Las Delicas, behind the luxurious Hosteria Las Quintas, a combined restaurant hotel in Cuernavaca, Mexico. He purchased this house as an investment with cash through his attorney Jorge Castillo under the name of Sam DePalma. He was currently refurbishing the house and was considering selling it in the future. In May of 1970, Mexican Immigration authorities began to show a renewed interest in locating Sam Giancana. They had become aware of his three residences, the two in Cuernavaca and the one in Mexico City, and began conducting an investigation. They proceeded to Giancana's residence at Nubes #2 in Cuernavaca and spoke to the servants of the house, who identified a photo of Giancana as the owner of the property; however, they claimed that he had not been there for months. Investigation by the Mexican authorities at the penthouse apartment failed to locate him. The Mexico City penthouse was a condominium listed under the name of Giancana's attorney, Jorge Castillo. The authorities again failed to locate Giancana in Mexico City, and if located living in Mexico, he would have been subjected to expulsion. Apparently, Giancana continued to depart and enter Mexico with ease. The authorities intended to reinforce stops at the Mexico City airport as well as the private flight terminals. The Mexican attorney general was also getting involved in the investigation of Giancana. It was later learned that it was the usual procedure of Giancana to sneak across the Mexican border by having two women who resided in El Paso, Texas, drive across the border to Mexico, pick up Giancana, and then drive back into Texas. This procedure caused a minimum of interrogation at the crossing point by the Custom Service, because the women would advise customs that all three had just come into Mexico from Texas for the purpose of having dinner and were returning home.

During September of 1970s, Giancana began suffering from a kidney ailment and reportedly visited a medical facility in Houston, Texas, for treatment. Giancana was now sporting a full beard and occasionally wore a mod-styled wig. He planned to spend the 1970 Christmas holidays and New Year's Eve at the Acapulco Towers in Acapulco. On January 29, 1970, Phyllis McGuire and her personal maid visited Giancana in Acapulco Towers. They spent the next few days deep-sea-fishing and dining in restaurants. They then went to Giancana's residence in Cuernavaca, where Ms. McGuire had a very serious disagreement with Giancana. In January of 1971, he was again visited by Phyllis McGuire at his penthouse in Mexico City for a brief period. It appeared that this relationship had ran its course, and their romance was over. Giancana subsequently sold his Nubes #2 home in Cuernavaca for $180,000 to a Mexican politician and was also believed to have vacated his penthouse in Mexico City. He reportedly left Mexico temporarily because of pressure from the Mexican authorities.

In August of 1970, Giancana reportedly had used his contacts to influence the sister of the Shah of Iran to obtain permission from her brother to establish a gambling casino in Tehran, Iran. The shah insisted that only Giancana and a few of his top lieutenants would be allowed in Iran, and all the other gambling operatives would be native Iranians. Giancana reportedly appointed Louis J. Lederer, a Chicago and Las Vegas gambling figure for the past two decades, to make arrangements for the operation of this casino. Lederer was reported to have purchased one hundred slot machines in London, England, for use in the casino, which was scheduled to open in the fall of 1970. Lederer was conducting a training school for Iranians as dealers and other casino employees for the scheduled opening of the casino. Lederer was an acknowledged expert on casino gambling. On November 30, 1970, the Ab-Ali Country Club and Casino opened in the Ab-Ali Hotel in the suburbs of Tehran with Lederer in charge. Giancana also maintained an apartment in Beirut, Lebanon, believed to be located in Jounieh, a suburb of Beirut where he reportedly set up a gambling operation at the Casino of Lebanon. No further confirmation had been received in this regard. Giancana's function had been to set up gambling casinos for organized crime in foreign countries, and according to reports received, they had not been as lucrative and as profitable as anticipated. Giancana reportedly made periodic visits to Beirut, Lebanon, from 1972 through 1974. With all of the turmoil in the Mideast and the overthrow of the Shah of Iran, all of Giancana's gambling investments there were subsequently abandoned.

On July 6, 1971, Sam Giancana appeared at the embassy at Madrid, Spain, and applied for a passport for continued travel abroad for three months. This passport was valid for five-year travel. He did not indicate any specific travel plans. He was sporting a beard and a moustache. Giancana had previously been issued a passport at Guatemala City, Guatemala, on August 5, 1966, which was due to expire. He apparently had need for a current passport.

In October of 1971, Giancana was back in Mexico and resided at his home in Las Quintas in Cuernavaca under the name of Sam DePalma. Giancana's post office box in Cuernavaca was still rented under the name of Richard Scalzetti. In the meantime, in October 1971, his former confidant and bodyguard chauffeur Richard Scalzetti Cain was released from prison, where he was serving a four-year sentence for conspiracy in a bank robbery case. His probationary period expired on April 5, 1972, and he left the Chicago area to join up with Sam Giancana in Mexico. In April 1972, Richard Cain appeared in Mexico City and contacted his former wife and took her and her family out for dinner. He had not contacted her for at least seven years. Cain was later reported to have been in Madrid, Spain, where he allegedly set up a small gambling casino operation along with a house of prostitution on behalf of Giancana.

Giancana continued to travel abroad extensively during the next several years. He maintained his apartment in Beirut, Lebanon, and made frequent trips to California, Las Vegas, New York City, Arizona, and various other places, including a few highly confidential trips to Chicago. In June of 1972, he returned to Mexico. His constant companion and golfing partner was his attorney, Jorge Castillo. They played golf frequently at the Churubusco Golf Club in Mexico City. On October 24, 1972, the Mexico City newspaper *La Prenza* carried an article about the "Chicago La Cosa Nostra" and mentioned the presence of Sam Giancana in Cuernavaca and that he was not being bothered by Mexican authorities. Apparently, this again caused renewed interest in Giancana by the Mexican Immigration authorities, and this prompted Giancana to leave Mexico temporarily. In July of 1973, Giancana was back in Mexico and was seen playing golf with several of his card-playing associates at the Churubusco Country Club in Mexico City.

On October 6, 1973, Sam Giancana entered the United States at New Orleans, Louisiana, from Montego Bay, Jamaica. His purpose in entering the United States was to visit his new girlfriend who lived in California. He had been in the Chicago area several months before to attend the funeral services of his aunt, Rose Flood. Giancana's current heartthrob was Carolyn Morris, an attractive, well-groomed, and cultured blonde woman in her late forties who resided in Santa Monica, California. She was the former wife of a prominent music publishing company executive. She was a former actress, and her closest friend was the well-known actress Lauren Bacall. Carolyn Morris has been dating Giancana for about the past two years and had received a large diamond ring, reportedly valued at about $50,000, as a gift from him. She had been a frequent house guest of Giancana in Mexico City and Cuernavaca and had carried on a worldwide romantic relationship with him. Giancana and Carolyn Morris considered themselves engaged to be married. During May of 1973, they traveled together to Athens, Greece, and toured the Greek islands for three weeks as Mr. and Mrs. Sam Morris. She was also the woman who was believed to have accompanied Giancana on a safari trip to Africa about a year earlier. On December 10, 1973, Giancana personally appeared at the passport office in Washington DC and applied for a new passport, claiming he lost his previous passport in Mexico City. A new passport was issued, which was valid for three months only. After leaving the Washington DC area, he departed for California to be with his fiancée Carolyn Morris in California for Christmas and to spend New Year's Eve with her in Hawaii.

Giancana's fiancée Carolyn Morris, 1972

Carolyn Morris

THE KILLING
OF RICHARD CAIN

In the meantime, at approximately 1:30 p.m. on December 20, 1973, Sam Giancana's confidant and bodyguard chauffeur Richard Scalzetti Cain, age 49, who had returned to Chicago, was murdered in a gangland fashion by two masked gunmen in Rosie's Sandwich Shop, 1117 West Grand Avenue, Chicago, Illinois. Inspection of his body revealed that he was carrying only $15 in cash and no identification. Cain was shot in the head, twice at close range, with a shotgun, which virtually decapitated him. Rosie's had been a prime meeting place for hoodlum leader Marshall Caifano, Richard Cain, and notorious members of a burglary gang. Caifano had been in daily contact with Cain at Rosie's and could have set him up, since Caifano left shortly prior to the killing. The reason for the killing of Cain was not established; however, it was known that Cain had a serious disagreement with Sam Giancana the prior year, which probably had to do with finances. From information developed, Cain returned to the Chicago area about several months earlier and was in desperate need of finances. He had talked to hoodlum boss Fiore Buccieri and Pat Marcy of the First Ward about obtaining a job for the mob, and nothing materialized. He felt that his close association with Giancana would be a valuable asset and would not be challenged. He knew that the Chicago mob was leaderless with Giancana out of the country and could do as he pleased. Cain began to involve himself in various activities that conflicted with organized crime. He became associated with two groups of burglars and thieves, and they met at Rosie's on practically a daily basis. Cain had been setting up scores for them and disposing of their loot. Several of these burglars were arrested by the Chicago police while in the process of leaving a burglary scene with a quantity of loot in their possession, and Richard Cain was suspected as being the informer. This occurred just days before Cain was murdered. This could have been the motive for his killing, but Cain was no informant. The thieves probably overlooked the fact that good police work could have been the cause of their arrest because the thieves were extremely active with their scores and had been under close police scrutiny for some time. It appeared to be a falling out among thieves, and Richard Cain became the fall guy. Anthony Accardo was obviously alerted to the problem and had to approve the hit contract. Giancana was probably notified as a matter of courtesy because of Cain's previous close association with him. The two gunmen carried two way radios to affect their escape without interference. They wore ski masks to hide their identities from the patrons. Cain was a very charismatic, devious, and manipulative individual who could not be trusted. Cain pretended to be cooperative at times with the FBI, CIA, and the IRS only to divert attention away from his own nefarious activities. Apparently, he miscalculated his source of power and fell out of favor with the Chicago mob and was dealt with swiftly and harshly.

Following Cain's murder, it was also reported in the press that Cain was an informant of the FBI. It was true that Cain had been contacted by C-1 agent Bill Roemer on several occasions who was attempting to develop information on Sam Giancana and the Chicago mob; however, Cain never provided the FBI with any worthwhile information that would have qualified him as a confidential informant. He received a few cash payments from Roemer with the hope and expectation of eventually becoming productive. Cain was completely untrustworthy and was a skillful con man with an unusually persuasive ability. Cain had convinced Cook County Sheriff Richard Ogilvie to hire him as his chief investigator over the objections of many, only to fire him later when he became involved in criminal activities. He also deceived and betrayed Chicago reporter Jack Mabley who was an ardent supporter of Cain and who offered to be a character witness for him in criminal court proceedings. Cain's life of double dealing was finally over.

DAVID P. KAYE, TEAMSTER LOCAL 714 (RICO)

David P. Kaye, nee Kaminsky, was the chief steward and business agent of Local 714 of the Teamsters Union since 1967. In 1974, C-1 Agent Raymond Maria, a CPA and a talented investigator, who was capably assisted throughout the investigation by SA Herbert Briick, initiated an extensive investigation into allegations that David Kaye was using his position as a union officer to extort wages from exhibitors at McCormick Place, Chicago's premier exhibition hall. Kaye was in charge of controlling the exhibitors and tradesmen at McCormick Place and had been forcing visiting exhibitors to place him on their payrolls as a union steward, while performing no work. This constituted a pattern of racketeering activity in violation of the federal racketeering statute (RICO). Agent Maria did an incredible job in identifying all of the exhibitors who were victims of this shakedown. He located and/or caused to be interviewed about one hundred persons in Chicago and in other cities during this complex investigation. During the FBI probe, it was disclosed in August of 1974 that six Chicago hoodlums had also been linked to Local 714 by being on the lucrative payroll of various outside service contractors at McCormick Place. Because their ties with organized crime had been exposed, they were permanently barred from union activity at McCormick Place. They were Rocco Potenzo, mob gambling boss for Sam Giancana; Rocco Infelice, mob enforcer; Americo DiPietto, convicted narcotics peddler; Wayne Bock, a former professional football player and enforcer; Charles "Specs" DiCaro, a former cartage thief and gambler; and Mario Garelli, a convicted narcotics peddler. Also reportedly linked to Local 714 was Joseph Nicoletti, who was convicted of perjury in the 1960 income tax trial of Anthony Accardo.

In December 1974, David P. Kaye was indicted by a federal grand jury in Chicago on seventy-four counts of racketeering and extortion. Count 1 of the indictment was a felony and charged Kaye with a violation of the federal RICO statute, which was the first time this statute was known to have been used against a labor official. Counts 2 through 74 were misdemeanor violations of the Taft Hartley Law. This case represented the largest single indictment ever returned against a defendant in the

Midwest area. Kaye was subsequently convicted on all counts of the indictment and was sent to prison. This case was prosecuted by Chief of the Strike Force Peter F. Vaira and AUSA James P. Walsh, a competent labor attorney. This RICO conviction was the first of many more RICO convictions to follow.

GIANCANA, JOHN ROSELLI, THE CIA, AND FIDEL CASTRO

During the early 1960s, C-1 Agent John Bassett and I had a chance meeting with Giancana's lieutenant Chuck English at the Armory Lounge in Forest Park, Illinois. English initiated the conversation and apparently recognized us as being with the FBI. English asked me why we were bothering his boss, Sam Giancana, because we were all part of the same team. I didn't quite understand what he was talking about and asked him to be more specific. He did not go into too much detail but implied that Sam was also working for the federal government and mentioned the CIA. I was stunned by the information. I could not believe that any federal agency would be working with Sam Giancana, the boss of the Chicago mob. I thought that possibly his comment may have had something to do with President Kennedy's 1961 Bay of Pigs fiasco because Giancana and the Chicago mob had gambling interests in Cuba before Fidel Castro took over. We reported this information to FBI headquarters, and they checked with the CIA to determine whether or not there was any validity to the information. I was not privy to the CIA's response to FBI headquarters at the time, but the bureau told the Chicago office that the CIA was no longer dealing with Sam Giancana. Little did we realize at the time that, thanks to Chuck English, we had unwittingly stumbled upon "Operation Mongoose," a covert operation of the CIA involving Sam Giancana and the Chicago mob's efforts to dispose of Fidel Castro.

We later learned that in 1960, the CIA originally contacted former FBI Agent Robert Mahue, a former aide to billionaire Howard Hughes in Las Vegas to solicit his help, in a plot to get rid of Fidel Castro in Cuba. Mahue recruited John Roselli, a former Capone-era mobster, who was the Chicago mob's chief representative in Las Vegas. Roselli, the former husband of motion picture actress June Lang, brought Sam Giancana into the Castro conspiracy. Giancana reportedly sought the assistance of Santo Trafficante Jr., the boss of organized crime in the Florida area who had previous connections in Cuba. Also in 1960, information had been confidentially received that Giancana had a conversation with Phyllis McGuire about Fidel Castro and Cuba. Giancana reportedly told Ms. McGuire that Castro was going to be disposed of in November of 1960 and that he had a person in

250

Florida who was arranging to have a woman poison the drink or the food of Fidel Castro and kill him. No further information was obtained in that regard. However, the Bay of Pigs invasion in 1961 may have aborted this plan. The efforts to kill Castro by Mahue, Roselli, and Giancana were unsuccessful and publicized in 1971. The Senate Select Committee on Intelligence conducted hearings into the matter in 1975, and John Roselli was subpoenaed to testify. Roselli testified for several hours and basically confirmed the CIA conspiracy plot to kill Fidel Castro, which involved Sam Giancana and the Chicago mob. It was believed that Giancana and Roselli had no serious plan to follow through with the killing of Castro but were going through the motions of being cooperative with the CIA for their own personal agenda.

In October of 1960, information was received that two individuals had placed a wiretap on the Las Vegas hotel telephone of Dan Rowan, a member of the comedy team of Rowan and Martin, allegedly at the request of Sam Giancana, who was checking up on his girlfriend Phyllis McGuire who was also dating Dan Rowan at that time. One of the wire tappers, a private investigator, was reportedly arrested by the Clark County Sheriff's office in Las Vegas. Robert Mahue reportedly contacted the CIA and told them that the wiretap in question was an effort of Sam Giancana to obtain confidential information for the CIA. The CIA apparently went along with Mahue's implausible pretext, and the case against the wire tapper was dismissed. Also, John Roselli, whose true name was Filippo Sacco, was born in Italy. In 1967, he was involved in a multimillion-dollar card cheating scandal at the Friar's Club in Los Angeles and was convicted. Because Roselli was an illegal alien, he was ordered deported to Italy who refused to accept him. The CIA may have interceded on Roselli's behalf, and he was allowed to remain in this country. It was also during the early 1960s that John Roselli reportedly introduced Giancana to an extraordinarily sexually desirable woman in Las Vegas by the name of Judith Campbell. She was a freelance artist. Giancana showered her with expensive gifts and loving affection, and entertained her on a number of occasions at his Oak Park, Illinois, residence. In 1977, Judith Campbell (Exner) wrote a book entitled *My Story*, outlining her affairs with Sam Giancana, Frank Sinatra, and President Kennedy.

On August 9, 1976, the decomposed body of John Roselli was found stuffed in a fifty-five-gallon steel drum off the coast of Miami, Florida. Even though the drum had been weighted down, it floated to the surface. Roselli had been strangled, stabbed, and his legs had been cut off. Apparently, Roselli created too high a profile for the Chicago mob, and this was their way of voicing their intense displeasure.

GIANCANA'S ARREST AND DEPORTATIONFROMMEXICO

On February 6, 1974, Peter Vaira, who had replaced Sheldon Davidson as chief of the Strike Force in Chicago, issued a federal grand jury subpoena for the appearance of Sam Giancana on February 26, 1974. Information had been received that Giancana was to appear in NYC on February 18, 1974, for a one-day visit. The subpoena was forwarded to the New York office; however, Giancana could not be located. Giancana had returned to Mexico where he entertained his fiancée Carolyn Morris as a house guest for a two-week period. In the event that Giancana could be located in the United States, he would be served with a grand jury subpoena. Giancana remained on the Mexican Immigration Exclusion list.

On June 28, 1974, Sam Giancana was present at a wedding reception for the son of Attorney Jorge Castillo at the Churubusco Country Club in Mexico City. Many Mexican dignitaries were in attendance and may have been aware of Giancana's presence as a guest. This may have caused renewed interest in Giancana by the Mexican authorities. On the evening of July 18, 1974, Mexican Immigration authorities advised that Sam Giancana was taken into custody at his residence at 7:00 a.m. on that date at his Quinta San Cristobal residence, Cuernavaca, Mexico. On a pretext, they were able to lure Giancana away from the house, and as he approached the outside gate, they took him into custody. He readily admitted his identity as Sam Giancana. His current fiancée, Carolyn Morris, was a house guest at the time of his arrest. He was scheduled to be deported from Mexico City the following morning at 8:15 a.m. for San Antonio, Texas. His expulsion was ordered by the undersecretary of the Mexican Government.

Peter Vaira, chief of the Chicago Strike Force, had received authorization from the US Justice Department to issue a subpoena for Giancana to appear before the federal grand jury in Chicago on July 23, 1974. The subpoena was dispatched to the San Antonio office for service upon Giancana's arrival in San Antonio. Upon arrival in San Antonio, Giancana was served with the subpoena and was allowed to proceed to Chicago. He was observed deplaning at Chicago O'Hare and was very docile in submitting to an FBI interview. He deplored the fact that as an "old broken down man," he was being subjected to the same type of treatment. He believed that he would have been left alone until Richard Cain was murdered in Chicago and said, "You guys started bugging me again and brought Carolyn (Morris) into it." He claimed that he had nothing to do with Cain's killing, "because he was messing around with too many people." Giancana was a completely different man than before, extremely polite, and answered all questions courteously. The officers of the Intelligence Unit of the Chicago Police Department were standing by and took him to police headquarters to interview him regarding the murder of Richard Cain. He told the police that he was a thousand miles away from Chicago as his alibi. He explained the circumstances of his expulsion from Mexico, being thrown into jail the previous night and taken across the border to San Antonio. He was put on a plane to Chicago without proper clothing, toilet articles, completely penniless, and could not call anyone because he had no money with him. He intended to remain in Chicago until he resolved his appearance before the federal grand jury. Upon completion of the police questioning, he was placed in a taxi cab and taken to his Oak Park residence.

When Giancana was expelled from Mexico as an undesirable person, he was not allowed to take any personal property with him. The Mexican authorities were not able to locate or recover any documents whatsoever at the time of his arrest. Giancana was seized outside the gated community in Cuernavaca in his robe and shorts and was taken directly to Mexico City for deportation. Giancana denied owning the home or any other property in Mexico. He claimed to be just a tourist. In the residence at the time of his arrest was Carolyn Morris, his fiancée, and three other unidentified women. No one in the household was aware of what had happened. While en route to Mexico City, Giancana attempted to bribe the agents to secure his release but was unsuccessful. Giancana was told that if he returned to Mexico, he would be subject to prosecution. Giancana's attorney, Jorge Castillo, was aware of his arrest and was taking steps to obtain a court order to prevent his deportation; however, Giancana's expulsion was expedited to prevent any legal action from being taken. Another contributing factor to the arrest and deportation of Giancana could have been that Mexican President Luis Echevarria was aware of recent media publicity linking Giancana to the alleged plot to assassinate Dictator Fidel Castro of Cuba on behalf of the CIA and would be very sensitive to any criticism of Giancana's illegal presence in Mexico.

On July 21, 1974, an article appeared in the *Mexico City Daily* newspaper entitled, "Government Deports Mafia Figure Sam Giancana as Undesirable," and detailed the events of Giancana's arrest and deportation from Mexico. It was pointed out that in April of 1967, Mexican authorities ordered Giancana to leave the country with the instruction that he should never return. Nonetheless, "Sam utilized another name and managed to return again to Mexico." Giancana's attorney, Jorge Castillo, was reported to have said that should Giancana return to Mexico, he would welcome him back with a big celebration. As of October 1974, the Giancana estate at Quinta San Cristobal, Cuernavaca, and the entire household staff remained intact; and there was no indication that the home was up for sale. Jorge Castillo continued to be the administrator of the estate, which was now valued at about $700,000. The property was purchased in 1969 by a company created by Castillo named "San Cristobal."

GIANCANA'sSecondGrant
of Immunity

A conference was held on July 22, 1974, between C-1 agents and the Chicago Strike Force attorneys regarding the material to be used for the grand jury questioning of Sam Giancana who was to appear on the following day. Giancana was to be questioned about three particular areas, namely, the gangland slaying of his associate Richard Scalzetti Cain in December of 1973; his mode of living for the past eight years, noting that his expenditures obviously far exceeded the $40,000 he had been claiming on his annual income tax returns; and his contacts during the past eight years with organized crime figures, including Carolyn Morris, his fiancée. While waiting for his appearance before the grand jury, Giancana complained about the large gathering of news media representatives at his residence and at the federal building on that day. He claimed that he had to resort to physical force to make his way into the building. On July 23, 1974, Giancana, accompanied by veteran hoodlum attorney George Callaghan, appeared before the grand jury and took the Fifth Amendment to all questions asked. He was continued under subpoena until September 17, 1974. This visibly upset Giancana because he desired to get this over with so that he could get out of town again. It was the present plan of attorney Peter Vaira to request permission of William Lynch, Organized Crime Section of the US Department of Justice, to grant immunity to Giancana.

On October 29, 1974, three associates of Giancana appeared before the grand jury in Chicago. They were Anthony Champagne, Giancana's attorney; James Perno, a relative who maintained Giancana's residence in Oak Park during his absence; and Robert C. Brown, the accountant who prepared Giancana's tax returns while Giancana traveled abroad. The purpose of the inquiry was to look into Giancana's income from the Lawrence-River Road Trust, which provided Giancana with most of his income. Champagne was the attorney who set up the trust based on the sale of the River Road Motel in Rosemont in February 1963. The motel was sold by Sam Giancana to Don Stephens, village president of Rosemont, Illinois, for $520,000. Champagne took the Fifth and claimed attorney-client privilege. Perno took the Fifth and Brown admitted he prepared the tax returns and relied upon information provided by Perno and Champagne.

On December 17, 1974, Giancana appeared before the federal grand jury in Chicago where he invoked the Fifth Amendment to all questions asked. He was brought before Chief US District Court Judge Edwin Robson, who granted Giancana immunity and ordered him to return to the grand jury and answer questions. Giancana then returned to the grand jury where he answered a few general questions about his relationship with Jorge Castillo. Giancana claimed that Castillo was never his attorney, that he was only a casual associate of his and never entered into any real estate dealings with him. Giancana obviously lied to all of the questions about his relationship with Castillo and claimed that he merely rented a different place in Mexico for a few weeks at a time. In view of his elusive and deceptive testimony, he was ordered to present himself for further grand jury testimony on January 14, 1975. As previously reported, Giancana had three residences, two in Cuernavaca and a penthouse suite that he rented for about two years in Mexico City. Castillo was not only his attorney but was the sole administrator for all of his properties. Giancana paid Castillo in cash for all his property transactions, and Castillo paid all the bills during the eight years Giancana lived in Mexico. In each of these transactions, Castillo formed a separate company to conceal the true ownership, which is a common practice for Americans buying property in Mexico. This testimony formed a good basis for perjury. In view of the fact that Giancana was now going to answer questions of the grand jury, it became vital to completely explore his entire criminal background and establish perjury if he continued to lie. Peter Vaira established an electronic surveillance (ELSUR) hearing on January 14, 1975, to ensure that any further questions asked of Giancana were not tainted by previous unlawful ELSURs.

On January 16, 1975, Giancana appeared in the chambers of Chief Judge Robson; and it was agreed that an ELSUR hearing would be waived until such time as questioning of Giancana by the grand jury relating to matters that may have been tainted by unlawful ELSURs. Judge Robson ordered Giancana to answer all questions under grant of immunity, which may be asked by the grand jury relating to events that occurred after May 1966 or during the period he was in self-imposed exile from the United States. Giancana reappeared before the grand jury on February 11, 1975, and answered a limited number of questions asked of him by Douglas Roller, Strike Force attorney. Giancana's answers were obviously evasive and undoubtedly perjured. Giancana now claimed he was mistaken when he previously testified that he did not purchase a residence in Mexico. He now claimed that he and Richard Cain (deceased) purchased a home together in Mexico, and that Giancana paid $35,000 as his share of the purchase price, which he borrowed from Cain. Giancana's appearance before the grand jury was continued generally until several additional witnesses could be interviewed and had testified. A conference was held between C-1 agents and Strike Force attorneys to review Giancana's perjured testimony and to formulate plans for future grand jury investigation. We felt that we had a good chance to bring perjury charges against Giancana based on his recent testimony.

On February 18, 1975, the following persons appeared in Chicago in response to subpoenas calling for them to appear before the federal grand jury:

Carolyn Morris, the fiancée of Giancana who took the Fifth Amendment privilege;

Max Gluck, an interior decorator who decorated Giancana's three residences in Mexico, testified about his knowledge of and dealings with Giancana. Gluck had even received a collect call from Giancana several years earlier from Beirut, Lebanon, with a request to contact attorney Jorge Castillo and have Castillo send him some money.

Albert Andreas, a businessman and former owner of Las Nubes #2, residence in Cuernavaca, sold his home to Giancana in August of 1966 for $125,000. Giancana gave Andreas a down payment of $5,000 in cash and wanted to pay the balance in cash. Andreas refused because he did not want to take the chance of receiving any counterfeit bills. They went to the Banco De National in Mexico City where they had the cash balance changed into a draft on a New York Bank. He furnished detailed information on the activities of Giancana in Cuernavaca. Andreas was interviewed only and not required to testify.

Justina Prince a.k.a. Nena Rico and her husband Franklin Prince advised that they were visitors to Giancana's residence in Cuernavaca. They were interviewed and not required to testify. Strike Force attorney Douglas Roller was very pleased with the results obtained to date from the above witnesses.

Roller then obtained permission from the US Department of Justice to travel to Mexico City. Bureau authority was granted for FBI Supervisor Vincent L. Inserra to accompany Mr. Roller to Mexico for the purpose of conducting additional pertinent interviews at the US embassy of individuals associated with Giancana's activities. The persons to be interviewed in Mexico were Giancana's attorney, Jorge Castillo; retired General Jose Ortiz, present owner of Nubes #2 Cuernavaca; Salvatore Castaneda, owner of the Hotel Restaurant in Cuernavaca in which Giancana was alleged to have a financial interest; and Mrs. Gerald Schultz, former owner of Giancana's residence in Quinta San Cristobal, Cuernavaca.

On March 31, 1975, Douglas Roller and I arrived in Mexico City. We checked into the Maria Isabel Hotel located adjacent to the US embassy in Mexico City. On April 2, 1975, with the assistance of the US embassy personnel, the interviews began. Mexican attorney, Jorge Castillo, who had been representing Giancana as a client for the prior eight years was relatively cooperative and furnished considerable information concerning the activities of Giancana and Richard Cain while in Mexico. When asked specifically about Giancana's residences in Mexico, Castillo respectfully declined and asserted attorney-client relationship. Noted that when

Giancana testified before the grand jury in Chicago, he emphatically denied any attorney-client relationship with Castillo whom he claimed was only a friend. Castillo had no objection to answering any other questions, which he felt were not based upon attorney-client relationship. Castillo identified a number of photographs of persons who were visitors of Giancana in Mexico. He would be willing to travel to Chicago and testify before the grand jury, as long as it would not affect attorney-client relationship. In the event that Giancana agreed to waive this relationship, he would be willing to testify to all of his dealings with Giancana.

Daniel Marquez, secretary to retired General Jose Ortiz, present owner of the Nubes #2 residence, Rancho Tetela, Cuernavaca, Mexico, was interviewed through an interpreter. He advised that he handled all of the arrangements for General Ortiz, regarding the purchase of the residence at Nubes #2 on June 18, 1971. He identified a photo of Sam Giancana as the owner, from whom they had purchased the residence. The seller of the Villa was a corporation known as "Las Nubes, S.A.," which was handled by attorney Castillo. The total purchase price was $171,000. Marquez pointed out that the contract reflected a price considerably less than the sale price to avoid paying the full amount of Mexican Transfer Tax, which is a common but improper practice. He made available a copy of the notarized contract regarding the purchase of Nubes #2, written in Spanish.

Mrs. Gerald Schultz, whose husband is now deceased, was the former owner of the villa residence known as Quinta San Cristobal, Las Quintas, Cuernavaca, that was sold to a Sam DePalma for $160,000 on November 28, 1969. Mrs. Schultz identified a photo of Sam Giancana as Sam DePalma. The closing on the sale of the San Cristobal residence was handled by Jorge Castillo.

Salvator Castaneda, owner of the Hosteria Las Quintas Resort and Spa, a luxurious hotel restaurant complex in Cuernavaca in which Giancana was alleged to have a financial interest, was interviewed, and was very cooperative. He claimed that the name, photo, and aliases of Sam Giancana and Richard Cain were not familiar to him.

The interviews were conducted at the US embassy in Mexico City, so that Mexican sovereignty would be respected. Strike Force Attorney Douglas Roller was extremely pleased with the results of the interviews and felt confident that the pertinent information obtained would establish an excellent foundation for a perjury violation against Giancana. Roller requested the Department of Justice to review the evidence submitted for a possible perjury indictment against Giancana. He was confident that the Department of Justice would soon authorize prosecution.

On May 12, 1975, Sam Giancana was admitted to the Methodist Hospital in Houston, Texas. He was under the care of the world famous surgeon Dr. Michael DeBakey. On May 13, 1975, Giancana had gall bladder surgery and was released from the hospital on May 21, 1975. He was readmitted to the hospital on May 24, 1975, with postoperative problems. Giancana's relatives and fiancée Carolyn Morris were frequent visitors to the hospital. Giancana was released from the hospital on June 17, 1975, and returned to his home in Oak Park, Illinois, the next day.

THE KILLING OF SAM GIANCANA

At about 7:00 p.m. on June 19, 1975, only one day after he had returned to his Oak Park, Illinois, residence from the hospital in Houston, Texas, Giancana sat down alone for dinner in the upstairs family TV room. The caretaker's wife, Ann DiPersio, had just prepared some chicken for him to eat; and he was in the process of having dinner when his daughter Francine and her husband Jerry DePalma and their young daughter arrived for a visit. They also joined him for a snack at the dinner table. Following dinner, they all proceeded to the basement area for conversation, where they remained until about 10:30 p.m. The DePalmas then departed. Because it was a pleasantly cool evening, Giancana asked his caretaker Joseph DiPersio to join him for a brief walk in the neighborhood. Giancana was still feeling somewhat weak from his recent surgery and wanted someone to be with him. They went for a fifteen-minute walk and returned to the residence through the cellar door entrance, which had been left open. It went down a flight of stairs to an open steel door that led to the kitchen basement area. Giancana appeared to be in good spirits and in a relaxed mood. He gave no indication that he was concerned about his safety. DiPersio left Giancana and proceeded to his attic apartment. About fifteen minutes later, Giancana called for him, and he went downstairs to see what he wanted. Apparently, there was a water leak coming from the ceiling and water was dripping onto the basement dining area. DiPersio was trying to determine the source of the leak when he noticed that Dominic Blasi, Giancana's most trusted friend and confidant, had entered the basement dining area and sat down at the table. Blasi asked for a drink of scotch, and DiPersio got him some ice for his drink. DiPersio finally located the source of the leak, removed some ceiling tile, and placed a bucket under the slow leak. He would try to repair the leak in the morning. DiPersio left Giancana and Blasi alone at about 11:20 p.m. and joined his wife in their upstairs apartment. About a half hour later, DiPersio noticed that Dominic Blasi's car was not in the driveway. He then called to Giancana, but there was no answer. He went downstairs to the basement dining room and noticed that Giancana was lying on his back on the basement kitchen floor in a pool of blood. He noticed that the gas burner on the stove was turned on high and that there was a small frying pan with sausage, spinach, and beans on the verge of burning. He removed the pan from the stove and burned his hand in the process. He called for his wife and told her to call for an ambulance and the police. Several minutes later, the ambulance arrived and declared that Sam Giancana was dead. Someone apparently had fired six shots into his neck and one into his mouth as he was standing at the stove in his basement kitchen preparing a late-night snack. Giancana was killed instantly. DiPersio had asked him, just minutes before finding the body, if there was anything he needed, to which Giancana replied no. No gun was found at the scene. Robbery was not the motive because Giancana had about $1,500 in cash on his person. Giancana usually left the basement door open and unlocked until he was ready to retire for the evening.

It was readily apparent that whoever murdered Sam Giancana had to be closely associated with him and knew the layout of his residence. The last person known to have seen Giancana alive was Dominic Blasi, and he had been there about twenty minutes or less before the killing. It was very rare for Giancana to be visited by anyone late at night, especially Blasi who generally visited Giancana during the daylight hours. There would have been only a twenty-minute window of opportunity for someone else to have entered the residence during this precise time and then to have murdered Giancana without being seen by Blasi or caretaker DiPersio. Blasi would have to be considered a prime suspect in the murder of Giancana; however, Blasi was not known to be a hit man. One other logical possibility existed. Blasi may have been ordered to set up the killing of Giancana for a hit man who was waiting in the wings to obtain the okay from Blasi as he left the residence. The Chicago mob had to select someone who was known to Giancana and would be acquainted with the kitchen basement at the Giancana residence. In any event, Blasi could have been the setup man for the killing of Giancana, and this killing had to be sanctioned by Chicago mob leaders Anthony Accardo and Joseph Aiuppa. The Intelligence Unit of the Chicago Police Department had been on surveillance at the Giancana's residence earlier that day and had left for the evening. They had observed Giancana's lieutenant, Chuck English, as a visitor during the day.

Giancana was waked on June 21 and 22, 1975, at the Montclair Funeral Home in Chicago. It was the request of the family to exclude hoodlum members of the Chicago mob from attending the memorial service. The wake was restricted to family and close personal friends of Giancana. Phyllis McGuire flew in from Paris, France, and was picked up at the airport by Chuck English to attend the ceremony. Popular vocalist Keely Smith was also reported to be in attendance. Several close hoodlum friends of Giancana attempted to attend the wake and were turned away and had to return at a later time to be personally admitted by Giancana's family members. Dominic Blasi served as a pall bearer. There were only a few dozen cars in the funeral procession. On June 23, 1975, Giancana was buried at Mount Carmel cemetery and placed in a mausoleum crypt with his wife, Angeline. Normally when a person of Sam Giancana's stature in organized crime dies, there is a huge outpouring of sympathy expressed by the entire hoodlum community as well political dignitaries. This was not the case with Salvatore Momo Giancana.

On August 19, 1975, two months after the killing of Giancana, a high-standard .22 caliber Duramatic automatic pistol with a homemade silencer was discovered by River Forest, Illinois, village employees as they were mowing the grass in the Thatcher Woods Forest Preserve, about two miles away from the Giancana residence. It was speculated that the killer, while fleeing from the scene of the murder, may have been startled by the sound of the police sirens and flashing lights responding to the Oak Park shooting and disposed of the weapon in the forest preserve. The gun had been positively identified as the murder weapon by ballistics experts. The serial numbers on the gun were traced from the manufacturer to a Miami gun dealer on June 20, 1965, and later sold to another gun dealer in Tamiani, Florida. That is where the trail ended. The barrel of the pistol had been shortened and threaded for the silencer. It had forty-two holes drilled into the gun barrel, which enhanced the effectiveness of the silencer. Recovery of a murder weapon was a highly unusual event, following a gangland slaying.

1974 photo of Sam Giancana

Giancana Murder Weapon

On June 24, 1975, the Cook County State's attorney's office obtained a search warrant and seized a desk, a file cabinet, and tape recorder previously observed in the residence of Sam Giancana during the crime scene search of his basement. Jerome DePalma, son-in-law of Giancana, filed a motion for an injunction to restrict the authorities from opening and processing the items seized. The motion was filed before Circuit Court Judge Daniel Covelli, who ruled in favor of DePalma's motion. It was noted that Judge Covelli had been linked with the Chicago criminal element over the years. The state's attorney's office finally persevered when it received a ruling from the Illinois Supreme Court that allowed them to inventory and review all documents seized. A combination safe was also drilled open with a court order, and all items were inventoried. The safe contained three small-caliber handguns, hundreds of American coins, and an IOU for $165,000, which was a loan from Giancana to a citizen of Mexico, probably attorney Jorge Castillo, who provided Giancana with cash as needed throughout his stay in Mexico. Found in Giancana's desk was a gift list, from the wedding of one of Giancana's daughters, and it contained hundreds of names of guests and the amounts of their cash gifts. Included in this list were many prominent politicians and public figures, along with a "Who's Who" of the Chicago mob. It just so happened that Judge Covelli's name was on the list with a gift amount of $500. Of course, Judge Covelli denied knowing anything about the wedding or having contributed a $500 gift. He refused to withdraw from the case involving the items taken from the Giancana residence. Covelli stated, "I'm staying on this case until the finish." Bernard Carey, Cook County State's attorney, claimed that Judge Covelli's actions were hindering the investigation of Giancana's murder. The Illinois Supreme Court eventually ruled against Judge Covelli. It was noted that in1966, Pat Marcy and John D'Arco of Chicago's First Ward attempted to assist the career of Judge Covelli by having him appointed to the federal bench. These efforts were thwarted, and Judge Alexander Napoli was appointed by President Lyndon Johnson to fill the vacancy. It was further noted that prominent mobsters such as Anthony Accardo, Gus Alex, Sam Alex, Murray Humphreys, Frank Ferraro, and Paul Ricca, each gave $2,500 as wedding gifts.

Meanwhile, a Cook County grand jury investigating the murder of Giancana issued subpoenas for Anthony Accardo, Charles English, Dominic Blasi, Mario DeStefano, a part-time bodyguard of Giancana, and several members of the Giancana family. The mobsters invoked the Fifth Amendment, and no pertinent information was developed as a result of the grand jury. On November 18, 1975, Dominic Blasi appeared before the grand jury and invoked the Fifth Amendment and was scheduled to reappear at a later date. On December 12, 1975, Giancana's housekeepers, Joseph DiPersio and his wife Ann, appeared before the grand jury. Both were granted immunity and testified.

The Chicago Strike Force also subpoenaed the documents and items obtained from the Giancana residence for review by the federal grand jury. These included various stock certificates, a series of trusts relating to the Lawrence River Road Trust, as well as properties in Melrose Park, Cicero, and Oak Park, Illinois. Profits from these rental properties were shared jointly with Charles English. Several documents were in Spanish, wherein several corporations had been set up during the period of time that Giancana was in Mexico, which indicated that Giancana had purchased Mexican bonds and several buildings rented as supermarkets, and Giancana's last residence at Quinta San Cristobal. All of these records were eventually returned to the family attorney. It was not believed that the Giancana family found a massive cash hoard as they probably had anticipated. Giancana apparently died without telling family members where he kept all of his cash other than those documented in the records. Giancana's most valuable assets in his estate would have been his Oak Park residence and all of his investments in Mexico. However, it would appear that Jorge Castillo would stand to gain inasmuch as all of the Giancana property and assets were in the name of companies administered by Jorge Castillo, Castillo's wife, and the Castillo law firm representing Giancana.

The killing of Sam Giancana had to be the most significant gangland slaying in the history of organized crime in Chicago. It also had to be sanctioned by the top leaders of organized crime, Anthony Accardo and Joseph Aiuppa. There had been much speculation over the reason for the killing of Giancana, and each explanation had a modicum of truth to it. In my opinion, it was a combination of a number of factors that led to the demise of Giancana who had outlived his usefulness and had become a huge liability to the Chicago mob. This began with the unprecedented civil suit brought by Giancana against the FBI in 1963 that was unsuccessful and brought excessive attention and exposure to organized crime. Also, the publicity surrounding Sam Giancana, Phyllis McGuire, and Frank Sinatra at the Cal Neva Lodge, which caused Sinatra to lose his gaming license and his financial interests in Nevada, was another factor. This was followed by the Chicago federal grand jury investigation of Giancana and his entire hoodlum hierarchy, along with their corrupt political associates, that resulted in the incarceration of Giancana for one year for contempt of court. The attention that was focused on these proceedings as a result of Giancana was enormous. This was followed by the revelation of Giancana's involvement with John Roselli and the CIA in a conspiracy to assassinate Cuba's Fidel Castro. Roselli paid the ultimate price for this misguided adventure. Giancana was absent from the Chicago scene for an eight-year period, as he appeared to be setting up gambling casinos for organized crime in foreign countries while operating out of Mexico. He was arrested and deported by the Mexican authorities to the United States where he faced another grand jury in Chicago and was in the process of being prosecuted on perjury charges. In addition, upon his return to the United States, he was short of funds because his money was tied up in Mexico. He then attempted to assert his influence back into certain hoodlum interests, much to the dismay of the leaders of organized crime. His flamboyant style of leadership had ran its course and had caused untold damage and turmoil to the Chicago crime syndicate. It was time for Sam Giancana to go. According to the records of the Chicago Crime Commission, who have been recording gangland slayings since 1919, Sam Giancana was listed as victim #1023. Sam Giancana finally joined the number of unfortunate gangland slaying victims that he helped to create over the years through his direct involvement in murders and those that were sanctioned by him.

My last confrontation with Giancana occurred in the mid-1960s in the lobby of the Drake Hotel in Chicago, where he had dinner at the Cape Cod Room with his intimate paramour, Bergit Clark. He was in a very friendly mood, and after exchanging greetings, Giancana's last parting words to me and agent Marshall Rutland were "You work for your living. I'll steal for mine."

Giancana's words came as no surprise. On March 27, 1965, there was an armed robbery of $467,000 in jewelry from the Laykin et Cie Company in Los Angeles, California. In September 1967, information was received from Peacock Jewelers in Chicago that a ring worth approximately $10,000 was brought into Peacock Jewelers by Bergit Clark, Giancana's paramour, and had been identified as having been stolen in the above robbery in Los Angeles. Ms. Clark was subsequently interviewed by C-1 agents on September 29, 1967, and although she refused to definitely identify Giancana as the donor of the ring, she left very little doubt during her interview that Giancana was the source of the ring. She claimed that she had broken off her relationship with him prior to his imprisonment and had not had any type of contact with him since his release from the Cook County jail on May 31, 1966. This situation had been discussed with the Chief of the Strike Force, Lawrence Morrissey, on several occasions; however, no further action was taken because Giancana was no longer in the country. It was noted that mob jewel thieves usually store their stolen property in vaults at key locations in the Chicago area for inspection by select members of the mob hierarchy, who would take possession of choice items as needed for their own personal use as a "street tax" imposed by the Chicago mob.

THE LAST OF
A VANISHING BREED

N ow that the Chicago mob had permanently retired Sam Giancana from his provocative role as boss of the Chicago mob; the Chicago hoodlum hierarchy decided to formally celebrate the retirement of two of their loyal members with a farewell luncheon during the summer of 1976. The luncheon was private and was held at the then-named Sicily Restaurant, 2743 N. Harlem Avenue, Chicago, Illinois, that was closed to the public for lunch. Ten of the most powerful mobsters of the Chicago outfit were in attendance. Never before had they allowed themselves to be photographed together.

Historic Photo of Luncheon Meeting of Chicago Hoodlum Hierarchy, 1976.

Seated closest to the camera in the front row are Anthony "Joe Batters" Accardo, Joseph "Black Joe" Amato, Joseph "Caesar" DiVarco, and James "Turk" Torello. In the back row are Joseph Aiuppa, Dominic DiBella the honoree, Vincent Solano, Al

Pilotto, and Jack Cerone standing with Joseph "The Clown" Lombardo. Dominick DiBella had taken over as boss of Chicago's North Side upon the death of Ross Prio in 1972. DiBella was stepping down because he was dying of cancer and was being replaced by Vincent Solano, president of Local 1 of the Laborer's International Union in Chicago. DiBella passed away several months later. Also retiring was Joseph "Black Joe" Amato, who was being replaced by James Torello, as boss of the far northwest suburbs.

Photo of Joseph Aiuppa, Dominic DiBella, and Anthony Accardo

On the right, a corpulent Anthony Accardo who had retained his position as chairman emeritus of the Chicago outfit, posed with Dominic DiBella, whose appearance had changed dramatically since his illness. Joseph "Doves" Aiuppa was acting boss at the time of this photo, which indicated his importance in the Chicago mob. The presence of Joseph Lombardo at this meeting was significant, because he was one of the youngest members in this group of VIP hoodlums. This was an obvious endorsement of Lombardo for future hoodlum responsibility, especially because he was reported to be a rising star in the Chicago outfit. Nine of the mob leaders in the photo are deceased at this time, and Lombardo is the only one still alive. Lombardo's future as a mob leader was to be filled with adversity, misadventure, and despair.

JOSEPH LOMBARDO ET AL.

Another significant C-1 investigation occurred in 1974 and concerned the misapplication of $1.4 million of loans from the Central States Teamsters Union Pension Fund by advisors to the fund to hoodlum-owned and—controlled businesses in Chicago, New Mexico, and Las Vegas. The C-1 case agent was Peter J. Wacks, assisted by SAs Frank Ford, Gus Kempff, Robert Malone, and other C-1 agents, all of whom did exceptional work in the preparation of this case. A federal grand jury indicted Joseph Lombardo; Anthony Spilotro, a mob enforcer; Allen Dorfman, who was associated with the Teamster union pension fund; Irwin S. Weiner, a Chicago bondsman who was caretaker of the financial interests of deceased hoodlum leader Felix Alderisio; Ronald DeAngeles, a mob enforcer; and two trustees of the pension fund. Just prior to the trial, a material witness named Daniel Seifert, age 29, was shotgunned to death outside of his plastics firm in Bensenville, Illinois, on September 27, 1974, by two masked gunmen. Unfortunately, as a result of the Seifert murder, Lombardo was severed from the case; and the rest of the subjects were ultimately acquitted. However, their good fortune would be temporary.

C-1 case agent Peter J. Wacks was not discouraged. He would later implicate Lombardo in the FBI's famous "Operation Pendorf" case, which was the code name for the penetration of Allen Dorfman. In 1982, Lombardo, Allen Dorfman, and others were convicted of conspiring to defraud the Teamsters Central States Pension fund on behalf of the Chicago mob. Following the conspiracy conviction of Allen Dorfman, he was murdered in a gangland fashion on January 20, 1983, just three days before he was to be sentenced. He was silenced to prevent him from cooperating with the government. Lombardo, however, was sentenced to fifteen years in prison in this case. Former C-1 agents Peter J. Wacks and Arthur Pfizenmayer were the principal agents behind the successful convictions obtained in the "Operation Pendorf" case.

Joseph Lombardo was again convicted in 1986 along with Chicago hoodlum leaders Jack Cerone and Joseph Aiuppa for skimming over $2 million in funds from the Stardust Casino in Las Vegas, Nevada. This was the FBI's famous "Strawman" case that involved mobsters from Kansas City and Chicago and ended the mob's skimming of Las Vegas casinos. Lombardo was sentenced to serve sixteen years in prison, later reduced to fourteen years. Aiuppa was sentenced to serve twenty-eight years and six months. Cerone was sentenced to serve twenty years. Lombardo was released in November of 1992, and Aiuppa and Cerone were released in 1996.

Joey Lombardo's notorious past was about to ensnare him again. In September 2007, Lombardo was again convicted in US District Court in Chicago on charges of racketeering murder conspiracy in connection with the Chicago FBI Office's landmark "Operation Family Secrets" investigation. Specifically, Lombardo and his partner in crime Frank Schweihs were charged with the 1974 murder of federal witness Daniel Seifert, who was scheduled to be a key witness in a trial against Lombardo, Spilotro, Dorfman, and others on charges of defrauding the Teamster Union Pension Fund. With the killing of Siefert, prosecution of the pension fund case was not sustainable. The two gunmen, who killed Seifert, were masked and abandoned a stolen 1973 Ford listed to a fictitious name and address on the registration. At that time, C-1 Agents Peter Wacks and Gus Kempff were primarily responsible for initiating a request of our Springfield FBI office to retrieve the original vehicle title application and registration on the stolen car, which was forwarded to the FBI Laboratory for handwriting and fingerprint analysis. At the 2007 trial, a former employee of the FBI Identification Division testified that he was able to identify a fingerprint of Joseph Lombardo on the fraudulent title application of the stolen 1973 vehicle, which contributed to the murder conviction of Lombardo. Frank Schweihs, who assisted Lombardo in the killing of Daniel Seifert, was dropped from the case because of serious health problems and has since died. Lombardo was sentenced to serve the remainder of his life in prison. C-1 Agents Peter Wacks and Gus Kempff, who passed away in 1990, would be pleased to know that they contributed in some small way to the murder conviction of Joey "The Clown" Lombardo, some thirty-three years later. The Chicago Division of the FBI did an incredible job in handling the "Operation Family Secrets" investigation, which ultimately charged fourteen current and former Chicago hoodlums with eighteen previously unsolved gangland murders since 1970.

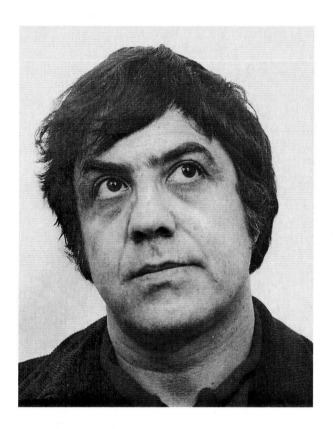

**Photo of Joseph Lombardo, arrested on February 24,
1974, by C-1 agents on charges of Teamster pension fund fraud**

ANTHONY MAENZA

Anthony "Poopy" Maenza was a well-known hit man and a brutal enforcer for the Jack Cerone hoodlum group. He had a long record of arrests and had been acquitted on three previous murder charges. A criminal intelligence case was opened on Maenza and was assigned to C-1 agent Richard Cavanagh, one of my more relentless investigators. SA Cavanagh determined that Anthony Maenza had made material false statements on a loan application at the National Bank of Chicago during July of 1966 in violation of the Federal Housing Act (FHA). The facts were presented to a federal grand jury, and Maenza was indicted on June 2, 1971. A fugitive arrest warrant was issued, and Maenza was subsequently arrested on June 4, 1971. He had about $1,000 in cash on his person and no identification papers. He was released on a $4,500 bond. On August 2, 1971, Maenza failed to appear for an arraignment in federal court. Judge Bernard Decker issued a bench warrant for Maenza's arrest for contempt of court, failure to appear, and ordered Maenza's $4,500 bond forfeited. On August 3, 1971, Anthony Maenza was rearrested without incident. Following a two-day jury trial, on November 9, 1971, Maenza was found guilty as charged on the FHA violation and was sentenced to one year in prison and fined $500. An appeal bond was set at $10,000.

During the fugitive investigation to locate and arrest Anthony Maenza in June of 1971, SA Cavanagh made an astute observation. He determined that Anthony Maenza was treated as an in-patient for several weeks at the Oak Park, Illinois, hospital while using his brother's name, Michael Maenza, and his Metropolitan Health Insurance Policy. Maenza's medical expenses exceeded several thousand dollars, which was billed to and paid for by his brother's insurance company. This matter was turned over to the Illinois Bureau of Investigation (IBI). On September 1, 1972, Anthony Maenza was indicted by a Special Cook County grand jury on charges of theft by fraud. Maenza was arrested by the IBI on September 6, 1972. Following a two-day bench trial, Maenza was found guilty as charged on September 24, 1974. C-1 agents provided detailed information about Maenza in local court. It was anticipated that Maenza, because of his previous criminal record, would receive a prison sentence for this local violation. On October 25, 1974, Cook County Circuit Court Judge Frank J. Wilson sentenced Anthony Maenza to four years on probation and ordered Maenza to make restitution. Maenza was defended in this case by Jack Cerone Jr., son of hoodlum leader Jack Cerone. It should be noted that Judge Wilson was also the presiding judge who acquitted mobster Harry Aleman of murder charges during a bench trial in 1977 because of an alleged $10,000 bribe. Judge Wilson later committed suicide after this bribe scheme was made public.

JAMES "THE BOMBER" CATUARA ET AL.

James "The Bomber" Catuara was a prominent leader of organized crime in southern Cook County, Illinois. He also operated one of the largest stolen auto and "chop shop" operations on Chicago's South Side. In 1972, information was received from a C-1 source that Catuara was planning to travel to Phoenix, Arizona, using his 1971 Cadillac Eldorado. Investigation into this matter determined that the Cadillac driven by Catuara was a stolen vehicle. He was allowed to travel from Chicago to Phoenix and return, and he continued to maintain possession of the stolen vehicle. On May 25, 1972, a federal grand jury in Chicago returned an indictment charging James Catuara with violating the federal interstate stolen vehicle statute. Catuara was arrested by Chicago agents at his Oak Lawn, Illinois, residence without incident and released on bond. Unfortunately for Catuara, he lost favor with mob rivalries in the chop shop operation; and on July 28, 1978, while seated in his red Cadillac, he was killed in gangland fashion at Hubbard and Ogden in Chicago.

WILLIAM DAUBER ET AL.

William Dauber, a.k.a. Billy, was a notorious hit man associated with the Chicago far south side hoodlum group of James "The Bomber" Catuara. Dauber was reportedly responsible for more than thirty gangland killings. In 1973, William Dauber and three of his cohorts transported a stolen Cadillac from Indiana to Illinois after they had reportedly murdered the car owner in Indiana. Dauber was part of Jimmy Catuara's South Side "Chop Shop" operation that involved the stealing of cars and the selling of cars with stolen parts to auto outlets. On March 30, 1973, Dauber, Steven Ostrowski, John Schnadenberg, and Joseph Malek were found guilty in federal court in Chicago for violating the federal interstate stolen vehicle statute. On April 3, 1973, Judge Julius Hoffman sentenced subjects as follows:

- Dauber: five years on each of two counts to be served consecutively with each other and consecutive with a prior six-year sentence plus fines of $7,500
- Ostrowski, Schnadenberg, and Malek: five years on each of two counts to be served consecutively plus fines ranging from $5,000 to $7,500

Judge Hoffman further imposed a $120,000 surety bond on each subject pending their appeals. Contributing to the success of the Catuara and Dauber cases were C-1 agents John Oitzinger, Frank Ford, William F. Roemer, and Merle Hamre. It should be noted that Steven Ostrowsky was killed in a gangland fashion on October 5, 1976. Also, William Dauber and his wife, Charlotte, were killed in their car in gangland style on July 2, 1980, after a high-speed chase, by convicted hoodlum murderer Frank Calabrese, now deceased.

LEONARD PATRICK ET AL.

Leonard Patrick had been one of the upper echelon members of organized crime and a gambling boss and enforcer on Chicago's North Side for decades. Patrick was one of the original ten top hoodlums selected for investigation under the Top Hoodlum Program in 1957.

In 1973, C-1 agent John Osborne, who had performed extraordinarily well in the Town Hall police corruption case, was also responsible for uncovering a multimillion-dollar Chicago North Side gambling operation under the control of Leonard Patrick. Agent Osborne, with significant assistance from SAs Robert Long, Robert Malone, Herbert Briick, Paul Neumann, Joseph Doyle, William Hermann, and other C-1 agents, obtained a court-approved Title III electronic coverage on a key wire room that was determined to be one of the largest of its kind. This group was handling an estimated $1,500,000 in bets each month. Search warrants were prepared by Strike Force Attorney Michael King and executed by C-1 agents. Suppressed grand jury indictments followed charging eight members of Leonard Patrick's operation with violating the federal gambling statute. Arrested on April 23, 1974, were well-known gamblers Anthony Tito, Harold Kasten, Stephen Price, Morris Klotz, Joseph Tognotti, Norman Rottenberg, Arthur Sommerfield, and Louis Kopple.

Additional federal grand jury hearings into this matter continued. Leonard Patrick was called before this grand jury. As a result of Patrick's testimony, the IRS filed a jeopardy assessment against Patrick's assets and the assets of his deceased bookmaking partner, Ben Epstein, in the amount of $865,000. Patrick also testified that he paid Chicago Police Lieutenant Ronald O'Hara $500 per month for protection against gambling raids in 1968 and 1969. Lieutenant O'Hara was called before the grand jury and denied he had ever received any money from Patrick. Lieutenant O'Hara was subsequently indicted for perjury, and Patrick was to be the key witness against O'Hara. During the trial of O'Hara, Leonard Patrick refused to testify. Patrick was granted immunity and still refused to testify and was subsequently held in contempt of court. According to Patrick's attorney, Patrick's refusal to testify was based on threats reportedly made by Lieutenant O'Hara against Patrick and his family. On October 22, 1975, Patrick was found guilty of contempt of court and was sentenced to four years in prison by Federal Judge Prentice Marshall. This case dealt a major blow to the Chicago mob's North Side gambling operation. The Chicago news media afforded this case considerable attention because of the prominent role of Leonard Patrick as a hoodlum gambling boss. This case culminated a four-year investigation by case agent John Osborne and other C-1 agents, and it was skillfully guided and prosecuted by Chief of the Strike Force Peter F. Vaira and AUSA Gregory Ward.

THEFT AT PUROLATOR ARMORED EXPRESS VAULT, CHICAGO, ILLINOIS

On October 20, 1974, Purolator Company officials and Chicago firefighters responded to a smoke alarm from inside the vault of the Purolator Security Inc., Armored Express Service at 127 W. Huron Street, Chicago, Illinois. It was determined that thieves had robbed the company vault of $4.3 million in cash, which was believed to be the nation's largest cash theft in US history. The thieves tried to set fire to the remaining contents in the vault to conceal the theft; however, the fire had burned itself out because of the lack of oxygen. The smoldering flames were extinguished, and the company was able to recover $36 million in cash that had been left behind. Investigation centered around Ralph Ronald Marrera, the lone Purolator guard on duty on the night of theft. He had failed a polygraph exam. Investigation determined that he had planned and executed this theft with three other thieves who were subsequently identified. C-1 agents Merle Hamre and Frank Ford assisted case agent Ramon Stratton and played a vital role in this historical case. They were able to obtain a detailed confession from one of the suspected thieves named Peter Gushi, a prominent member of organized crime and a close associate of hoodlum leader James "the Bomber" Catuara. Gushi pleaded guilty to twelve counts of bank burglary, bank larceny, and interstate transportation of stolen property. The C-1 agents also convinced Gushi to testify as a government witness against the other subjects in US District Court in Chicago. Gushi was the star witness against Ralph Marrera, James Maniatis, and Pasquale Marzano; and all received prison sentences. Marzano was the expert who was able to beat the locks on safes and vaults. Peter Gushi and his family were placed under the Federal Witness Protection Program by the US Marshal's office. All of the $4.3 million in cash had been recovered and/or accounted for, with the exception of about $600,000, in what had been described as the biggest cash heist in US history.

THE KILLING
OF VALERIE PERCY

Valerie Percy, the lovely twenty-one-year-old twin daughter of former Illinois Senator Charles Percy, was brutally murdered during the early morning hours of September 18, 1966, at the Percy mansion in Kenilworth, Illinois. According to recent news accounts, the murder of Valerie Percy remained unsolved, and a reward of $100,000 was being offered by the Percy family for any information leading to the arrest and conviction of the person or persons responsible for the murder. Senator Percy had purchased this spacious seventeen-room, three-acre lakefront Kenilworth estate in 1950. It was later sold to an executive of Baxter Labs when the Percy family moved to Washington State. The property was again sold in 2008 and was demolished in 2010 by the new owner, who developed the land for a new home. The demolition of the Percy home reawakened national attention on one of America's great unsolved murder mysteries. Senator Percy had five children. He married Lorraine Percy after the death of his first wife Jeanne, who was the mother of the twins Valerie and Sharon, and their son, Roger. Sharon, an identical twin, married John "Jay" Rockefeller IV, a US senator from West Virginia. Percy's daughter, Valerie, was a charming and vivacious young lady in the prime of life. She was a graduate of New Trier High School in Winnetka, Illinois, and completed her studies at Cornell University. During the summer of 1966, she was campaigning with her father Charles Percy, who was running as a Republican for the US senate in Illinois in the fall. Charles Percy had been employed at Bell & Howell and eventually took over as president and chief executive officer at the age of twenty-nine. He was described as a boy wonder. Following the murder of his daughter Valerie, Charles Percy was elected US senator in Illinois in November 1966. He was considered by some to be a future candidate for president of the United States. Senator Percy died on September 17, 2011, in Washington State at the age of ninety-one.

Sometime around five o'clock on a quiet Sunday morning on the eighteenth of September, 1966, an intruder apparently entered the Percy estate through the patio French doors. Access was gained by breaking a glass panel of the door. The intruder proceeded to the second floor and entered the bedroom of Valerie Percy. It appeared that he may have awakened Valerie from her sleep, and she was brutally beaten with a blunt instrument and then stabbed more than a dozen times as she lay in bed. She fought back, but in vain. Valerie's stepmother, Lorraine Percy, told police that she was awakened that morning by moaning sounds coming from Valerie's bedroom. As she entered Valerie's bedroom, she observed the outline of a man standing over Valerie's bed with a flashlight in hand shining on Valerie's bloodied body. The intruder fled the house through the same French doors leading to the patio.

The police were immediately summoned, and an intensive and exhaustive investigation was conducted in an attempt to identify the intruder, with no positive results to date. Nothing of any value was reportedly taken from the Percy mansion. The police gathered evidence at the scene, which included several unidentified palm prints from the residence. The Chicago office of the FBI made the services of the FBI laboratory available and offered their services to the police in the handling of any investigative leads as needed on an interstate and nationwide basis. As supervisor of the C-1 Organized Crime Squad in Chicago, our confidential sources were alerted to report any and all information that could assist in the solution of this high-profile case. Following several years of extensive investigation by the Kenilworth police, no subjects or suspects were identified as being involved in the murder of Valerie Percy. Because of the relatively small size of the Kenilworth Police Department and to alleviate the tremendous investigative burden of such a major criminal case, it was decided to transfer the primary investigative responsibility of this major case to a special Illinois State Police Task Force headed by Sergeant Robert Lamb in Lake County, Illinois.

During February 1973, the Chicago office of the FBI at 219 S. Dearborn Street had a very unusual visitor who identified himself to the receptionist as Mr. Leo Rugendorf. He asked to speak with Agent Lenard Wolf or Mr. Vince Inserra. Because Len Wolf was not available having been recently transferred to the San Diego office of the FBI, I was somewhat surprised to learn of Leo Rugendorf's presence at the FBI office, especially because he appeared on a voluntary basis and was not accompanied by an attorney. Leo Rugendorf was a prominent member of the Chicago mob who had been convicted along with three of his associates in a large bankruptcy fraud conspiracy case involving the Sterling-Harris Ford Agency in Chicago during the late 1960s. Rugendorf received a sentence of one year in prison, which was later reduced to six months because of his poor health. The case received nationwide attention because of the magnitude of the fraud, when three hundred cars disappeared from the agency car lot over one weekend in 1961. The mastermind behind this case was reported to be mob boss and enforcer "Milwaukee Phil" Alderisio, to whom Leo Rugendorf reported.

Rugendorf had also been recently arrested by the FBI in connection with an interstate jewelry heist in which he participated and the case was pending. Not knowing what to expect I went out to the reception area and greeted Rugendorf and escorted him back to my private office. Rugendorf remembered me from the

Sterling-Harris Ford Agency fraud case because I had testified in this case against him. He told me that agent Lenard Wolf, and I had always treated him courteously, and he wanted to return the favor. Rugendorf said that he was going to make me "famous" by providing me with information on a matter that would make me a "hero." I was flattered by his remarks and had absolutely no idea what he was talking about. He said that he was going to tell me who murdered Valerie Percy in the late 1960s. He then identified Frank Hohimer (true name Francis Leroy Hohimer), a notorious career home invader, as the person being responsible for the break-in at the Percy residence and the murder of Valerie Percy. Rugendorf claimed that Hohimer had admitted this crime to him. He explained to me that Valerie was awakened by Hohimer during the early morning hours, and he beat and stabbed her to death to silence her. As further proof of Hohimer's involvement, Rugendorf said that Hohimer had placed a phone call from the Percy residence sometime prior to the time of the murder to Rugendorf's Twin Foods Products Company in Chicago, when Hohimer was actually casing the Percy residence. Rugendorf claimed that Hohimer spoke to him from the Percy residence and that a check of the phone records from the Percy residence would reveal this fact and place Hohimer at the scene of the crime. It was later reported by the Illinois State Police that a phone call was in fact made from the Percy residence to Rugendorf's place of business in Chicago.

It was noted that Twin Foods was a hoodlum-dominated enterprise and that Chicago hoodlum mobsters Sam Battaglia, Milwaukee Phil Alderisio, Albert "Obie" Frabotta, and Marshall Caifano reportedly held a financial interest in the company along with Rugendorf. Rugendorf was asked why he chose to report this information on Frank Hohimer after all these years. It was obvious to me that Leo Rugendorf, who had the reputation of being a major mob fence of stolen jewelry and property, apparently had a falling out with Hohimer and was seeking some sort of retribution. It was highly unlikely that a person of Rugendorf's reputation with the Chicago mob would suddenly turn informant and openly volunteer to cooperate with the authorities against a top jewel thief and home invader like Frank Hohimer. Rugendorf claimed that he was terminally ill and did not have much longer to live and wanted me to get credit for the solution of this case. I thanked him for the information and the trust he placed in me; however, it was explained to him that the FBI did not have primary jurisdiction in the Percy case because the crime of murder was primarily the responsibility of local and state authorities. Also, this information would be turned over to the Illinois State Police, who were now handling the Percy murder case, and that they would undoubtedly want to talk to him further on this matter. Rugendorf expressed no objection in cooperating with or giving a statement to the Illinois State Police, and he departed on very friendly terms.

It was readily apparent that Leo Rugendorf was not providing this information to me and the FBI out of the kindness of his heart, but he obviously had a falling out with Frank Hohimer, and this was his way of seeking revenge. This obviously had to do with a case in which Frank Hohimer and his burglary associates Leonard B. Ricketson and Colin W. Green were involved. It was a home invasion of an Indianapolis executive on June 16, 1967. Jewelry and other valuables totaling about $200,000 were stolen. Just prior to the expiration of the federal statute of limitations in this case, Chicago FBI agents were able to identify the subjects of this interstate theft. On January 25, 1972, the federal grand jury in Chicago returned a three-count indictment charging Leo Rugendorf, Frank Hohimer, Leonard Ricketson, and Colin Green with violating the Interstate Transportation of Stolen Property statute. All subjects were subsequently arrested by the FBI. Hohimer and Green entered guilty pleas and became government witnesses. Hohimer implicated Leo Rugendorf, whom he claimed planned the home invasion. According to Hohimer, on the day following the theft, Rugendorf visited Hohimer's apartment in Chicago and gave him $20,000 in cash for the jewelry. Hohimer then paid his brother Wayne $50, Green $200, and Ricketson $700, and kept the balance. Ricketson was found guilty and received a three-year sentence to run concurrent with a five— to ten-year state charge for burglary. Hohimer also implicated Leo Rugendorf in a similar home invasion robbery in Denver Colorado. Rugendorf was eventually severed from the Indianapolis robbery theft trial because of bad health, and he died before his trial took place. It was obvious that Leo Rugendorf was retaliating against Frank Hohimer for implicating him in these two major home invasion thefts. His information, however, about Valerie Percy was very credible; and he was willing to testify against Hohimer. It was a falling out among thieves. Also, since his hoodlum boss Milwaukee Phil Alderisio had died in prison in September 1971, Rugendorf had no compunction about testifying as a government witness.

Immediately following the departure of Leo Rugendorf from the Chicago FBI office, I phoned Sergeant Robert Lamb of the Illinois State Police, whom I knew on a personal basis, and relayed all of the details of my conversation with Leo Rugendorf about the Valerie Percy murder. I also told him that Rugendorf was in poor health and had agreed to cooperate with the Illinois State Police as soon as possible. Sergeant Lamb assured me that this matter would be given his personal, immediate, and continuous attention. Leo Rugendorf was subsequently interviewed by the Illinois State Police and basically confirmed the same information that I had provided to him.

A short time later, I learned from Art Petacque, a prominent *Chicago Sun Times* crime reporter, that Leo Rugendorf had also contacted him at the newspaper. Rugendorf was also interviewed by Art Petacque and his partner Hugh Hough. Rugendorf told them all about the alleged involvement of Frank Hohimer in the Valerie Percy murder. Art Petacque was a good friend of the Chicago FBI office and was an excellent source of intelligence information on the Chicago mob. Petacque was also personally acquainted with Rugendorf, and we compared notes on the information provided by Leo Rugendorf. We were both convinced that Rugendorf's information was very credible and that Rugendorf would not have informed on

Hohimer unless he had personal knowledge of Hohimer's involvement in this crime. Petacque was also alerted to the fact that Rugendorf's information had been referred to the Illinois State Police, and they were pursuing Hohimer as a key suspect. Time was of the essence because Rugendorf was in poor health, and according to Rugendorf, he did not have too much longer to live. Rugendorf was suffering from heart disease and had a serious diabetic condition.

The *Chicago Sun Times* subsequently conducted an extensive investigation and published a series of articles that named Frank Hohimer as the alleged killer of Valerie Percy. Art Petacque, Hugh Hough, and the *Sun Times* won a Pulitzer Prize for reporting on a series of articles on the Valerie Percy case. Frank Hohimer was currently serving a thirty-year sentence for a series of home invasions in Denver and Indianapolis, both FBI cases in which Rugendorf was involved. According to Art Petacque, Hohimer's brother, a used car salesman, also told Petacque and the *Sun Times* that Frank Hohimer had confessed to him that he, Frank, was involved in the Valerie Percy murder. Petacque also advised that he and Hugh Hough interviewed Frank Hohimer in prison, and he denied the killing of Valerie Percy but conveniently identified his partner in crime, Fred Malchow, as being responsible for the Percy murder. Malchow was a known vicious home invader and a hard-core career criminal from Buffalo, New York. The only problem with the Hohimer revelation was that Malchow was already dead and had died while fleeing from a prison break in Pennsylvania along with his cellmate, Jimmy Evans. Malchow had been described as a psychopathic cold-blooded killer. During his prison escape, he fell while crossing a train trestle and was killed. Jimmy Evans reportedly claimed that Malchow admitted to him, while in jail, that he was involved with the killing of Valerie Percy. It was also reported that Fred Malchow once boasted of having been involved in a jewel burglary at the home of actress Zsa Zsa Gabor in California. In 1978, Frank Hohimer wrote a book entitled *The Home Invaders: Confessions of a Cat Burglar*. It was the basis of a 1981 film named *Thief*, starring actor James Caan.

Today, the Valerie Percy killing may be largely forgotten but remains as one of America's notable unsolved murder mysteries. The Kenilworth, Illinois, Police Department still considers the case open and unsolved. With the passing of Leo Rugendorf, shortly after divulging pertinent and critical information in this case, and with the death of Fred Malchow, it is not very likely that this murder case will ever be solved with a conviction. It is unfortunate that the state or local authorities did not consider the timely impaneling of a local grand jury to investigate all aspects of the Percy killing by placing key witnesses under oath and documenting all of the facts in this case so that the truth could be determined. Leo Rugendorf, a prominent Chicago mobster, was ready and willing to testify under oath, including the phone call he received from Hohimer from the Percy residence. There were other potential witnesses who reportedly made claims about the notorious home invaders, Frank Hohimer and Fred Malchow, as being involved in this murder conspiracy. I think we missed a great opportunity.

Various Gangland Slayings According to Leo Rugendorf

Upon the conclusion of my conversation with Leo Rugendorf in the Chicago FBI office regarding the Valerie Percy murder, I casually asked him if he had any information on any other killings in the Chicago area that he would like to share with me. Rugendorf did not hesitate and voluntarily furnished the following information:

David Zatz (murdered on May 5, 1952), a local North Side bookmaker, was the bag man for the police commander at the Wilson Avenue Police District. Zatz was demanding more protection payoff money from Phil Alderisio and Albert "Obie" Frabotta for allowing gambling to operate in that district. They refused to increase the monthly police payoffs, and the police began to close down some of their operations. The mob retaliated against Zatz and killed him at his residence. He was on his knees crying for mercy when Alderisio and Frabotta took care of him. Zatz was stuffed in the trunk of his car. Walter Spritz took over for Zatz as the bag man for that district and has since passed away.

Paul Labriola a.k.a. "Needle Nose" and James Weinberg (murdered March 15, 1954) were small-time hoodlums who used the outfit's reputation to muscle in on certain activities. They were set up by Gerald Covelli, a well-known Rush Street hoodlum and hit man, and Joseph "Ruffy" Lisciandrella, a North Side enforcer. (Labriola and Weinberg were found stuffed in the trunk of a car. They had been drugged, strangled, and shot.)

Roger Touhy (murdered December 16, 1959), a rival gang mobster, who was killed immediately following his release from prison as he was leaving his home in Chicago, accompanied by his bodyguard, a retired Chicago police officer. Phil Alderisio and Obie Frabotta took care of him because he was a potential threat to their operations.

Arthur Adler bought the Trade Winds nightclub in the Chicago Rush Street area during the early 1950s. John "Mimi" Capone, brother of Al Capone, muscled his way into the nightclub; and the ownership was a front for the mob. The Trade Winds was a nightly meeting place for many prominent Chicago hoodlums. Adler was stealing from the club, and the club was in serious financial condition. Adler sold the club in 1959. No money was exchanged at the time of the sale, only the assumption of debts. Marshall Caifano, Phil Alderisio, Obie Frabotta, and Sam Battaglia were responsible for the demise of Arthur Adler. (Adler disappeared on January 20, 1960, and his nude body was discovered stuffed in a sewer on March 28, 1960, by two city sewer inspectors at 1625 N. Neva Street, Chicago, Illinois.)

Kenneth Gordon (murdered June 7, 1963) was an ex-convict and Chicago thief, whose father, Meyer Gordon, was one of the biggest fences of stolen jewelry in the country. Kenneth Gordon was known to have set up dozens of jewelry scores and was suspected of tipping off the police on one score. Chicago enforcer and well-known hit man, Frankie "The German" Schweihs, was responsible for the killing of Kenny Gordon.

Gerald Covelli (murdered June 18, 1967) was a well-known Chicago Rush Street hoodlum and enforcer. He became involved as a government witness in a federal case and left the Chicago area for California. Milwaukee Phil ordered the hit on Covelli. Ronnie DeAngeles, the Chicago mob's electronic expert, located Covelli in Encino, California, and rigged his car with a bomb that killed him.

Arthur "Boodie" Cowan (murdered July 12, 1967) was a Chicago bookmaker and loan shark collector for hoodlum North Side gambling boss Leonard Patrick. He was suspected of stealing mob funds from his collections. He was found in the trunk of his car with a bullet in his head. This killing was performed by Leonard Patrick and his partner and enforcer, Dave Yaras.

Alan Rosenberg (murdered March 17, 1967) was a loan shark collector and a "scam" operator who was a close associate of Milwaukee Phil Alderisio. Rosenberg was brought into the hoodlum organization by Irwin S. Weiner, a Chicago bail bondsman and close associate of Chicago hoodlums. Alderisio was the best man at Rosenberg's wedding, but he became a huge liability and fell in disfavor with Alderiso with all of his swindles. Alderisio and Obie Frabotta were responsible for his killing. (Rosenberg's 325-pound handcuffed body was found in the backseat of his car with six bullet wounds in the chest and one in the back of the head.)

TOP ECHELON CRIMINAL INFORMANT PROGRAM (TECIP)

It is a well-established fact that live, confidential informant coverage or confidential human sources are an absolute necessity when it comes to dealing with criminal, national security, or counterterrorism matters. Confidential informants have been the lifeblood of the FBI in developing cases within the areas of investigative jurisdiction. The successes achieved over the years far outweigh the occasional unfortunate setbacks received along the way. In August of 1963, the bureau initiated the Top Echelon Criminal Informant Program (TECIP) in an effort to further penetrate the upper echelon of organized crime. The program had several inherent flaws. Normally, informants had to be advised of, and agree to, a number of conditions prior to being designated as an informant of the FBI. Some of the conditions were as follows:

> Their relationship with the FBI would be held in the strictest of confidence.
> They would not involve themselves in any criminal activity.
> A certification had to be made that the informant had shown no indication
> of emotional instability or unreliability.

The conditions set forth above were difficult to adhere to on its face, because you're attempting to infiltrate or penetrate the upper echelon of organized crime by telling potential informants not to become involved in criminal activity. It was logical to assume that any important member of organized crime would already be involved in criminal activity, and to tell him not to get involved in criminal activity was questionable.

BOBBY RUSSO

With regard to the development of informants under the TECIP in 1963, I received a telephone call from an individual whom we will refer to by the pseudonym of Bobby Russo. He was calling from the local Cook County, Illinois, jail where he was being held on bad check charges. He offered his services to the FBI in return for help in effecting his release from jail. I assigned C-1 agent Dennis Shanahan to contact Bobby Russo, so that we could evaluate his value to the FBI as a possible confidential informant. Following the interview with Russo, SA Shanahan reported that Russo could be useful to the FBI under the TECIP because of his knowledge and association with members of organized crime in Chicago. Bobby Russo was subsequently released from jail and provided a wealth of criminal intelligence information on the Chicago mob and their gambling activities. He had agreed to all of the conditions as required of a criminal informant under the TECIP. I was the alternate contacting agent with Dennis Shanahan as the principal handler. As time went on, Bobby Russo preferred dealing with me, so I took over and became his primary handler, which was an unusual situation for a supervisor. From 1963 and for the next thirteen years, until my retirement from the FBI in 1976, Bobby Russo developed into one of the most productive informants in the Chicago Division and had received cash payments from time to time based on the value of the information furnished. It was a mutually beneficial relationship over the years. Russo provided voluminous information on organized crime and their gambling activities as well as official corruption matters that resulted in hundreds of arrests and convictions in state and federal courts. His infiltration of various criminal elements and the gathering of highly sensitive information, while exposing himself to great physical danger, was truly remarkable.

In about 1966, he and his partner testified as government witnesses in federal court in Chicago in a large jewelry bankruptcy scam operation. Convictions were obtained on his testimony without disclosing Russo's relationship as an FBI informant. Russo's partner also testified and was subsequently killed in gangland fashion. Russo and his family had received numerous threatening phone calls on their lives. Notwithstanding this intimidation, Russo courageously continued his confidential relationship with the FBI and continued to provide outstanding information on all phases of organized criminal activity that was not available through other sources.

In 1973, Bobby Russo provided information regarding an independent insurance claim adjuster whom we will refer to as Tony, who was involved in a counterfeit money operation that was printing $20, $50, and $100 bills. This information was provided to the US Secret Service and resulted in five arrests in the Cleveland, Ohio, area based solely on information provided by Russo. Tony, the insurance claim adjuster, was also reportedly involved in an arson ring conspiracy to burn down buildings and collect fire insurance. Tony, as a claim adjuster, reportedly had contacts in the Bomb and Arson squad who would give him a favorable police report when needed. The adjuster would handle the fire loss for the benefit of the claimant. In 1974, Bobby Russo identified three arson fires that were connected with Tony the adjuster. I warned informant Russo several times not to get personally involved in these arson cases because the repercussions from these crimes could be devastating, and there would be little I could do to help him. He reassured me that he was only acting as a disinterested outsider and was not involved in any way. Based on specific information provided by informant Russo, I opened a new interstate arson case for investigation on Tony, the insurance claim adjuster, and others involved in this conspiracy. I assigned the case to C-1 agent Joseph P. Doyle, who was one of my more proficient and accomplished investigators on the squad. After months of intensive investigation into the arson case, SA Doyle reported to me that informant Bobby Russo not only was involved in the arson conspiracy but was also acting as the "agent provocateur." This information stunned me. I knew that it could be a huge problem for me as Russo's handler for thirteen years and for the FBI. It could not have come at a worse time, because I was in the process of retiring from the FBI after twenty-five years of service. I immediately closed the informant file and had no further contact with Russo. I knew that this case would eventually come back to haunt me. My fears would be realized shortly after my departure from the FBI. For the time being, I decided to let the arson conspiracy case run its course without any interference on my part.

JAMES "WHITEY" BULGER

One of the most tragic and egregious cases of informant development under the TECIP had to do with James "Whitey" Bulger," who was prosecuted in 2013 in the Boston area on numerous counts of racketeering including nineteen murders. This case was a classic example of the perils associated with the development of confidential informants and for FBI agents who become too closely attached to their informants. Whitey Bulger was the leader of the Winter Hill gang, an Irish mob from South Boston, Massachusetts, who became a longtime informant of the FBI beginning from about 1975 to 1990. His handler was an FBI agent named John Connolly. Over the years, Connolly claimed that Bulger was providing the FBI with vital information about the Italian mob in the Boston area. In the meantime, Bulger and his notorious gang members were obviously involved in widespread criminal activities including narcotics, gambling, money laundering, and more than fifty brutal gangland murders, while enjoying the apparent protection resulting from their FBI informant status. Bulger and agent Connolly, as well as Connolly's organized crime supervisor, John Morris, developed a close personal relationship with Bulger and others that made Connolly and Morris vulnerable to being exploited by Bulger and his associates. This included dinners, lavish gifts, and cash payoffs to the agents, reportedly totaling more than $200,000. In return, Connolly was reported to have leaked information to Bulger and his lieutenant Steven "the Rifleman" Flemmi, about government witnesses who were going to testify against them. Several of these witnesses were subsequently murdered. In 2002, agent Connolly was convicted of racketeering and obstruction of justice for furnishing confidential information to Bulger, which caused Bulger to flee from the authorities. While agent Connolly was serving a ten-year sentence, he was also convicted in 2009 on a second-degree murder conspiracy charge in Florida and was sentenced to an additional forty-year prison term. Bulger, having been alerted by Connolly of impending charges against him, fled from the Boston area to avoid prosecution and had been a fugitive for sixteen years. The FBI offered a $1 million reward for information leading to his arrest. On June 22, 2011, Whitey Bulger was located and arrested in Santa Monica, California, in the company of his longtime girlfriend Catherine Greig. An arsenal of weapons was also seized hidden in his apartment. Bulger was subsequently tried on a thirty-three-count indictment in Boston, which included racketeering and nineteen charges of murder. Bulger's seven-hundred-page FBI informant file, which was originally declared confidential and had never been seen before by the public, had been introduced by the defense as evidence. Bulger claimed that he was never an FBI informant. That claim was contradicted by the volumes of information furnished to the FBI by Bulger as well as the testimony of his accomplices. The defense claimed that these files were a fabrication and focused primarily on the corruption of the FBI agents. Even though the prosecutors presented over seventy witnesses who testified against Bulger, the defense attorneys hammered away on the corruption of the two FBI agents that allegedly allowed the murders and criminal activities of Bulger and his henchmen to take place. The Boston news media unfairly characterized the entire Boston FBI office as corrupt and did an injustice to all of the dedicated and hardworking agents and personnel in the Boston office. Bulger claimed that a former prosecutor, now deceased, gave him immunity to commit crimes, which was totally absurd. The judge refused to allow it as a defense. Former ASAC Robert Fitzgerald of the Boston FBI Division, who had been called as a witness by the defense, had previously recommended that the informant file on Whitey Bulger be closed for obvious reasons; but he was overruled by his superiors. It was unfortunate that his sage advice to delete Whitey Bulger as an informant was not heeded. The reputation of the FBI office in Boston had been unfairly tarnished by the revelations resulting from the continuing saga of the Whitey Bulger case. On August 12, 2013, the jury found James "Whitey" Bulger guilty on a thirty-two-count indictment that included a pattern of racketeering involving murder, extortion, money laundering, drug dealing, weapons charges, and conspiracy; and that Bulger took part in eleven of these murders. On November 14, 2013, Bulger, who was eighty-four years of age, was sentenced to serve two life terms, which guaranteed that he will spend the rest of his life in prison because Massachusetts is not a capital punishment state.

FBI informants should never be allowed to involve themselves in violent crimes under any circumstances. Former Boston ASAC Robert Fitzgerald was obviously aware of the perils associated with the notorious criminal activities of Bulger and his gang and received no support from any of his superiors to delete Bulger as an informant. Whitey Bulger, a ruthless and major organized crime figure and his gang, should have been subjects of an intensive criminal investigation by the FBI rather than treated as FBI informants under the TECIP. Where was the oversight by those who provided supervision to this program? It appeared that they failed to adhere to their own guidelines. Even more disturbing had been the conduct of the prosecuting attorneys in Boston for negotiating the release from prison of Bulger's partner and confessed killer John Martorano after having served only twelve years for committing twenty murders. That's incredible. That was Martorano's reward for having testified in court against Whitey Bulger and former FBI agent Connolly. They even reportedly supplied Martorano with government funds to help him get started upon his release from jail. Martorano had been glamorized by the news media for having written a book with movie rights about his twenty murders and criminal activities. The book was entitled *Hitman: The Untold Story of Johnny Martorano*. It had been reported that Martorano profited by more than $300,000 from slaying others. In addition and equally as bizarre, Kevin Weeks, another Bulger enforcer who testified against Bulger and agent Connolly, only served five years in prison for having committed five murders. Incredible! Meanwhile, former FBI agent John Connolly, while serving a ten-year sentence for obstruction of justice in Boston, was also sentenced to forty years in Florida on a second-degree murder conspiracy charge. Agent Connolly languishes in jail probably for the rest of his natural life on murder charges that he had relatively little to do with. He was convicted solely on the testimony of these vicious convicted murderers and has been subjected to excessive and unreasonable punishment that vastly exceeds his indiscretions. Agent Connolly's offenses have been bloodless and pale by comparison to Bulger and his gang of killers. Is there truly equal justice under the law when the fairness of the criminal justice system is most seriously questioned? To lessen the likelihood of these informant incidents from happening, FBI headquarters issued new stringent guidelines regarding the handling of confidential informants or confidential human sources. The problem remains, however, because these criminal informants are a different breed of individual. They are extremely difficult to manage or control and are not completely reliable or emotionally stable. Because information is the lifeblood of the investigative process, informants remain a critical necessity for the FBI, but with proper supervision and oversight.

Addendum—Immediately prior to the publication of this book, a Florida state appeals court made an astonishing, but a long awaited decision on May 28, 2014, regarding the 2009 second-degree murder conviction, of former FBI agent John Connolly, with a gun, for which he is serving a forty year sentence in prison. In a 2 to 1 decision the court reversed the murder conviction and ruled that Connolly was wrongly convicted because the jurors relied too much on flawed charges against him. In addition, the court pointed out that Connolly did not carry or fire the weapon that was used to kill victim John Callahan, president of World Jai Alai in Florida in 1982. It was previously established that mobster, John Martorano, who confessed to twenty murders, and who has since been released from custody, admitted that he used his own gun to kill Callahan. Hopefully, John Connolly will soon be released from jail pending an appeal by Florida prosecutors. It appears that justice for John Connolly may finally prevail in this case.

FBI Retirement

In 1976, retirement for FBI agents was allowed when one reached the age of fifty and had completed at least twenty years of satisfactory service. Mandatory retirement also became effective when an agent reached the age of fifty-five. So when agents became eligible to retire, they were actively seeking another job as a second career before the FBI terminated their services. Those were the cold hard facts. I had received a number of job offers from various local and federal agencies, which I had turned down, because they were temporary in nature or politically connected. I was looking to find employment in the private sector. In 1975, I received a call from James Harding, a casual acquaintance of mine who at the time was the chief financial officer of the Kemper Insurance Companies in Long Grove, Illinois. He invited me to lunch and offered me a position with Kemper as director of Internal Security. He explained that the former director passed away about three years prior and had not been replaced. Financial problems were occurring internally at Kemper that were consuming too much of the time of the top executives addressing these problems. The job sounded promising; however, we could not agree on a starting salary and parted company. One year later, James Harding called me again and said that he was still looking for a director of Internal Security. He had interviewed a number of law enforcement officers and was not completely satisfied with their credentials. I told him that we had been down this road before. He told me to come on out to Kemper and we would work out the details. In February of 1976, I met with James Harding and Rudolph Landolt, then president of Kemper Insurance, and they made me a generous offer as director of Internal Security, which I accepted without any hesitation. This was precisely the type of employment I was seeking as a second career. They made me an officer of the company, provided me with a company car, and gave me the responsibility and full authority to handle all matters involving internal fraud, theft, and embezzlement on a national and international basis. Little did I realize at the time that I would be spending the next twenty-seven years with Kemper after having completed twenty-five years of service with the FBI.

KEMPER INSURANCE COMPANIES, LONG GROVE, ILLINOIS

$\mathbf{M}$y very last day with the FBI was February 17, 1976. On the very next day, I reported for work at the Kemper Insurance Companies in Long Grove, Illinois. I didn't skip one day. I was anxious to start my second career. What a huge change in the environment, from the bustling congestion of the downtown area of Chicago to the beautifully landscaped suburban headquarters of the Kemper complex, occupying almost one thousand acres of scenic property, with lakes, ponds, and har-tru tennis courts, located about forty miles north and west of Chicago. Just the sight of the property lowered my blood pressure. James S. Kemper Sr. founded the company in 1912 and served as the US ambassador to Brazil under President Dwight Eisenhower. His son, James S. Kemper Jr., took over as chairman and CEO in 1969 and expanded the traditional property and casualty business to include risk management services, reinsurance, health and life insurance, and a major financial services company. It employed almost eight thousand employees and operated countrywide and in many foreign markets. In 1971, it was James Kemper Jr.'s decision to move Kemper's headquarters from a Chicago location to this magnificent sprawling suburban complex. Jim Kemper was certainly a man of vision for Kemper Insurance.

It did not take long for my FBI past to catch up with me during my second career at Kemper. About one year after my retirement, my former confidential informant Bobby Russo, whom I developed under the TECIP, was indicted by the federal grand jury in Chicago on federal arson conspiracy charges, along with Tony, the insurance claim adjuster, and others. The trial was scheduled for July 1977, and I was served with a subpoena to testify and give evidence for the defense. I knew that spelled trouble. The defense had subpoenaed the voluminous FBI informant file of Bobby Russo to show the court that Russo had been furnishing confidential information to the FBI for the past thirteen years and that Russo involved himself in this case at my direction and the FBI. The confidential file was now available for everyone to see. All of my assurances that our relationship would be kept confidential were empty promises. My immediate concern was for the safety of Bobby Russo and his family, because various elements of organized crime would certainly want to seek revenge for his role as an informant for the FBI. I did not want to be responsible for Bobby Russo becoming another casualty of the FBI's war against organized crime as we had painfully experienced many times in the past. I was required to testify at the trial about our long relationship and his value to the FBI over a thirteen-year period. There were no secrets in court; and all of the details of Russo's relationship with the FBI, including payments made to him over the years, were made known. I concluded my testimony by stating that without Mr. Russo's information, the formal investigation leading to his arson conspiracy indictment would not have been possible, because the original investigation was based solely on information provided by Mr. Russo. That was the best I could do to mitigate the situation. No one else from the FBI or the US attorney's office came to his defense or considered using Russo as an unindicted co-conspirator or using him as a government witness because of his service to the FBI. Russo was found guilty and was sentenced by Federal Judge Thomas McMillan to serve three years in prison. He was sent to the Federal Correctional Institution at Seagoville, Texas.

In April of 1979, I received a personal letter at Kemper from Bobby Russo, who served about a year of his sentence and was led to believe that he would be paroled after serving one-third of his time. He found out that this was not the case and that he had to serve his full term. He made a plea for help because he felt that he was a victim of circumstances and that his longtime service to the FBI should have been taken into consideration for a reduction of sentence. His pregnant wife had lost her baby and was undergoing a traumatic period in her life. He desperately needed help to be eligible for parole and to be reunited with his family. He had no one to turn to for help. I felt a strong moral obligation to help Bobby Russo with his parole in any way that I could. His relationship with the FBI had been exposed and publicized, and his personal safety was in jeopardy. On April 18, 1979, I sent a letter to Russo's case manager at the Federal Correctional Institution at Seagoville and provided him with all of the details of Russo's relationship with the FBI and how he was one of the most productive, confidential informants in the Chicago area. He provided information that resulted in hundreds of arrests and convictions in state and federal courts. I also pointed out that Bobby Russo originally furnished the information that culminated in his conviction and resulted in his present confinement. The purpose of my letter was not to pass judgment on the guilt or innocence of Bobby Russo but for the US Parole Commission to have the benefit of all of the facts of his background that would have a bearing on his parole. It did not take long for the US Parole Commission to contact me. They requested that I appear in person before the Commission in Seagoville to give testimony at the parole hearing for Bobby Russo on June 5, 1979, at 10:30 a.m. I took time off from my Kemper position and paid my own expenses to travel to Seagoville, which is a small community just south of Dallas, Texas. I was the only witness to be called. I appeared before the parole commission as scheduled and testified in detail for about one hour about Bobby Russo's long relationship with the FBI. I answered all of their questions and concerns, and the hearing seemed to go well. It did not take long for the parole commission to make their decision, since Bobby Russo was released on parole in early June of 1979. Shortly after he received the good news of his release, Bobby Russo sent me the following letter:

> Dear Vince   June 8, 1979
> "Words can only reflect my gratitude for all that you have done for me, and my heart will always possess a sincere thanks. A truer friend I have never had and for this I will always be thankful. Knowing that my wife and I will be able to put this horrendous experience behind us and face life with a great appreciation of its realness is a beautiful thing. My case manager told me that in all of the hearings that he has been party to, and there have been many, never has any representative presented themselves as you did. He and the examiners, were quite impressed, as was reflected by their decision. It only proves that 'truth' will always overcome most of life's adversities. I will never forget the look on my wife's face when I broke the news, such happiness after all that she had been through was rewarding. And of course, your excitement added to hers and mine presented a beautiful picture of the day. Once again, words can never truly describe how we feel, and my sincere appreciation for all that you have done, you have been great to us and we will never forget this."
>
>   Sincerely your friend,
>   Bobby

That letter was the last time I heard from Bobby Russo. We have never communicated with each other for almost thirty-five years. I guess no news is good news. I wish him the very best. That had been quite an experience for both of us during all of those years, and it appears to have had a happy ending. My primary concern was for his personal safety in view of the dangerous role he played for the FBI. The Chicago Division of the FBI and FBI headquarters had been unaware of the events experienced by me following the incarceration of one of the FBI's top echelon criminal informants, whose symbol number was known as CG 6722-CTE, under the TECIP. My problems with Bobby Russo were miniscule when compared with the tragic events encountered in the Whitey Bulger matter. Now that this chapter in my life was finally behind me, I was ready and eager to return full time to my challenging second career at the Kemper Insurance.

James S. Kemper Jr., chairman of Kemper, was an avid golfer who had a great passion for the game of golf. This led him to use the sport effectively to promote the insurance business through the utilization of the "Kemper Open," an annual golfing tournament for professional golfers held in strategic parts of the country. In 1979, he converted about three hundred acres of choice property at the Long Grove complex to launch a challenging eighteen-hole championship golf course and called it the Kemper Lakes Golf Club. The architects for this golf course were Dick Nugent and Ken Killian, and they did an incredible job.

Unfortunately for James Kemper Jr., he did not consider purchasing the property located on a one-acre-plus site at the south entrance of the Kemper Lakes Golf Club in Long Grove, which was immediately adjacent to the first tee area. At that time, this property could have been purchased for about $80,000, an insignificant amount of money when compared with the overall investment at Kemper Lakes. It was eventually acquired by Albert Sarno, a former Chicago police officer who had been a loan shark collector for Chicago West Side mobster Joseph "Gags" Gagliano, an associate of Sam Giancana. Al Sarno's partner in the loan shark operation had been Chris Cardi, also a former Chicago police officer and West Side mobster who was killed in a gangland fashion in Melrose Park, Illinois, shortly after he was released from prison on a narcotics charge.

Al Sarno owned and operated the Elmwood Sewer and Water Company from his residence in Long Grove, Illinois. It was not uncommon for Sarno to store many of his large excavating machines and equipment on his property such as tractors, cranes, backhoes, and the like. Not only were these machines an eye sore on the property located at the entrance of the Kemper Lakes championship golf course, but they also became a noise pollution problem, especially for golfers who were teeing off at the first tee. Jim Kemper Jr. became very concerned over this situation. He planned on having many golf tournaments at Kemper Lakes, including professional tournaments, and the Al Sarno situation had become a huge annoyance. Sarno was well aware of the dates of these tournaments, and he would start up his machines during the tee-off times just to attract attention and simply to be obstinate. Because Al Sarno had the reputation of being a Chicago mobster, the Kemper Executives designated me to act as liaison between Kemper and our neighborhood nuisance Al Sarno.

During the mid-1980s, I paid my first visit to Al Sarno at his home in Long Grove, Illinois. He remembered me from my FBI days and seemed a little nervous to see me at first but remained friendly. He introduced me to his live in companion named Tammie Ruff, who was a pleasant young lady. We discussed the noise problem at the first tee, and I asked him if he could hold down the noise during certain scheduled golfing events. He did not turn me down but implied that he wanted something in return. I asked him what he wanted. I was startled by his response. He said he wanted permission to fish at Kemper Lakes with his children. Fishing at Kemper Lakes was restricted to employees and their guests who were required to obtain fishing permits from Kemper's Building Security department. I then made arrangements for Sarno to have fishing privileges at Kemper Lakes and that seemed to resolve the noise problem for a period of time. I would occasionally drop in on Sarno to say hello and to ensure that we maintained a good relationship. On one occasion, I told him that I was sorry to hear about his former partner Chris Cardi, who had been shotgunned to death, and he just rolled his eyes and quickly changed the subject. Sarno knew that he had the upper hand with Kemper, and it was just a matter of time before he took advantage of his strategic location. In the meantime, Kemper had built a high fence between the two properties to conceal the many visible excavation machines stored on the Sarno property. Kemper, however, had no defense against the clamor of these machines once they were operational. As expected, the truce between Sarno and Kemper did not last very long. Sarno resumed his noise pollution at the first tee. Jim Kemper Jr. had retired from Kemper Insurance and cofounded a company called Kemper Sports Management, along with Steve Lesnik, a former Kemper Insurance executive. They contracted to handle the management of the Kemper Lakes Golf Club and insisted that Kemper Insurance find some way to restrain Al Sarno from being a continuing annoyance at the first tee. Further contact with Sarno was to no avail. He implied that he would consider selling his property to Kemper to alleviate the problem. It was obvious that he was holding Kemper hostage for the purchase of his property at a highly inflated price. He was asking for a buyout of $1.4 million, which was absolutely outrageous. Sarno let it be known that his asking price included a substantial nuisance value, and he knew it. This problem could have been avoided if Kemper had purchased the property in 1971 for a fraction of the cost. Kemper Lakes had just negotiated with PGA officials to hold the prestigious 1989 PGA golf tournament at Kemper Lakes, which would be the first major golf championship tournament to be held there. Something had to be done before the PGA tournament was to take place. I was assigned to negotiate for the purchase of the Sarno property for Kemper Insurance. Sarno claimed that he made many improvements to his home since he purchased it, including additional bedrooms and baths and that it had greatly increased in value. After much haggling over the price, he finally agreed to reduce the price to about $1.2 million, which was pure and simple extortion. I presented the proposed sale price to the Kemper Executives, and they were willing to buy out Sarno just to get rid of him. The legal department prepared the sales contract, and Sarno was told to leave as soon as practical with all of his excavating equipment. Shortly after the departure of Al Sarno, Kemper Insurance was uncertain about what to do with the vacant home on the property, so they eventually demolished it to reduce the amount of the property tax. Al Sarno made a huge profit on the sale of his home. It did not take him long to build a 4,100-square-foot, single-family home on three and one half acres at a cost of about $250,000 at Long Meadow Court, Mundelein, Illinois. Sarno enjoyed fishing and boating, and he invested part of his windfall profits in a luxury fifty-five-foot power boat and called it *The Cod Father*, a clever play on words. He maintained his boat at Winthrop Harbor, Illinois. Sarno passed away in January of 2012.

The men's PGA golf tournament was held at Kemper Lakes Golf Club in 1989, and it was a huge success. The late Payne Stewart was the winner of the tournament, his first win of a major golf championship. Many other successful golf tournaments were held at Kemper Lakes over the years. Stan Mikita, the Chicago Blackhawks Hall of Famer, served as head golf professional at Kemper Lakes for about eight years following his retirement from the Blackhawks in 1980. He was succeeded by Emil Esposito, a fine professional golfer and a gentleman. The Chicago Bears' players were frequent golfers at Kemper Lakes, including Mike Ditka, Jim McMahon, Kevin Butler, and many others. Kemper Lakes Golf Club was eventually sold by Kemper for about $18 million to a private group and currently operates as a private golf club.

My title with Kemper Insurance Companies was subsequently changed to director of Corporate Security, to more accurately describe the nature of my work and to include the handling of additional external fraud matters as well as all of the Internal Security problems. I hired two former FBI agents to assist me, namely Harold Johnson, who served with me on the C-1 squad, and Robert Buckley, a former FBI counterterrorism supervisor in Chicago. Their performances were outstanding, and each year, our savings and recoveries for Kemper far exceeded the amount of our budget. We were actually a huge profit center. I also hired Robert Geist, a former Evanston, Illinois, police officer following the retirement of Harold Johnson. Geist was an excellent investigator and had an expertise in performing many of our physical security surveys throughout the country. We added former FBI agents Charles Blossfield and Thomas Wronski to the Special Investigations Unit of the Claims Department, and they were very effective in resolving many fraudulent insurance claims. My secretary, Mrs. Carol Ploog, who later became my administrative assistant, did an incredible job in handling all of the many details and functions that were required of our small but very effective financial investigative unit. I retired in February 2003 at the age of eighty. I had two incredibly enjoyable and rewarding careers and it was time for me to call it quits and spend what time I had left with my family and for recreation and travel.

Unfortunately for Kemper Insurance and its many dedicated and loyal employees, the company was on the verge of bankruptcy. Our chairman of the board and chief executive officer was David B. Mathis, and his handpicked president and chief operating officer was William D. Smith, both of whom were very optimistic about the financial future of Kemper Insurance just prior to its financial collapse in 2003. Mr. Mathis spent the next ten years liquidating the company, while Mr. Smith retired suddenly with his severance package and took off for the wine vineyards of Argentina. Also on the Kemper Board of Directors at that time was Jim Edgar, former governor of the state of Illinois. It was an unimaginable and tragic collapse of one of the most respected and successful insurance companies in the world that had been in business for more that ninety years. It was, however, a most enjoyable and challenging experience for me while it lasted.

EPILOGUE

Following my retirement from the FBI in 1976, the C-1 squad was in a state of flux and was slowly being downsized from its original complement with key agents reassigned to other investigative squads, as well as transfers to other field divisions. The organized crime field was losing some of its priority and fervor. There was a general reorganization within the Chicago Division, and because the C-1 squad had the most agents, it was only logical that the C-1 squad personnel would be most affected. The C-1 squad and its Criminal Intelligence Program no longer exist today as we knew it in the past.

Upon retirement from the FBI, Agent John Dallman became manager of Investigative Services for Northrup Grumman in El Segundo, California, and has since retired. Bill Roemer was transferred to the Tucson, Arizona, office of the FBI where he retired. He authored several books on organized crime and has since passed away. Marshall Rutland had been transferred to FBI headquarters and died at the age of forty-five. Jim Annes, upon retirement, started his own private investigative agency in Irvine, California. Richard Cavanagh was transferred to the Sacramento FBI office and upon retirement became a tax attorney. He has since passed away. Herb Briick became a security representative for American Airlines and had retired. Bobby Gillham later became SAC of the Houston FBI Office and now has his own consulting firm. John Roberts retired to California. John Osborne was transferred to the Philadelphia FBI Office and later became the township treasurer of Radnor, Pennsylvania. Peter J. Wacks, whose father and brother were FBI agents, started his own private investigative agency in Chicago. John Bassett passed away as a result of an accident. Dennis Shanahan, my gambling coordinator, was transferred to the FBI office in Knoxville, Tennessee, and has since passed away. Richard Kusserow was appointed by President Ronald Reagan as the inspector general of the Department of Health and Human Services, and had a staff of about fourteen hundred. Raymond Maria became a very successful CPA in the Washington and Virginia areas. And the list goes on and on. Most of the C-1 agents upon retirement from the FBI took prestigious positions of employment in the private or public sector of Chicago or went into business on their own. During the nineteen-year period that the C-1 Organized Crime Squad was in existence, over one hundred agents had been assigned to the squad at one time or another. To list them all would be virtually impossible; however, all had contributed significantly to the overall accomplishments achieved by the C-1 squad against the Chicago mob, a portion of which has been set forth in this book.

These agents were the pioneers who paved the way for other agents to follow in the field of organized crime. They were required to wage war against the glory days of one of the most powerfully entrenched organized crime organizations that ever existed in this country since the days of Al Capone. No one person was responsible for the many successes achieved during this nineteen-year period. Rather, it was a complete and unified team effort, and it was my good fortune to have been part of it for nineteen years. Granted, organized crime will always be with us, but certainly on a much smaller scale. It has been dealt a savage blow from which it will never completely recover. Their activities and contacts have been exposed, exploited, curtailed, and relentlessly pursued and prosecuted. Another factor that had a devastating effect on the Chicago crime syndicate was the loss of influence as a result of the exposure of public officials, members of the judiciary, law enforcement officers, and labor leaders, with whom they had a close working relationship, all of which was further evidence of our effectiveness. The Chicago mob has been greatly reduced in size, and their ability to function as before will never be the same. Their organization has dwindled to just a shadow of their former empire. The status of the hierarchy of organized crime in Chicago had been one of confusion and disarray, following the incarceration of mob leader Sam Momo Giancana. His self-imposed exile in Mexico for eight years was a landmark achievement. Other hoodlum leaders that replaced Giancana were also prosecuted and incarcerated. The hoodlum comments set forth in this book give expert testimony of their plight as a result of the relentless intervention of the FBI. The words of Paul "The Waiter" Ricca, former Capone mobster and former boss of the Chicago mob, said it all when he was arrested by the FBI on charges of perjury in 1966: **"The good old days ended when the FBI stepped in."**

INDEX

Edwards Brothers Malloy
Thorofare, NJ USA
October 7, 2014